PAGE TO PAGE

To Anne
With love from
Janet

7.25.2007

From Bainbridge
Island off the
coast of Seattle, WA

PAGE TO PAGE

Retrospectives of Writers from
The Seattle Review

Edited by Colleen J. McElroy

A McLellan Book

University of Washington Press   *Seattle & London*

This book is published with the assistance of a grant from the McLellan Endowed Series Fund, established through the generosity of Martha McCleary McLellan and Mary McLellan Williams.

Support for this book has also been provided by The Seattle Review, the University of Washington English Department's Pollock Endowment, the Grace P. Kameros Fund, the Friends of English and the Graduate School at the University of Washington, and the Janis Jaonni Murphey Memorial Fund.

University of Washington Press
PO Box 50096, Seattle, WA 98145
www.washington.edu/uwpress

Library of Congress Cataloging-in-Publication Data

Page to page : retrospective of writers from The Seattle review / edited by Colleen J. McElroy.
        p.   cm.
    Includes profiles, interviews, and works by David Wagoner, Denise Levertov, Sonia Sanchez, Nelson Bentley, Richard Hugo, Larry Levis, Diane Wakoski, Carolyn Kizer, Lynda Barry, Yusef Komunyakaa, Marilyn Chin, Ivan Doig, William Stafford, Sharon Olds, Rick Bass, and N. Scott Momaday.
    ISBN 0-295-98518-6 (pbk. : alk. paper)
    1. American literature—20th century.   2. Authors, American—20th century—Biography.   3. Authors, American—20th century—Interviews.
I. McElroy, Colleen J.   II. Seattle review.

PS536.2.P28   2005
810.9'0054—dc22   2005042210
[B]

CONTENTS

Rick Bass

N. Scott Momaday

PREFACE

A*CTOR STEPHEN FRYE*, interviewed during the making of the film *Wilder,* noted that among all aspects of writer Oscar Wilde's life, the act of writing was the most difficult to portray. "There's not much to show when a writer is writing," he explained; "just the sitting down and silence is all." And yet we, as readers, are fascinated by what goes on outside the pages, the ways in which the life of the writer acts upon and is acted upon by the process of writing. Every writer can recall the blunt, sometimes painfully obvious questions volleyed from the audience during a Q-and-A session: Do you write every day, every morning, all day? Do you use a pen, a pencil, a computer? Who reads your work before you send it to the publisher? What writers have influenced you? How do you get started? These are questions that audiences seemingly never tire of asking, and all of them are set to unhinge a mystery: How different is the writer's life?

In 1997, I added to *The Seattle Review* a feature called "Retrospectives," which I hoped might answer some of those questions. Between 1997 and 2004, *The Seattle Review* published sixteen retrospectives of both poets and prose writers. It is a diverse and experienced group, spanning the country from the East to West Coast and representing a wide range of voices. Through photographs, interviews, essays, and a sample of the writer's work, these retrospectives offer a glimpse into a writer's life. They are not biographical in the strict sense, nor are they critical pieces in the pedagogical sense of literary criticism. The "biographical" slant is most evident in the photographs—from candid images of family and child-hood to more recent shots—which allow readers to see a fragment of the writer's private world. The point is not to offer a life history, but to bridge the gap between a work of writing and the life that produced it. Similarly, the criticism offered makes little or no attempt to fit the writer into a particular school of writing. We find that most writers show a rather casual concern for their theoretical position within a genre and are instead more amenable to taking a look back at their particular (and peculiar) hurdles, as the term "retrospective" implies.

That was the easy part. The difficult task was asking writers to do what most of us dread: sort through family photos, often stored in shoeboxes, attics, or dusty corners of closets. Some would comply only after I had promised to personally hand-carry each print to the photographic stu-dio for reproduction and to return the originals as quickly as possible. I have accumulated a long list of people to thank for entrusting their photos to me, to Ivey Photographic Reproductions, and to the vagaries of express mail. No photograph was lost and each played an essential role in setting "Retrospectives" into motion by giving added weight to the essays, interviews, and writing samples. One reader sent a note: "After reading Carolyn Kizer's retrospective, I went out and found her books. Thanks for the introduction." Another said, "It's amazing that Lynda Barry writes with crayon and paint brush. It's like having an escape kit when you're stuck."

This anthology is also unique in content and design in that it com-bines a variety of perspectives on each featured writer's life and work. The retrospectives that were completed posthumously include essays from other writers, thumbnail sketches from friends, and, of course, those invaluable photographs from the family and the estate of the writer. The essays range from the personal to the explicative, but always we come back to the writer as a person.

I offer my heartfelt thanks to the graduate students in the MFA Pro-gram at the University of Washington for their excellent contribution. Interviewers are honor-bound to field the questions that will inspire the most evocative responses without treading too heavily on the respondent's point of view. "The trick is to be deeply familiar with the work," Linden Ontjes once told me. It is to their credit that the interviewers represented here—some of them completing their first interviews—were meticulous in becoming familiar with the writers' work.

Despite the hours of transcribing interviews, the nail-biting tension of collecting photographs, the endless quest to identify all the photographs, the forest of copyright releases, and the ongoing layout and placement glitches, I would do it all again. For one brief moment, we have brought to life on the page the real person who lies behind a work of writing. These writers and their families have graciously shared a bit of their lives. When reading these retrospectives, we find ourselves amazed, saddened, and always hopeful. Words persist. Without them, we have lost the nuances of our existence. In *Page to Page*, we have the privilege of viewing the writers as well, and we understand, as poet Andy Sullivan writes, *"that the stare you smile at / is the original."*

ACKNOWLEDGMENTS

I wish to thank all of the students, editors, and writers who made possible the production of *The Seattle Review* during my tenure as editor-in-chief. A special thanks to those students who accepted the position of coordinating editor, for the hours of letter writing, Xeroxing, and proofreading, and for their generous donation of time and energy to *The Seattle Review*, in general, and *Page to Page*, in particular. You helped me keep my sanity as I wandered through a forest of typesetting, CD-Roms, photographic reproductions, and printing. I will be forever grateful.

And for their generous donations, I wish to thank the University of Washington Friends of English Endowed Fund, the Grace Posner Kameros Fund, the University of Washington Graduate School Fund, Dr. Steve Sumida, Dr. Johnnella Butler, and the support in memory of Janis Jaonni Murphey, who ardently believed that poems were meant to be read aloud.

In addition, I want to recognize the many friends and colleagues who also have been a part of this project: Rob Weller, computer specialist extraordinaire; Lou Oma Durand and Marisis Nelson for their faith in saving the *Review;* and to Johnny Horton, Philip Sorenson, Meredith Cole, Marcia Woodard, Vicki Angel, and Peter Aaron, who offered their time and resources. Special thanks to Dr. Steve Sumida, Tyler Meier, and Dr. Michael Faucette, and to Irene Wanner for collecting the materials for the N. Scott Momaday retrospective. Without them *The Seattle Review* and these retrospectives would not have survived. I also want to acknowledge all the people at the University of Washington Press who worked so hard to reconstruct the individual retrospectives into a collection, especially Michael Duckworth and Marilyn Trueblood. And, of course, a huge thanks to all the authors who allowed me to reprint the material included in this collection.

Colleen J. McElroy
Seattle, May 2005

INTRODUCTION

*I*MAGINE THE SEATTLE REVIEW as a spacious beach cottage here on the Salish Sea, sheltering writers as they build their own houses of words. Contributor Ivan Doig might call this shelter a "house of sky," and N. Scott Momaday might name it "a house made of dawn" or a bear's house in which "I shall preside with wild, disinterested kindness."

Here are writers who have found a home in *The Seattle Review.* In their own work and through astute interviews, photos, and biographical articles, the prominent writers in this retrospective (1997–2004) come vividly to life. It is as though we join them for an instructive tea; or visit with them to the creaking descant of a porch swing, often looking out over water, that deepest Northwest reflection. This collection offers us intimacy, even companionship, with these well-known writers, glimpsing the diverse worlds their words create.

Many writers here, such as David Wagoner, N. Scott Momaday, Richard Hugo, Ivan Doig, William Stafford, and Rick Bass watch daily details of tides, clouds, the velvet-shed antler—a mesmerizing natural world, what poet Denise Levertov has called "a brusque, flame-lit earth." Others, such as Yusef Komunyakaa, Diane Wakoski, Lynda Barry, Nelson Bently, Marilyn Chin, Sonia Sanchez, and Larry Levis, keenly study self, society, body, culture, history, and more distinctly human landscapes—as Sharon Olds writes in her poem on Auschwitz survivors, the "human hills and mountains, the intimate crowning of a private life."(p. 328)

"I am one of the few Northwest poets who is not a nature poet," Carolyn Kizer notes, distinguishing herself as "primarily occupied with character." Her far-ranging interview embraces feminism, physics, and politics, as well as the classical Chinese poets' passion for friendship. Kizer also describes dreams as "instructions on how to live" and assigns her students to keep dream journals and exchange dreams as they would poems. "If dreams don't mean anything," she concludes, "poems don't mean anything, either." (p. 137)

Kizer talks insightfully about "metaphor as history," the power of Jungian archetypes, and the poet's—especially the woman poet's—role in changing consciousness. She praises the importance of the mother-daughter relationship in the work of all poets, citing in particular her own mother, who "made a poet out of me."

Denise Levertov also writes about her mother and her garden: it was "never prim . . . but suggested a foreign opulence, especially when the California poppies—later to delight homesick G.I.s billeted down the road—were in full orange glory." (p. 18) This maternal garden, a feminine flowering alongside the soldier's war-fatigue, offers the solace that so haunts many of Levertov's later poems addressing war, as well as "neighboring with eagles" here in the Northwest.

This collection is a harmony of women and men's voices, a melodious balancing. Among its distinctive pleasures is the unfolding on the page of friendships and dialogues between writers. It's as though we're at a dinner party listening to Ivan Doig quote a Richard Hugo poem written to Denise Levertov:

[N]o matter what my salary is
or title, I remain a common laborer, stained by the perpetual
dust from loading flour or coal. I stay humble. (p. 230)

We are likewise privy to a poignant letter and poem Larry Levis writes for his friend—and the editor of this collection—Colleen McElroy:

Birth & Death own the little walled cottages:
Since one's illiterate, the other always speechless,

There's no real way of meeting either.
And what did you come here for if not to hear
Finality in the soft click of a latch
Or in the long *thou* of the empty wavebreak? (p. 91)

In this cottage of a collection Carolyn Kizer reminisces about studying with David Wagoner, and James Welch tells stories of how much Richard Hugo loved baseball and Montana. Seeming to speak for everyone in the collection, Welch observes: "A true poet is a person who lives the poems, who is so obsessed with the world of the imagination and the need to write that it guides his or her life as surely as the stars guided that ancient mariner." (p. 73)

It is exhilarating to hear the stories behind the work, to see childhood photos of Marilyn Chin in Hong Kong, or a portrait of Sonia Sanchez as a young woman trying on a bathing suit at Gimbel's in New York City. A smiling girl, Sharon Olds shows off her huge new mittens, and a bespectacled Diane Wakoski hides behind a huge, flowering amaryllis. We feel at home with these photographs, as though leafing through a family album. One of my favorite photos shows Rick Bass as a boy, his grin crooked, his eyes squinting as he holds up a fish caught in Texas. Later we glimpse this boy in the man casting his fly-fishing rod into a Yaak river, as if he must make a study of this water flowing with his stories.

For many of these writers, nature is what grounds and inspires the human quality of their work. David Wagoner writes of his Midwestern childhood, "I grew up in a kind of graveyard for anything natural." (p. 6) He experiences the epiphany of Northwest wilderness when studying with Theodore Roethke, who invited him to teach at University of Washington in 1953. "The first time I . . . drove up a former logging road into one of the last two stands of virgin rain forest in North America," Wagoner writes, "I thought I'd found where God lived." (p. 8)

William Stafford, one of our great voices and a man profoundly rooted in Oregon since 1948, sets his novels and poems in our far-flung, mist-hidden territory. In his poem "Lake Union," Stafford summons up Seattle, a city shaped by water:

. . . a fog gathers in every
scrap of skyscraper, and the crowds and bridges.

And we—noted or not, numbered and then
passed over, a census where nobody counts—
we stand unjudged and unjudging,
open and serene and ready,
quietly jubilant like a pier in the tide
or a wisp of moss caught on a thorn.

We merge with that lost whistle groping
And the long erasing swish of the rain. (p. 298)

Ivan Doig, another Northwest transplant who took deep root here,
reveals that his writing habits echo his earlier ranching work. He is up
always before dawn, "starting to milk the thesaurus about the time I
would have been milking cows on a Montana ranch." (p. 233) The chosen lands of Montana and the Salish Sea suffuse his fiction so deeply
that the landscape itself becomes a character. At the same time Doig
strives for a "cool remove," or distance from self and place, so that he
might see more clearly.

Many of the authors write about beloved country or homeland, but
from far away. Marilyn Chin writes of "the nature of displacement" and
the longing for human community, country, or tribe. As an immigrant
issue, this "story of leaving one's motherland to be absorbed by a new
culture" is seminal. "Some days, I may feel homeless," Chin says. "Some
days I feel like a citizen of the world. . . . Home now is my art, my poetry."
(p. 205) Speaking as a "post-colonial, Pacific Rim, feminist Chinese-
American poet" and a so-called "minority poet," Chin declares, "Our
voices are necessary. We keep the literature honest. . . . We are the ones
who are 'making it new.'" (p. 211)

Chin also talks about the music of her poetry, her "fusionist aesthetics" (p. 212) of melding "two types of songs . . . the Chinese folk lyric
and the western limerick . . . folk ballads east and west" in such poems
as "Miami." Here Chin's immigrant character is drawn from life: a Japanese scholar, one of the "forgotten women," displaced in Ohio's Miami
University and teaching Japanese:

She teaches Japanese to Business minors
Each night she dims the stone lanterns
She lives there alone without a lover. (p. 205)

In Yusef Komunyakaa's poems, as in Chin's *Rhapsody in Yellow,* we hear the syncopations of jazz, echoes of Miles Davis' "old sorrow songs," ballads, the "liquid architecture" of poetry. (p. 188) Komunyakaa has even written lyrics for a libretto, "Shangri-La," for the opera *Slipknot.* Its main character, John Wong, is a "Metaphysical Detective," an ex-Ph.D student in philosophy investigating an embezzlement case against Takeover, Inc., a company in Thailand. As Komunyakaa explains, "I learned from jazz that one can incorporate almost anything into a poem"—or a song. (p. 182)

Whether in cross-cultural fusions or Whitmanesque verses, several other poets here share songs of self and human nature. Scrupulous self-revelation—awakening readers to other cultures and, often, silenced voices—is the work of Sonia Sanchez, Diane Wakoski, and Sharon Olds. In the *Seattle Review* interview "Let us Begin to Sing: A Poet and Her Mountain," Edward Jenkinson profiles Wakoski. It's not surprising to hear that her student years at Berkeley (1956–1960) were divided between "practicing the piano about five hours a day and writing poetry." (p. 109) But, to our good fortune, Wakoski chose to focus on the latter, sensing that the world would "acknowledge" her poetry more than her music. Her exhilarating public performances of poetry draw upon this musical background and foreshadow the current fascination for performance poetry, its revitalizing peer-to-peer and ear-to-ear oral tradition.

When William Stafford writes in his journal, "The world is a long poem I am falling through—I just tell about it" (p. 293), or when Denise Levertov writes, "Poets owe to Poetry itself a loyalty which may at times be in conflict with the demands of domestic or other aspects of life" (p. 23), they could be describing Sharon Olds and Sonia Sanchez.

Sharon Olds turns a clear, unblinking eye on domesticity and family in what Linden Ontjes calls "somatic poems." Olds "knows the world through her body," and her startling and often harrowing stories of surviving family invite us into a "conscious or subconscious awareness of the nature of good and evil.... Nothing less is at stake than the apprehension of the sacred, nothing less than the definition of beauty." (p. 312) This knowledge of the sacred, for Olds, comes through the familiar, the family, the body:

> How do they come to the
> come to the   come to the   God   come to the

still waters, and not love
The one who came there with them, light
rising slowly as steam off their joined
skin? (p. 314)

Sonia Sanchez also writes of family in her books, including *Home-coming* and *Wounded in the House of a Friend*. "I write to offer a Black woman's view of the world," Sanchez explains, "how I tell the truth is a part of the truth itself." As a mother, poet, activist, and professor, she is always moving, because "motion is life." Juggling these demands upon her time, Sanchez often writes late at night, when "words come drifting back like some reverent lover." In *Does Your House Have Lions*, Sanchez faces family—sister, brother, father, and ancestors—and this intimate dialogue brings her to a realization that "it is never too late for forgiveness . . . never too late." (p. 41)

Whether it is Sanchez writing that African Americans "finally realized that in order to begin writing truth, they had to first go home" or David Wagoner, Ivan Doig, William Stafford, Richard Hugo, Denise Levertov, or Carlyn Kizer finding home and work in this Western landscape, or Chinese American Marilyn Chin finding home in her poetry—all the writers in this retrospective bring us home, not only to share the shelter of this *Seattle Review* retrospective but also to reach out to a wider world. "I'm always traveling," Sonia Sanchez writes in what could be a mantra for the twenty-first century. On this endless journey, it is wonderful simply to rest inside the pages of this gracious book and follow N. Scott Momaday's counsel to an aged bear:

Translate yourself to spirit;
Be present on your journey.

Keep to the trees and waters.
Be the singing of the soil. (p. 382)

Brenda Peterson
Seattle, Washington, May 2005

PAGE TO PAGE

David Wagoner, age 3, 1929

DAVID WAGONER

SLIGHTLY DIFFERENT WAYS OF THINKING: AN INTERVIEW

Kate Gray

*T*HE POSH HOUSE in the cul-de-sac newly built north of Seattle threw me off. I had expected to find David Wagoner in an old Seattle bungalow, set in the woods overlooking Puget Sound, where he could study the sea and capture nature in its essence. As formally and warmly as ever, he greeted me at his door, and immediately I was immersed in a different world: I had entered his collection of poems, *Who Shall Be the Sun?* (Indiana University Press, 1978). Staring at me from the walls of the living room were masks, pointed and painted, from coastal Indian legends and ceremonies.

I asked him about that collection of poems and the compliment Hayden Carruth had paid him years ago, saying that Wagoner was "close to Indian sensibility. He knows enough to write in his own language, English . . . yet the feeling in his work has been distinctly learned. More, it has been *earned,* and the effort of that is power in its own fruition" (Gunton and Harris, 559). Wagoner had never heard of the review and confessed that he had felt a kind of compunction about invading Indian territory and wondered at that time how he had had the gall to write those poems at all. But no one else seemed to know those stories. At that time he alone was writing about native traditions. Then, he added

3

Ruth Banyard Wagoner with David, 1930

that he used to have above his desk a huge poster of the great Sioux chief, Gall, looking down at him while he wrote those poems. He chuckled, grew silent.

As in nearly everything he writes and certainly in the way he talks about his writing, David Wagoner seems humble. Having published fifteen collections of poetry, written a play and a series of one-acts, having written twenty-three novels and published eleven, Wagoner worries "about where the next poem is coming from. That is," he says in his soft and lilting voice, "enough of a burden for any writer." But he does not carry just one burden. Wagoner wears three hats, those of the writer, teacher, and editor, and has added a fourth: he is a father to two girls. "You know, the responsibility of bringing up two little girls is awesome, and I am trying to be good at it. It is very hard," he admits. At age seventy-two this tall, lean Midwesterner seems not to realize how good he is at so many things.

In the plush carpeting and soft furniture of the living room, I imagine David Wagoner telling his children legends of the Northwest, reciting poems, and singing them to sleep. His voice has the richness of Garrison Keillor and the subtle inflections of a stage actor. In 1926 David Wagoner was born in the rolling hills of Ohio. When he was a child, his parents took their two sons and daughter to musicals, both parents played the piano and sang. Then, in 1933, he and his family moved, when his father lost his job in the steel mill, to Whiting, Indiana, a place between Gary and Chicago that was heavily industrialized.

In collections of his work, like *Sleeping in the Woods* (Indiana University Press, 1974) and *Through the Forest* (Atlantic Monthly Press, 1987), Wagoner describes the natural world so precisely that I thought he had spent nearly every day of his youth exploring wilderness. In poems such as "A Guide to the Field," he writes:

Some (this ryegrass) like caterpillars spinning
Cocoons out of sunlight,
And some (this lavender bluegrass) a waist-high forest
Of slender fir trees,
Still others (cheatgrass, wild barley) plotted like flowerbeds
Under flights and counter-flights
Of swallows and field sparrows. Each blade, each spikelet,
Each glume and awn, each slowly
Stiffening stem, no matter what may come
In the next wind—hail or fire—
Will take its beheading, will give up this year's ghost
With less than a murmur . . . (*Through the Forest*, 210)

But instead, he lived next to a dead swamp. Reviewers imply that Wagoner learned his sense of compassion for living things in a similar way that William Stafford did, by walking in the outdoors as a child. But Wagoner contends that his compassion "may be in reaction to the Midwestern attitudes of that time. I came from a place that was so heavily

Walter S. Wagoner with David, Turkeyfoot Lake, Ohio, 1931

polluted," he says, "that it was so difficult for anything to grow that maybe I felt that those things that did flourish had something or knew something that the people I grew up with didn't know and yet I could learn from them. It was tough even for weeds to grow where I grew up." He adds, "I grew up in a kind of graveyard for anything natural."

When he was ten or eleven, he started writing poems modeled after Longfellow and other ballad writers. He also read everything he could get his hands on: comics, pulp magazines, detective novels, travel pieces. He listened avidly to comedy and drama on the radio and started at a young age to train his ear. He became nearly obsessed with magic, and practiced magic tricks more than he played sports with other boys (*Autobiography*, 400).

In an autobiography, he writes, "The imagery of stage magic took its place early in my vocabulary as a writer, along with the imagery of crime and imprisonment. Several of my closest friends went to reform school instead of to Standard Oil or college, and I could easily have done the same if I hadn't been lucky" (*Autobiography*, 400). Wagoner attributes a great deal to luck, but he learned hard work from his father, who spent his whole life working in steel mills while holding a degree in classical languages. His father was too shy to teach. His mother, Ruth Calder Banyard, was selfless and self-effacing. Wagoner's ability to deflect compliments and find comfort in silence even in conversation seems to have come to him honestly.

As he describes his life, Wagoner glides over his accomplishments: graduating from Naval ROTC at Penn State in 1944, publishing his first short story and first poems while still in graduate school, and becoming the first graduate of the writing program at Indiana University and then hired to teach creative writing at the age of twenty-two. In 1952 his first book of poems, *Dry Sun, Dry Wind* was accepted for publication by Indiana University Press, and his first novel was sent to Viking Press for possible publication.

But it was a workshop with Theodore Roethke at Penn State that changed his life. He writes, "It suddenly dawned on me that the nebulous future I'd half-imagined with myself in the roles (they shifted weekly) of stage magician, chemist, ship's officer, high school basketball coach, spy, or alternately, writer of spy novels, had become a much more firmly outlined pattern: I would be a college English teacher and a poet" (*Autobiography*, 403).

And he did. He also became a novelist. From the very beginning of his career, Wagoner alternated between writing fiction and poetry. If anything unifies his writing, it may be, as he puts it, that he is "heavily intrigued by the folktale. . . . A majority of my novels are . . . dealing with legendary material. To that extent, it may simply be that in a poem, I just don't have enough room for dialogue or other ways that my ears tempt me."

Much like two of his mentors, Theodore Roethke and Dylan Thomas, Wagoner uses the subtlety of sound to enhance meaning and comments that he has "an affinity for the dramatic lyric, in tones ranging from the loud and satiric through the quiet and conversational." In 1949, Wagoner spent two days with Dylan Thomas, when he and some cohorts kidnapped Thomas who had come to Indiana to read while Wagoner was teaching at DePauw University. They spent the night drinking, reading poems to each other, and imitating voices. Wagoner was surprised at how well Thomas could imitate a ghoulish mobster from Chicago.

Then, in 1953 Wagoner was around Thomas for a few months when he was rehearsing "Under Milk Wood" at the YMCA. They used to drink together, and Wagoner recalls, "in fact, I was drinking with him the night . . . he went into his fatal coma late September, 1953. He accepted me right away because I was a student of Roethke, whom he admired. He used to bellow things out in the bar like, 'The sons of Roethke never eat when they can drink,' which was pretty accurate."

After taking the workshop with Roethke at Penn State, Wagoner kept up a close correspondence and dedicated his first book of poems to Roethke. And it was Roethke who wrote Wagoner to invite him to teach at the University of Washington in 1953. For Wagoner the trip across the country was at once frightening, exhilarating, dreadful, and mind-altering (*Autobiography*, 405). He had never seen such open space or raw beauty. Soon after arriving in the Pacific Northwest, he visited the Olympic Peninsula and wrote:

The first time I . . . drove up a former logging road into one of the last two stands of virgin rain forest in North America (the greatest weight of living matter per square foot on earth, the guidebooks say) I thought I'd found where God lived. But the god waiting for me in that tangle of moss, wildflowers, nurse-logs, swordfern, and huckleberry turned out to be Pan. I became disoriented in something under ten minutes and spent the next hour relocating my car. By the time I did, I was no longer a Midwesterner. I didn't know what I was, but I was certain I'd been more or less lost all my life without knowing it. It was the beginning of my determination not to be lost in any of the woods, literal or figurative, I might explore after that.

Though I write about many different kinds of experiences, I've been called a nature poet, and to the extent that's true, I began to be one then. (*Autobiography*, 406)

Having taken a poetry writing workshop with Wagoner, I found it difficult to imagine him lost; his manner in the classroom was shy but self-assured. It is hard to imagine him lost. After moving to Seattle, Wagoner found a sense of belonging with such Roethke devotees as James Wright, Richard Hugo, Carolyn Kizer, and Stanley Kunitz. They worked together at the University of Washington, socialized and read their work to each other. They read the same poets and went to the same readings. Now, many of them serve as chancellors of the Academy of American Poets together. The process of knowing each other continues. As Wagoner says, the position of chancellor has been both interesting and challenging because the Academy "helps poets. We give away money, or help to [give away money]. And we get to know each other better, too. We get to have office meetings now and then, give readings. It's all very amusing," he says with a bit of a smirk.

While Wagoner rails against the devastation of nature, he also writes with humor and satire. He spent quite a few years in the theater and felt influenced by the Theatre of the Absurd, particularly by Harold Pinter and Samuel Beckett. From them he says he learned "understatement and mockery of inappropriate diction and silence when you expect something else, the half-said, the apparently irrelevant." In 1965 Wagoner was awarded a Ford Fellowship in Drama and became playwright in residence at Seattle Repertory Theater, then in its second year. He was allowed to go to any rehearsal or any performance, backstage or up front. Timidly, he adds, "I wrote one [play], too, and they were going to perform it in 1967. . . . And I am since very grateful that it didn't happen because I think it would have been awful. . . . No, I am not a playwright. . . . They go through hell."

He believes that play writing is almost as hard on the writer as writing movies. He should know. In 1982 Francis Ford Coppola turned his novel, *The Escape Artist* (Farrar, Straus, 1965) into a screenplay. Of that process, Wagoner says, "That was grisly; it was sobering. Some of it was fun to watch. You can have no idea when you watch the makings of a movie what the results will be because most of it gets thrown away." The film was produced and received some reviews, but it petered out, he believes, because it was released the same summer as *E.T.* and was designed for the same audience.

Even though Wagoner had not met huge success in play writing, he has carried some drama into his fiction and poetry. As X. J. Kennedy writes, Wagoner "reminds us that a poem, while it may well be a passionate outcry from the heart, inevitably has an element of theatricality" (Gunton and Harris, 558). In his classroom, he would often refer to a poem to illustrate a significant point, and then recite it. I told him how mesmerizing it was to hear him recite such poems as "Dulce et Decorum Est" by Wilfred Owen. Demurely, he pointed out that "a lot of teachers do this because it is so exasperating not to have the right books along. . . . And if you have what could be called a referential style, or a need to cite examples, you almost have to have a bundle of quotations ready. I think I developed that out of need." After pausing, he adds that memorizing was a way to absorb the poems he admired. He remembers standing in the Indiana University Bookstore and seeing for the

David Wagoner (age 34) with Dylan Thomas (age 36)

first time Dylan Thomas's "The Force that Through the Green Fuse
Drives the Flower." He says, "I didn't own the book although I bought
it soon after, but I read that [poem]. And I went back to my room, and I
realized I knew it. I recited it to a friend." He had a knack for memorizing.

Having taught for so many years, Wagoner feels that some of his
brightest moments in teaching have come when he has seen young poets
improve dramatically. Often he sees this because of his editing *Poetry
Northwest* and receiving submissions from former students. He feels his
own teaching has improved as well, and he describes some risks he has
taken in the classroom:

In recent years I've done what I used to feel afraid to do. I have actually
on a page rewritten some student poems by people who are very intelligent, very gifted, who are well on their way to becoming the best poets
they can be as it stands, and I have used them in class with fear and
trembling and have, I think, not offended. I have had them agree with
me. I would never have done that as a younger teacher. That was sacred
territory; that was theirs. But in a final effort to illustrate what I mean
about effective line breaks and maintaining a voice through the entire
poem [I felt I had] . . . to put this down on paper . . . and they haven't
thrown anything at me.

David Wagoner in 1981

I doubt he realized he had done this to one of my poems, and I had to agree there was much to learn from him.

In his workshop, Wagoner referred not just to submissions but to *boxes* of submissions. He took over the duties of editor of *Poetry Northwest* from Carolyn Kizer in 1966. For thirty years he has read all submissions, turned out letters, made selections, and put the magazine together. Wagoner's wife, Robin Seyfried, is the managing editor and sometimes offers a second reading when he is in doubt about his own judgment. He feels good about having published many local and national writers, but feels he does not deserve any credit in developing the large and distinguished community of writers in Seattle.

As teacher, editor, and writer, Wagoner balances three professions, each of which could potentially drain the other. At first he worried about atrophying, but as he wrote, he developed a strategy. "Before long I learned to recognize those times of the week or day when I could exercise whatever judgment I had without apparent cost to my poetry. . . . No matter how much energy I seemed to put into those two tasks, I made an equal amount available to myself as a writer, and the three jobs became just slightly different ways of thinking" (*Autobiography,* 408). Wagoner believes that he would not have worked as well had he not balanced all three professions:

[Within] teaching, editing and writing, there is some circular process. There is some cross-feeding: if you work hard in one, no matter how hard you work in one, and neglect, appear to neglect, the others, at the same time you are preparing yourself to do the others, so that there is a kind of relief instead of a sense of burden. When you go from one to the other, you go to a full pool or you yourself have been filling yourself, for a purpose. That is, the harder you try to write, the more you learn about teaching and the more thoughtfully you try to edit, the better writer you become, and so on. They are interconnected in some phantom way. For me, so far, I add, though . . . I have known those editors who have apparently edited themselves dry as writers, and a lot of teachers have complained that the burdens of teaching prevented them from writing, I listen to these serious people who know themselves and I have to believe them, but so far, it hasn't apparently happened to me. I don't know why. I feel lucky. I have edited warily for years; I have got to pay close attention to how I feel because this could kill me. This could be very bad for me. It is the same with all that analysis you have to do as a teacher. Well, at any rate, though I have had dry periods . . . I come back with a feeling of plenitude. I've been very lucky.

He adds almost under his breath, "I also may be fooling myself."

As he notices what time it is, I know the responsibilities of his fourth hat beckon: one daughter has a doctor's appointment. I know Wagoner has not fooled himself, and for his hard work and immense skill, he has earned the Ruth Lilly Prize, and the Levinson Prize from *Poetry* magazine. He has been nominated twice for the National Book Award, and received many other prizes. Some believe, as Leonard Neufeldt did in a review in 1980, that Wagoner

. . . is, simply, one of the most accomplished poets currently at work in and with America. . . . His range and mastery of subjects, voices, and modes, his ability to work with ease in any of the modes (narrative, descriptive, dramatic, lyric, anecdotal) and with any number of species (elegy, satirical portraiture, verse editorial, apostrophe, jeremiad, and childlike song, to name a few) and his frequent combinations of a number of these into astonishingly compelling orchestrations provide us with an intelligible and convincing definition of genius. (Gunton and Harris, 560)

Truly he is a man who balances near contradictions: he writes fiction and poetry, edits and teaches, writes reclusively, and raises a family, sits as a chancellor at the Academy of American Poets and prizes the framed version of a poem called "Closing Time" which appeared in the *New Yorker* and now hangs in the back of the Blue Moon Tavern in Seattle. His writing ranges from sublime observation to biting satire to quirky characterization. He has mastered three professions. As he walks me through the living room to the front door, beneath the beaks and noses of the coastal Indian masks, he thanks me for all my kind words. He is so adept at deflecting the compliments, I did not think he had heard me. I realize that there, indeed, had been an exchange. I understood more fully his lines from "Wading in a Marsh" (*Through the Forest: New and Selected Poems, 1977–1987*):

I see what to say: this marsh that holds me
Is the climax of a lake, shallowing, dying,
Filled with the best endeavors of pondweeds,
The exploring and colonizing shapes of a world
Too good at living for its own good,
But in this man-made silence, while wrens and kinglets
Decide what I am and slowly excuse me
For being a moving object with much less use
Than a stump, I learn why I came here
Out of order: in order to find out how to belong
Somewhere, to change where all changing
Is a healing exchange of sense for sense. (36–37)

WORKS CITED

Gunton, Sharon R., and Laurie Lanzon Harris, eds. *Contemporary Literary Criticism*. Detroit, MI: Gale Research, 1980.
Wagoner, David. *Contemporary Authors Autobiography Series*. Adele Sarkissian, ed. Detroit, MI: Gale Research, 1988.
———— Personal Interview. September 24, 1996.
———— *Through the Forest: New and Selected Poems, 1977—1987*. New York: The Atlantic Monthly Press, 1987.

Ride Toward the Sound of Gunfire

—General Custer's standing order
to his cavalry patrols in Indian territory

As a strategy, back then or now, it leaves
Something to be desired. When you arrive
At the scene of gunfire
You'll be behind the times, not having *been* there
To see the cause or the lost cause and effect.
With bullets whistling
Dixie past your ears, you are almost certain
To confuse the voices of command and reason,
Vengeance and near-panic,
Till you've become a god in the wrong machine
Whose white flag-waving logic-choppers and outposts,
Whose spitters-and-polishers
And very loud speakers will seem purely offensive,
Whose terribly friendly fire will put you at war
With hosts of believers
And non-believers and their second cousins.
Those riding can't shoot as straight as those in hiding,
Yet if you dismount
And stand your ground, which is somebody else's ground,
You make a much more economical target,
And if you sprawl at length
Behind the barricade of your flashy charger,
Your future in your own society
May lie in a charmed circle
Of enemies where you'll need no introduction
To the last man you ever wanted to meet:
Yourself out of action.

TV Editorial

The man square in the middle of the screen
Otherwise blank is making a hard pitch
For blankness, while his eyeballs, way off-center,
Scan the idiot board, which better not
Blank out or he won't remember how to deplore
The scrawlers of graffiti. He likes blank walls.
He wants all citizens who notice delinquents
Marking up somebody else's valuable space
To call the cops. Those ignorant abusers
Of privilege should be wiped out like their names
And alien slogans and philosophies.
He's all for freedom of speech but who's to pay
For the paint to paint them out? How many hours
Do they make us waste that might be better spent
On learning a little something for a change
Instead of scribbling nonsense? *It narrows down,*
He says and narrows his eyes to a blank, transfixed,
Under-rehearsed look, *to human values.*
He disappears. The screen goes blank, then fills
With a gang of bargains slashing across prime time.

Elegy for Some of My Poems

Some were stillborn. For them, a moment of silence.

Others died so soon after birth
(Siamese triplets, microcephalic odds
Without ends, the offspring and outfall
Of incompatible species) their freakishness
Is half concealed now by their innocence.

Some died early, victims of malnutrition,
Overexposure, and gross neglect. A motherless few
Were smothered by strangers.

And two consisted wholly of parts from the graves
Of the recently dead. When brought dimly to life
By heat lightning and static electricity,
They merely jerked and shuddered a moment,
Then fell off the gurney.

Of those who lived to hear their voices break,
Some throttled themselves and died in fits of outrage,
And some drowned in a rapture of the depths
At the shallow end of the pool of Narcissus.

Several in mid-career escaped hanging
By the skin of their wits and died later
Of a lingering green-sickness. Some breathed their last
Blindfolded, up against the wall, half-shot at dawn.

Of the rest, the less said, the better,
Since they had almost nothing to say themselves.

My once dearly beloved, you are gathered together here
In the sight of your maker, under the covers
Of a common grave, in rows, now left to your own devices,
With the sure uncertain hope you may go back
To the loam of the mother of language
To be rearranged for the seeds of a better father.

DENISE LEVERTOV

AUTOBIOGRAPHICAL SKETCH (1984)

WHO ARE YOU? And how did you become what
you are?" are questions which, when I try to answer them honestly,
increase my awareness of how strong, in my case (where in others place
and community often play a dominant part), were inherited tendencies
and the influence of the cultural milieu—unsupported by a community—
of my own family. My father's Hasidic ancestry, his being steeped in Jewish and Christian scholarship and mysticism, his fervor and eloquence
as a preacher, were factors built into my cells even though I rarely paid
conscious heed to what, as a child, I mostly felt were parts of the embarrassing adult world, and which during my adolescence I rejected as restric-
tive. Similarly, my mother's Welsh intensity and lyric feeling for Nature
were not just the air I breathed but, surely, were in the body I breathed
with. Reading, at 60, the out-of-print or manuscript pages of my father's
theological writings, or the poems my mother took (shyly) to writing in
her late 70s and 80s, I see clearly how much they, though not dedicated
to the vocation of poetry, were nevertheless protopoets.

When I say the cultural atmosphere of our household was unsupported by a community I refer to the fact that my parents—he a converted Russian Jew who, after spending the First World War teaching at

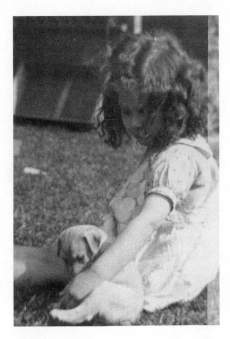

Denise, age 3, ca. 1926

the University of Leipzig (though under semi-house arrest as an "enemy alien"), settled in England and was ordained as a priest of the Anglican Church; she a Welshwoman who had grown up in a mining village and later in a North Wales country town, and subsequently traveled widely—were exotic birds in the plain English coppice of Ilford, Essex. Even though our house was semi-detached and exactly like its neighbors architecturally, it looked different because it had no half-curtains or venetian blinds like the others, only side-curtains on its large windows, so passers-by could look right in. What they could see included bookshelves in every room, while in the bay window of my father's upstairs study was an almost life-size stone statue representing Jesus preaching, which caused strangers to stare and cross the street to get a better look at it. And my mother's front garden, though more restrained than the larger back garden, was never prim like many of the others along the street but suggested a for-eign opulence, especially when the California poppies—later to delight homesick G.I.s billeted down the road—were in full orange glory.

The Levertoffs lived in Ilford because my father had been given (in the mistaken supposition that he would want to proselytize a Jewish

Denise, age 7

neighborhood) a church in Shoreditch that had no vicarage and no local congregation. Ilford, though in Essex, was then at the eastern extremity of London; its own western end was still country, though rapidly being "developed" into monotonous row upon row of small "mock-Tudor" houses I early learned to despise as jerry-built architectural monstrosities.

I didn't go to school, nor had my sister (nine years older) done so except briefly, another thing which set our household apart from others. Dissatisfied with my sister's one year at a convent boarding school during my infancy, and unimpressed by local day-schools, whether private or council, my mother (who had been teaching at a Constantinople high school run by the Church of Scotland when she met my father in 1910) taught me herself until at 12, enamored of the de Basil Russian Ballet to which my sister had taken me, I began daily classes at a school of ballet on the other side of London. At that point I was put on my honor to continue reading some history, and went also for weekly French, piano, and art lessons in London; my other formal education ceased.

Romantic and beautiful Wanstead and Valentines parks, frequent expeditions into the Essex countryside with my sister, and my mother's very strong sense of history, developed in me a taste for seeking-out and exploring the vanishing traces of the village Ilford which London had engulfed. The reading I did myself, and the reading aloud, which was a staple of our family life, combined to give me a passion for England—for the nuances of country things, hedges and old churches and the names of wildflowers—even though part of me knew I was an outsider. Among Jews a Goy, among Gentiles (secular or Christian) a Jew or at least a half-Jew (which was good or bad according to their degree of anti-Semitism); among Anglo-Saxons a Celt; in Wales a Londoner who not only did not speak Welsh but was not imbued with Welsh attitudes; among school children a strange exception whom they did not know whether to envy or mistrust: all of these anomalies predicated my later experience. I so often feel English, or perhaps European, in the United States, while in England I sometimes feel American—and certainly as a poet have been thought of for decades as an American, for it was in the United States that I developed, though my first book had been published in England before I crossed the Atlantic. But though I was quick to scornfully protest anti-Semitic remarks, or references to the Welsh language as a "dialect," these feelings of not-belonging were positive for me, not negative. I was given such a sense of confidence by my family, *in* my family, that though I was often shy (and have remained so in certain respects) I nevertheless experienced the sense of difference as an honor, as a part of knowing (secretly) from an early age—perhaps by seven, certainly before I was ten—that I was an artist-person and had a destiny. I did not experience competitiveness, because I was alone. The age gap—nine years—between me and my sister was such that my childhood was largely that of an only child. I was given a great deal of freedom to roam about outdoors as soon as I'd learned to cross streets safely; only the loneliest depths of Wanstead Park were out of bounds. The house was full of books, many of them late seventeenth- and eighteenth-century volumes. Everyone in the family did some kind of writing; my mother and sister always seemed to be helping my father correct galley proofs. My mother sang *Lieder,* my sister was a really fine pianist. The church services I attended were, despite the frequent childish embarrassment I've mentioned and my teenage doubts, beautiful with candlelight and music, incense and ceremony and stained glass, the incomparable rhythms of the King James Bible and the Book of Common Prayer.

All of this sounds idealized *ad nauseam,* I'm afraid. There were also tremendous domestic arguments and periodic full-scale "rows" and even

real tragedy (my gifted but erratic sister's life and her conflicts and rec-
onciliations with my parents were complex). But all in all I did grow up
in an extraordinarily rich environment which nurtured the imaginative,
language-oriented potential I believe was an inherited gift; and gave me—
or almost seduced me into—an appreciation of solitude. Since writing
poetry is so essentially a solitary occupation this has always stood me
in good stead and perhaps I would not have developed it if I'd gone to
school (unless I'd *hated* school, of course) for I have a sociable, gregar-
ious tendency too, that might have taken away too much time and con-
centration and necessary daydreaming. Or I might have become caught
up in aggressive competition, to the certain detriment of my creative
possibilities.

While it is true that I was not competitive because I had no peers to
compete with (my playmates, whether neighbors or kids I met in the
park, were altogether separate from my beginnings in literature), I did,
once I'd read Keats's letters, have hope of Fame; but I thought of this as
posthumous, and thus was saved from careerist ambition. And misin-
terpreting, to some extent, the gists of Mann's *Tonio Kroger,* I rather lux-
uriated in the protagonist's wistful alienation—though it was really his
friend Lisaveta Ivanovna, the painter, the artist who was getting on with
doing her art, who most excited me; especially since when I first read the
story at thirteen, I had the *chutzpa* to believe I would be a painter as well
as a poet. (I never deeply believed I would be a dancer despite the five
years of my life when I took two ballet classes a day, shedding many tears
in the process.)

Though my favorite poets were all men, I had enough faith in myself,
or more precisely enough awe at the magic I knew sometimes worked
through me, not to worry about that. Boys seemed, in fiction, to have
more adventures; but in the "pretend-games" I made up and got my sister to play with me in my later childhood, some daring young female
spies and messengers worked to combat Fascism and Nazism and to
assist the government side in the Spanish Civil War (which was then
going on). I didn't suppose my gender to be an obstacle to anything I
really wanted to do.

Humanitarian politics came into my life early—seeing my father on
a soapbox protesting Mussolini's invasion of Abyssinia; my father and
sister both on soapboxes protesting Britain's lack of support for Spain;
my mother canvassing long before those events for the League of

Denise Levertov, Colorado, late 1970s

Nations Union; and all three of them working on behalf of German and Austrian refugees from 1933 onwards. When I was eleven and twelve, unknown to my parents (who would have felt, despite their liberal views, that it was *going too far,* and was inappropriate for my age, as indeed it was), I used to sell the *Daily Worker* house-to-house in the working-class streets off Ilford Lane, down towards Barking, on Saturday mornings. Oddly enough I was never questioned, despite knee-socks and long plaits (or pigtails, as one said then) though I had many a door slammed in my face.

I've written here only about my childhood, and not at all about the rest of my life and all its experiences of people, places, events; nothing about the mind's later journeys in literature and the other arts which mean so much to me; nothing about "intellectual stance," aesthetics, philosophy, religion. But there is, after all, no mystery about all of that:

it's either in my poems or of little interest beyond the merely anecdotal. All that has taken place in my life since—all, that is, that has any bearing on my life as a poet—was in some way foreshadowed then. I am surprised to sound so deterministic, and I don't mean to suggest that the course of every life is inexorably set, genetically or by childhood experiences, for better or worse; nor that my own life had no options. Possibly I might have been a better person, and certainly a more efficient one in several respects, if I'd had a more disciplined and methodical education, more experience of economic struggle (never rich, and not extravagant, our household nevertheless never lacked for anything), and had not so early felt a sense of vocation and dedication to the art of poetry. But since I *did* have a vocation, to which some interesting genes contributed, it seems to me that I was fortunate in an upbringing favorable to their development; and this strongly affected my response to subsequent events and opportunities.

Poets owe to Poetry itself a loyalty which may at times be in conflict with the demands of domestic or other aspects of life. Out of those conflicts, sometimes, poetry itself reemerges. For example, the impulse to reconcile what one believes to be necessary to one's human integrity (such as forms of political action) with the necessities of one's inner life, including its formal, aesthetic dynamic, motivates the attempt to write engaged or "political" poetry that is truly poetry, magnetic and sensuous— the synthesis Neruda said was the most difficult of any to attain (b which our strange and difficult times cry out for). Yet sometimes ' poems one is able to write and the needs and possibilities of day to life remain separate from each other. One is in despair over the cu manifestation of malevolent imbecility and the seemingly invi power of rapacity, yet finds oneself writing a poem about the trou in the spring woods. And one has promised to speak at a mee help picket a building. If one is conscientious, the only solut attempt to weigh conflicting claims at each crucial moment, ar eral try to juggle well and keep all the oranges dancing in the a

NOTE: In 1984 Jeni Couzyn asked each of the living poets included ogy, *The Bloodaxe Book of Contemporary Women Poets,* to provide an a graphical sketch and some sort of statement about poetry.

Denise Levertov, *New & Selected Essays.* Copyright 1984 by Der reprinted by permission of New Directions Publishing Corp.

CONVERSATIONS
AND TEA WITH DENISE
Colleen J. McElroy

"*T*HERE'S A POINT*,*" she said, "there's a point where all of this begins to make sense." We were talking about woman things, Denise and I, because, as is my way, I had been complaining about how hard it was to think poetry when my personal life kept taking up my time. "Enjoy it now," she said, "but never stop writing." We had met for tea, at my house that year though we never stuck to any one place in all the years we made a date for tea. And we usually met in January, close to the new year, which may be why our conversations often turned to how we'd weathered the past year and what might lie ahead. We compared the years, the thickening waists and reluctant muscles, and how time seemed so elusive when there was so much to do. We would meet later, after she'd moved to Seattle, again in January, a rare season where snow would fall on the city the first day of the year.

"I need to leave," I said. "If it's snowing, I won't be able to get up the hill to my house, much less in the driveway."

"It's a light snow," Denise had said. And poured another cup of tea. Something English of course, brewed precisely. The aroma of tea mixed with the wet mulch scent of rain in the trees outside the kitchen window. Pine and eucalyptus and budding crocus caught by surprise.

"You learn to count the decades," she said, "not because ten years have passed but you've made leaps inside your head." I remember I kept trying to push the conversation forward, that cautious side of me envisioning my house shrouded in snow, the road to it impassable. While the romantic side lulled in the images of England during the War, the snow that fell on bomb craters, the lovers in between, the years ahead that she

Denise Levertov with Race Newton in Yorkshire, 1983. Photo by Ian McDonald

and I would still have to recall it all. "I could tell you a few things," she said. "Love and sex stay with you a long time."

Once, at a reading, when I'd brought a new love, handsome in his salmon-colored suit (no joke, he was), she'd smiled that famous Levertov smile, a little mischievous, and looking at him, asked me, "Where'd you pick this up?" But later, she told me she'd left that all behind, the need for desire, the tangle of romance. Looking at her last collection of poems, I don't think she left it all behind.

"You'll see how the years collect," she told me. She told me to remember how turning thirty had seemed so final after the endless possibilities of being twenty, where, she said, "Everything was possible and sex was absolute." I'd laughed with her, the two of us, poets recalling the foibles of our youth. But I did not miss her note of caution as she reminded me how the time between thirty and forty was more like sleepwalking. "No," I had admitted, "I can't really recall being thirty except that was when I started writing poetry. That time seemed enchanted." "And forty," she asked. I stalled. She described how time begins to play tricks, how, in your forties, your body seems more urgent and more unpredictable.

Denise Levertov, Maine, early to mid-1960s

"Then surprise, you're fifty," she said. "I'd had a party," I told her. She said that she'd just let it slide by of its own accord, a hard ten years to follow. But between fifty and sixty, those same ten years are more like twelve to fifteen, she told me. While the body accelerates, using up its energy and resilience at a faster pace, the mind seems to regenerate. We know more, we think, but we have less time to use it. Then there's sixty to seventy, and the ten years are more like fifteen or twenty. "The body ages faster than the brain," she said, "and after seventy, you stop calculating time in the same way. It finally makes sense that what you are is not just the physical self."

We greeted the next year in a tea shop. I wondered, for a fleeting moment, if she avoided my house because I never really learned the art of brewing tea, English style. But there was much to be said about meeting somewhere else, in the peacefulness of a place among a thousand aromas of spiced tea and green tea, of full leaf and split leaf, of peppermint and Chinese Pu Erh, and watching her eyes brighten to the possibility of a new blend. I believe that was the year we talked about my travels, all the stories I'd told her of places I'd visited. "Get out and see everything," she said, "the whole world. Then write about it. None of it makes sense unless you write about it. And you have such wonderful stories." I'd protested. Who was I to have wonderful stories to tell to a poet who'd seen more than I'd ever seen, who'd taken more risks than I would ever take? Still I promised I'd write them down, those stories, knowing my promise was more vague than real.

Denise never forgot. Each year after that, she'd ask how the writing was going. "I've been thinking about it," I told her. "I'll get around to it in time." She'd laughed. "Make the most of these days," she said, "and take notes on everything. The way the mountains turn pale at sunset, the insistence of flowers blooming in winter." It sounded so concise, so terse in that Levertov way she had of speaking. But I took her advice and scratched out bits of conversations I remembered, hers included.

Another year. We met at her house, the season closer to spring. We sat in the garden. Nikolai joined us. We talked about old friends and familiar places. She talked of aging. Twelve years separated us by age, not much in my estimation, but she insisted it was more distance than I could imagine. That year she talked about the delights of living in the Northwest, the mountains and water, the sunsets that make you feel closer to God. I remember a small flock of geese passing overhead. I told her that when I'd first moved here, I'd seen larger numbers of birds. "But the smell never changes," I told her. "The smell of rain."

I would not join her for tea again for over two years. This time, my travel memoirs had been published, the first line of dedication addressed to her. This time, poets were dying and husbands, and the light in her living room was dim even with a fire in the grate and the lamps turned on. She gave me photos of herself for the *Seattle Review* retrospective. I told her that one pose reminded me of the movie star, Greer Garson. She said, "I don't think so. There's too little to remind us of anyone." This time, for once, she was wrong. There was too much to allow me to forget.

Feet

I

In the forties, wartime London, I read
an ode by Neruda I've never found again,
about celery—celery the peasant, trudging
stony Andean ridges to market on poor
frayed feet.
        I could search out the *Obras Completas*
I know . . . But even if I never find it again,
those green fibrous feet, upholding
the tall stooped form with its flimsy cockscomb
of yellowing leaves, plodded
through me as if through the thin
mountain air, maintaining
their steady, painful, necessitous trudge, and left
their prints in my dust.

I I

Travestied by Disney, the Mermaid's real story
has gone underground for now, as books do
if they're abused. As Andersen told it, the tale
was not for young children, not even called
"The Little"—just, "The Mermaid." It's about love and grief,
a myth of longing and sacrifice, far closer, say,
to Goethe's *Parable* than to any jovial folktale,
much less to today's manufactured juvenile distractions.

The Mer-folk live for three hundred years, then dissolve
in foam of the wave, and forever vanish
into non-being; humans, the mermaid learns, rarely live
for even one hundred years, often far fewer, but they possess
immortal souls, and rise to continue living
in starlit regions merfolk can never see.
        In her resolve to love and be loved

by the human prince she had rescued once
from storm and shipwreck, and gain for herself
such a soul, the mermaid goes to the terrible
ocean witch, and obtains a potion to turn her golden-scaled
fish-tail into legs and feet—
and gives up her voice in payment. She does this
knowing each gliding, graceful step she will take
will bring her the pain of walking on knives.
She does this for love, and the dream
of human joys and a deathless soul.
                                There's more,
much more to the story—even a kind of
happy ending, after the final sacrifice, a concession
Andersen made to his time and place. But what endures
along with the evocation of undersea gardens,
of moonlight, of icebergs and coral, and of that same yearning
we find in the Silkie tales and in *The Forsaken Merman*,
are the knifeblades under her feet, unguessed-at
by any who see her glide and dance; and the torment
of having no tongue to speak her love, to speak
her longing to earn a soul.
                            Something in this
made my mother shed tears when she read it aloud,
her voice for a moment baffled—
and this when her closet was still full of elegant shoes
with the pointed toes of fashion. Did she foresee (and forget
till the next reading) the misery
old age and poor circulation and years of those narrow shoes
would bring her? Certainly she had no doubt
of her own soul; no, what hurt her
was the mermaid's feet. Her agony without complaint,
her great love, courage, unfathomed sorrow,
would not have equally moved my mother
without that focused sense of each step the mermaid took
being unbearable, yet borne, the firm support
we count on torn away, invisibly shredded.

III

I watched a man whose feet were neatly wrapped in green plastic enter
the restaurant that advertised a $2.00 special. Sloppy Joes. And I saw
him immediately come out again. It was cold and wet, and I was sheltering under the canvas awning till my bus was due. He stood there too,
and I could sense that he was fuming. "What happened?" I ventured.
He looked at me. Good eye, I thought. "No shoes," he said.

I know the rule, "no shoes, no service" is supposed to be in the interests of hygiene, but I've never understood how. Whatever dirt and germs
bare feet bring in, shoes bring too. Why anyone would want to walk barefoot on filthy sidewalks is another mystery—but that's a matter of personal choice. In this instance the man was, in any case, not barefoot:
several layers of heavy-duty green garbage-bag plastic hid his feet and
were tied firmly at the ankles. The arrangement made me think of Russian serfs, birchbark shoes . . .

"I've got the money," he said, and showed it me in his hand—
two bucks, and a few pennies for the tax. How *unfair!* He fumed, I fumed,
the rain poured off the awning, a steady curtain. He looked quite young,
under forty. Did I say he was Black? He hadn't the look of a drunk or a
druggy; looked a bit young for a Vietnam vet. When I offered to go in
and protest to the manager he didn't like the idea, and I saw he would
feel it a humiliation. I shouldn't have suggested that.

"What happened to your shoes—did they fall apart?" I asked shyly. "A
guy stole them in the night." I acknowledged, silently, the naiveté of my
own shock at this robbery of one destitute man by another. He could
get some second-hand shoes at Goodwill or the Salvation Army, he told
me, but he was hungry, had wanted to eat before the long walk to the
missions. I guessed he had spent the night under the freeway. This street
where we stood, near the college, was mostly upscale—this "luncheon
special" at a place which referred to itself as an "Eatery," was the only
thing of its kind. I thought with disgust of Sloppy Joes, trying to imagine being hungry enough to want one.

I offered him the price of a pair of the cheapest shoes you could buy;
I'd noticed them in the window of an Outlet store. He accepted with dignity. When I found myself wondering if in fact he would spend the money on shoes, I realized he might do better with good hand-me-downs than cheap new ones. By then the rain let up and we went our ways.

If affluent Whites took it into their heads to wrap their feet in plastic, a new fashion, how long would the "eateries" exclude them?

IV

Still in her 80s when she first lived there,
    she loved
        to tramp over the *cerro* above the town;
it reminded her.
    of Wales and the freedom
        of long girlhood walks in all weathers.
Here as there, the hills and mountains,
    —layer beyond layer,
        ranged themselves like advancing breakers,
though they broke on no shore;
    cloud-shadows stroked them, brightness
        flowed in again as the shadows
moved on. But in time
    her strength failed her.
        She walked only down to the town's
mercado to buy the fruit she craved,
    and exchange a word or two
        with the market women,
the vendors of juice or trinkets, and give her letters
    into the hands of sourfaced
        post-office clerks. In the *zocalo*
she could watch with pleasure the playing children
    or with amusement
        the foolish antics of tourists. Everywhere
the familiar faces of strangers.
    Then, climbing back up the hilly streets,
        ill-paved, high-kerbed, often,

by her mid-80s, she needed to pause,
    to stop and rest in a cool dark church.
            Once, and more than once, perhaps,
her feet pained her so much that weakness
    overcame her,
            she sat there crying,
desolate in the need to rise and walk on,
    four or five blocks to her room,
            her bed, her books, her patio—
accidental pilgrim
    in a strange land.
            When, my next visit,
I'd found her slippers padded and soft
    yet sturdy enough for the *calle*
            you'd think I'd brought her the moon and stars. . . .
We begin our lives with such small,
    such plump and perfect
            infant feet, slivers of pink pearl for toenails,
it's laughable to think of their ever sustaining
    the whole weight of a body.
            And end them sometimes
with gnarled and twisted objects
    in which are inscribed
            whole histories—wars, and uprootings,
and long
    patient or impatient sufferings,
            layer beyond layer,
successions of light and shadow, whole ranges.
    But no recollection
            of what our feet were like
before we put them to work.

V

Certain phrases recur—not main motifs but occasional
mini-cadenzas on flute, curling
brief as foam above stir and onrush of waves.
'Beautiful are the feet of the swallow
folded unseen past the mountain'—
or, 'Blesséd are the feet
of him who brings good tidings.'

Beautiful, too, one's own feet if they've stayed
more or less straight and strong through decades,
and one walks for miles by the sea or through fields and woods
or spends a joyful day in a great museum, arriving
at opening time, staying till closing, grateful to be so upheld.

Yet what prevails is harsh. The mermaid's knives.
My mother's tears. Or the shame
an aging poet felt when, bulky in body, diabetic,
she had to call upon someone to cut her toenails, and not just anyone,
someone (small and deft) in whose country we were guests,
a country our own was bombing, defoliating, attempting,
with all its mechanical power,
                                                    to obliterate.
With exacting care the Vietnamese nurse performed the procedure,
a doctor checked to see all was as close to well as possible,
and Muriel obediently stretched out her long thin legs, submitting,
grateful but deeply embarrassed: these ministrations
were given by those accustomed to dress the wounds
of footless or armless children,
of peasants whose hands were gone. Her feet
felt better, her soul was mortified.

And still those brief cadenzas
recur—'Blesséd are the feet
of him who brings good tidings,'—'Beautiful
are the feet of the swallow
folded unseen past the mountain.'

VI

Maundy Thursday. As prearranged, twelve chairs
are placed in a row before the altar, and twelve parishioners
seat themselves, and take off their shoes and clean socks.
As the old priest and the young one bend to their task,
one stiff, one supple, and carry the shining bowls of fresh warm water
to each presented pair of prewashed feet,
and wash them again and dry them on white, white towels,
the humble ritual, so ancient, so much an act of the body,
a sanctification of flesh (even though, at times,
proud prelates and small bigoted men have been the enactors)
stirs the heart, as true theater must, even in an age
with so loose or lost a connection to symbolic power.

But this is a good time to reflect on how dusty,
scarred by worn sandals, dirty between the toes, grime
on the calloused soles, the apostles' feet would have been.
And mine moves on to worse: old winos stumbling along,
unwashed their long nails thick as horn, shoes wrong-sized, broken.
And not just winos—anyone homeless, who has to keep moving
    all day
with no place to go, even if shelter at night
gives them a chance to bathe their blisters, must know
week by week an accretion of weariness, once-good shoes
grown thin; must know a mounting sense of frayed and helpless
fiber at the ends of swollen legs, although they have never imagined
the endless foot-after-foot journey of peasant celery.

SONIA SANCHEZ

A RETROSPECTIVE MOVEMENT AND THE WRITER'S LIFE: AN INTERVIEW

Lauri Conner

*T*HE FIRST TIME I met Sonia Sanchez I was a senior in college trying to find my own voice as a poet. She had just given the opening address for the Big Eight Black Student Government conference and upon returning to her hotel room, snuggled under the covers and prepared herself for an interview for the school's literary supplement. I remember I had asked about her experiences in school and she began her story by telling us both never to let anyone make us not want to write. Five years later, I am beginning to understand the weight of her statement.

Connecting with Sanchez by phone is difficult. Between her family, classes, chairing a department, readings, lectures, and writing, spare time is rare. What has always amazed me most about Sanchez is that she is always moving. "You do know that if you stop, you're dead," she says in a playful seriousness. "Motion is life. That what you have to do at some particular point is understand that from the moment of birth, we move towards death." She assured me that this movement towards death was not a negative movement as long as I understood that between those two defining moments can be some very illuminating and joyful moments that can have a great impact. She explained this movement

School days, 1943–44

in terms of aging, constructing and often reconstructing one's life. "There are certain things that you did when you were ten and when you got to twenty you didn't do those things again; there were things you did when you were twenty that at thirty you understood the nonnecessity of doing them." It is with this type of knowledge and growth that Sanchez has shaped her life.

Born in 1934 in Birmingham, Alabama, Sanchez is the author of more than fourteen books and five plays and the editor of two anthologies and several children's books. Her many accomplishments are a testament to her writing life. Recipient of numerous awards, including the Lucretia Mott Award, 1985 American Book Award, Governor's Award for Excellence in the Humanities, National Endowment of the Arts Award, a Pew Fellowship in the Arts and most recently, nominated for the National Book Critics Circle Award for *Does Your House Have Lions*. Poet. Mother, Activist. Professor. Each of the many hats she wears deserves their own punctuation.

In collections like *homegirls & handgrenades* (Thunder Mouth Press, 1984), *Under a Soprano Sky* (African World Press, 1987), and *I've Been*

Sonia Sanchez and Geraldine Driver

a Woman (Third World Press, 1978), which includes a retrospective of earlier works from *Homecoming* and *We a Baddddd People,* Sanchez maintains her resistance to stasis. In "Poem at Thirty," Sanchez writes:

it is midnight
no magical bewitching
hour for me
i know only that
i am here waiting
remembering that
once as a child
i walked two
miles in my sleep,
did I know

then where I
was going?
traveling. i'm
always traveling . . .
  (*I've Been A Woman,* 4)

It is this knowledge of movement that has shaped Sonia Sanchez's life. In discussing the idea of movement we began speaking about her last two books, *Does Your House Have Lions,* and *Wounded in the House of a Friend.* She told me how her first book, *Homecoming,* was only one of many books that came out with that title or with references to "home" in the title. Recalling a conversation with Ngugi wa Thiong'o, who also had a book titled *Homecoming,* she discussed how it was that as Africans or African Americans, that they finally realized that in order to begin writing truth, they had to first go home. "That's what we had to do," she said somberly, "that's how we had to deal." Sanchez's writing is informed by this dealing as well as the indefinite cycle of life shaping writing shaping life.

Often having to create her writing time, Sanchez has breathed life into language by using simple language to express large ideas. In using the term simple, I am implying that Sanchez writes and stakes claims in language and all its vernacularisms to dispatch complicated and sometimes difficult messages.

I write to offer a Black woman's view of the world. How I tell the truth is a part of the truth itself. I've always believed that the truth concealed or clouded is a partial lie. So when I decide to tell the truth about an event/happening, it must be clear and understandable for those who need to understand the lie/lies being told. (*Black Women Writers,* 416)

As we began discussing the importance of truth, we began talking about demanding singularity from ourselves and the importance of not letting anyone pour you into a box. Sanchez is always surprised when people approach her in amazement about how different one book is from another. "It makes no sense at all," she says of the amazement, "to be startled by that kind of difference." It is with this sensibility that Sanchez has moved through literature being the voice of many while spreading the truth of one.

"Universality?" I asked.

"All poets are universal poets." She said with amusement, "I can read Keats. I can read Neruda. I can read Shakespeare. I can read Rich. I can

Posing in Gimbel's, New York, 1950s

read anybody, and the poem moves beyond the page." She described how she could clearly write a poem from the Black perspective, the African perspective, but by the time she puts in on the page and gives it to the world, it goes beyond the page. "It loses the whole idea that this is just the Black stuff. It becomes a universal poem. It is the poem about love as opposed to a poem about a Black woman who wrote about love." She explained how the readers are claiming what they recognize in themselves that was opened up by the author's specificity. Universal.

As one of the leaders in the Black Arts Movement, Sanchez also resists being a prisoner of people's conditions.

People always want to place you in a box. People box you into a period or into a certain kind of writing. And the joy for me about writing is that you are independent. When you're an independent thinker and writer you can't get boxed in. No, some of us can't be boxed into the Black Arts Movements although they try to do that. Can't be boxed in for being a woman poet or a Southern poet or an urban poet. But when people do that I smile. I say: Okay, fine. But you go on and do what you have to do.

It seems that Sanchez has constantly surrounded herself with a supportive group of writers, from Imamu Amiri Baraka (LeRoi Jones), Nikki

Giovanni, and Haki Madhubuti (Don Lee) to Audre Lorde and Toni Cade Bambara. In realizing the company she has kept, and continues to keep, I wondered about the younger writers. Mostly I have noticed that she is open to spending time and helping a new generation of writers outside of formal programs. She has performed on D Knowledge's CD *All That and a Bag of Words,* written a review used for the back jacket of Kevin Powell's book *Recognize,* and helped Open Minds, a Seattle-based reading series for African American Poets, celebrate an anniversary. She explained that she doesn't expect anything from young writers except for us to take the time with writers who will follow: "I expect you to give something to the people coming behind you. That's the whole point of this."

As someone she has kept in communication with, I know too well this expectation; I have watched her speak to junior high, high school, and college students and what impresses me most is her distinctive manner in which she speaks to all levels. She mentioned a recent encounter with junior high and high school students who were sitting in their chairs waiting for her to prove herself for them. She abandoned her speech and began with a poem dedicated to Tupac Amaru Shakur: "I took it to where they lived. Always doing it with love and a sense of respect while telling them how bright they are; how beautiful they are." Ultimately, Sanchez lets youth know that although they are programmed for destruction, they have the ability and the skills to break those kinds of societal molds. What she expects the next generation of writers and teachers to do is let those that follow know that they cannot let anyone destroy them in the classroom. "We have to get these kids out of an arena of death." We talked about how we need these kids alive: "Our ancestors didn't make that middle passage, come here and go through slavery to have you end up in a place with no windows, no air, no light, no human touch; back into a middle passage. A modern-day Middle Passage." There's no power in an arena of death.

While discussing the Middle Passage, I began wondering about inheritance. How it is we claim those things that aren't necessarily ours. Sanchez mentioned how as a people we have always passed information on. Our great grandmother's stories were told to the grandparents told to the aunts and uncles who told it to us. "We are always passing on information about ourselves," she said, "and those pieces of information were passed on as a road map to how you get to where you get to." It was in this statement that we returned to the next generation of writers: "You see, what I do indeed pass on to the younger poets is their heritage, that they must pass on to the next generation." This kind of passing of information is what Sanchez actively does in *Does Your House Have Lions*. A book done in rhyme royal, it is a conversation between sister, brother, father, and ancestors. A pure navigation through inheritance, one voice could not have dominated the pages. The stories had to be set down next to each other so that a dialog could occur: "I realized that I truly didn't understand my brother's life until I allowed him to talk. And so my brother then brought his inheritance." The dialog continues with the father's voice in the third section: "I never truly understood my father, I realize, until he said in his own voice, 'I was a southern Negro man.' Think of those words. Think of the inheritance of a southern Negro man living and all the restrictions." In this conversation and discussion of inheritance she reminded me that forgiveness is a part of all of our inheritance. "It is never too late for forgiveness," she says, "never too late."

The form in which Sonia Sanchez writes *Does Your House Have Lions* stems from her knowledge of forms, first introduced to her by Louise Bogan at New York University. "I am a poet who has from the very beginning written in free verse, but there have been times in my life when I have retreated to form" (Finch, 195). Because of her understanding of the "rules," Sanchez has broken them in her free verse, where her poems, often echoing the sound of African drums and ancestral incantations, have come alive on the page and in the ear. She has expanded on many forms, sometimes creating her own forms as in the sonku: "When I have had to deal with formal pain, I have written in the sonnet. When I have thought I had very little time to put some of my thoughts on paper, I've retreated to haiku and tanka and felt a world of form that allowed me to live and breathe out my pain and joy" (Finch, 195). In "Sonku," from *Wounded in the House of a Friend* (89), we can see where the activity of creation occurs for Sanchez:

> have mercy on the
> woman who can't hold
> her breath cuz the man's

Morani Sanchez, Sonia, and Mungu Sanchez,
New York. Photo by Merrill A. Roberts Jr.

> gon take her for a
> long ride to the deep.

"Form makes you understand that you are responsible for the words you write. I don't feel concerned about any political implications of form. I'm a poet, and the form is not going to form me" (quoted in Finch, 197). Five years ago, this is what she meant: Learn the rules. Break them when you know them. Write what you want and tell the truth as you see it. Give back. Resist the boxes that people will want to pour you into without resisting the desire to write. I was too young then to understand that a writer's life isn't made, it is shaped by the life that is led, and that life is shaped by the choices you make as a writer. It is always about progression, movement, and truth.

As a mother, teacher, writer, and friend, Sanchez's work is never done, but it has been constant. The routine of movement is what keeps each

Sonia Sanchez with Toni Morrison

Sanchez with her father, Wilson L. Driver

role balanced for her. In *Black Women Writers (1950–1980): A Critical Evaluation,* Sanchez writes:

. . . I'll tell you how I get things done.

I must work a full-time job. Take care of a house and family. Referee or umpire at Little League games. Travel. Carry books when I travel. Work some more. Deal with illnesses and injuries. Help build the political organs within the Black community. Work on the car. Run for trains and planes. Find or create breaks. Then, late at night, just before the routine begins again, I write. I write and I smile as the words come drifting back like some reverent lover. I write columns for newspapers, poems, plays and stories in those few choice hours before I sleep.

And they say leisure is the basis of culture. (417–18)

The only change in that routine seems to be based on her sons being past the age of Little League. With a new book of poems titled *Like Singing Coming Off the Drums,* her plate is definitely full.

The movement that is created, both in her writing and her life, is based on continuity. Both continue to move, to progress, to dialog with her readers and herself. It is no surprise that she has chronicled her movement through her work. In "Prelude to Nothing" she begins:

I am trying to drain my mind
of all secretions only then
will I be able to remember
just what it was I said and did.
that made you paint your face
until it disappeared
in pale blue noise.
I acknowledge the diseases
of the brain; adolescence,
uncaring minds carrying too
many unexplored hills to hum.
forgetfulness. sadistic brains
that genuflect then chant
no hailmarysfullofgrace
the world is too much with us . . .
    (*I've Been A Woman,* 35)

It is here, in this prelude, this acknowledging of the self and the out-side world that shapes the life and writing of Sonia Sanchez. In the course of our interview she let the electrician in, paid him, made tea, waited for her graduate assistant, made plans for the movies, answered the door (twice) and didn't skip a beat in our conversation. "Negotiating the world," she laughed and we joked that life doesn't stop.

I began to understand the importance of our initial conversation days before the interview, when she asked me if I was writing.

"Yes," I replied.

"Are you teaching?" she asked.

"Yes," I replied. "I don't think I was prepared for the amount of energy that it takes. But I'm enjoying it now. Very much."

"It does take a lot out of you. Especially if you are doing other things. . . ." There was a small pause between those words and her strong, mellifluous voice.

"Welcome Sister. Welcome."

This was classic Sanchez.

WORKS CITED

Evans, Mari, ed. *Black Women Writers (1950–1980): A Critical Evaluation*. New York, NY: Anchor Books, 1984.

Finch, Annie, ed. *A Formal Feeling Comes: Poems in Form by Contemporary Women*. Brownsville, OR: Story Line Press, 1994.

Sanchez, Sonia. Personal interview. January 17, 1998.

———. *I've Been a Woman: New and Selected Poems*. Chicago, IL: Third World Press, 1978.

———. *Wounded in the House of a Friend*. Boston, MA: Beacon Press, 1965.

Sister's Voice

this was a migration unlike
the 1900s of black men and women
coming north for jobs. freedom. life.
this was a migration to begin
to bend a father's heart again
to birth seduction from the past
to repay desertion at last.

imagine him short and black
thin mustache draping thin lips
imagine him country and exact
thin body, underfed hips
watching at this corral of battleships
and bastards, watching for forget
and remember, dancing his pirouette.

and he came my brother at seventeen
recruited by birthright and smell
grabbing the city by the root with clean
metallic teeth. commandant and infidel
pirating his family in their cell
and we waited for the anger to retreat
and we watched him embrace the city and the street.

first he auctioned off his legs. eyes.
heart. in rooms of specific pain.
he specialized in generalize
learned newyorkese and all profane.
enslaved his body to cocaine
denied his father's signature
damned his sister's overture.

and a new geography greeted him.
the atlantic drifted from offshore
to lick his wounds to give him slim
transfusion as he turned changed wore
a new waistcoat of solicitor
antidote to his southern skin
ammunition for a young paladin.

and the bars. the glitter. the light
discharging pain from his bygone anguish
of young black boy scared of the night.
sequestered on this new bank, he surveyed the fish
sweet cargoes crowded with scales feverish
with quick sales full sails of flesh
searing the coastline of his acquiesce.

and the days rummaging his eyes
and the nights flickering through a slit
of narrow bars. hips. thighs.
and his thoughts labeling him misfit
as he prowled, pranced in the starlit
city, coloring his days and nights
with gluttony and praise and unreconciled rites.

Brother's Voice

there is nothing i do not comprehend
i have become a collector of shouts
hold my ears father, i have come to mend
our hearts raise a glass celebrate root out
lyrical slaughters become your only son devout
i have become a lover of sweet water
i worship stone i will not betray you father.

Father's Voice

steady your hand old man do not trouble
yourself with language, stalk his wound
he is listening to your corpuscles cradle
the clap and thunder of a new sound
he has called your name and old teeth are found
can you hold me son, as i rise from this whimper
can you hear me son, as i cross over this river.

i am preparing for his coming, i sit on my flesh
i am wealthy my limbs free of moths
i am in praise of convalesce
i will stand free of the walking sabbaths
i will return sermons crowded with cloths
i am learning how to talk to my son's dust
i have tossed my net toward a future trust.

Dancing

i dreamt i was tangoing with
you, you held me so close
we were like the singing coming off the drums.
you made me squeeze muscles
lean back on the sound
of corpuscles sliding in blood.
i heard my thighs singing.

From *Like the Singing Coming Off the Drums*

Haiku

i have caught fire from
your mouth now you want me to
swallow the ocean.

Haiku

FOR YOU

love between us is
speech and breath, loving you is
a long river running.

Haiku

i turn westward in
shadows hoping my river
will cross yours in passing.

Sonku

i collect
wings what are
you bird or
animal?
something that
lights on trees
breasts pawnshops
i have seen
another
path to this
rendezvous.

Blues Haiku

am i yo philly
outpost? man when you sail in
to my house, you docked.

Haiku

my womb is a dance
of leaves sweating swift winds
i laugh with guitars.

Sonku

FOR NNEKA AND QUINCY

love comes with
bone and sea
eyes and rivers
hand of man
tongue of
woman love
trembles at
the edge of
my fingers.

NELSON BENTLEY

A BIOGRAPHICAL SKETCH

Sean Bentley

*I*HAD WHAT I gather was an unusual childhood. All the while I was growing up, both my father Nelson and mother Beth read, wrote, and taught poetry. From birth I was steeped in poetry—I was read Milton in my crib, for example. My father insisted that my first words were, "Of Man's first disobedience . . ." I loved to identify the photos of the authors on the Oscar Williams anthologies, and knew Yeats and Auden by sight as some kids know sports stars (I still can't tell one sports personality from another).

Approximately forty-eight weeks of the year my father taught days and nights, hosted TV and radio poetry shows—on which I often appeared, thinking nothing of this media exposure, hosted student and professional readings at the library, bookstores, and the university, handled correspondence courses, edited *Poetry Seattle* and *Seattle Review,* and juried poetry contests for everything from the Pacific Northwest Writers' Conference to Mother's Cookies. He couldn't say no. Well, he said no to Mother's Cookies the second time around. In what few off hours were left he wound down after class in coffee houses and pizza joints with adoring students.

Every quarter Nelson would show the film made about Theodore

Nelson, age 12, ca. 1930

Roethke just prior to his death, "In a Dark Time." Ten years down the road, students who hadn't known the man had only those few minutes to absorb his voice, his gestures—otherwise they were forced to rely on his highly stylized poetry, or on others' reminiscences, which admittedly were fairly colorful. This poem is about that film.

After Screening "In a Dark Time"

FOR NELSON BENTLEY

SEAN BENTLEY

Your friend's been telescoped; how often have you
studied the icons, his simple conducting arms,
the stifled waltz abstract before his hearth?

Soon we all will only know the same
gestures, inflections, dogmatic as propaganda:
this emblem, this inspected idol, Roethke.

This single token of ten years might remind you
of the dig, Makah fragments sluiced from mud;
their old day lost its shackle. With the joy

of detectives, poets Linda and Greg scoured
at Greg's own tribal past. And now a workshop
of poets puzzles together a shard of life

celluloid's preserved, no less thoroughly.
His character's the intrigue: maddening as half
a potlatch bowl. We can only come to know

the artifact, try to decipher what runes we see,
make bright the essence of your obscured friend.

Most people might not apprehend from the film Roethke's fairly frequent
journeys off the deep end—I recall at least one episode when during a
party at our house, my mother brought our mantel clock down the hall
to my bedroom, wrapped it thoroughly in one of my sweaters, and buried
it at the bottom of my toybox. The ticking was getting to Ted.

Now, seven years after my father's death, the situation is much the
same—although no film was made of Nelson (and he was happy with
that, thinking that both Roethke and poet Vernon Watkins had been
jinxed; Watkins survived only a short time after "Under a Bright Heaven"
was filmed). Students can hear about him from the old fogies like me
who were in his workshop, and they can read his work, which although
intensely, encyclopedically autobiographical, is still only a partial picture
of the man. Take for example, an early poem, "Zero Tide."

You see for all his civic and academic activity, he still was compelled
to take a brief vacation every year, between summer and fall quarters.
The family usually demanded it, even if he wanted to keep on teaching.
This is when he typically allowed himself to get sick. He never took a
sabbatical but taught for about 140 consecutive quarters. We often went

Nelson and his mother, Jessie Bentley

to the ocean. Even here—perhaps especially here—poetry remained foremost in his mind.

Zero Tide

I walked from our cabin into the wet dawn
To see the white caps modulating in,
The slow wash of the word in the beginning:
Wind on the bowing sedge seemed from Japan.
A cloud of sandpipers wavered above the dune,
Where surf spoke the permanence of sun.
Back inside, I sat on my son's bed
Where he sweetly slept, guarded by saints and poets,
Oceanic sunrise on his eyelids;
I whispered "Sean, get up! Its a clamming tide,"

Nelson Bentley with son, Sean, at the KCTS studio
in Seattle, 1958

And thought of chill sand fresh from lowering waters,
Foam-bubbled frets across the hard-packed ridges.
"Sean, it's zero tide!" From a still second,
He came out of the covers like a hummingbird.
"Don't wake up Julian." In the ale blue light
He dressed in whirring silence, all intent.
Along the empty coast the combers hummed:
Sleepy gulls mewled in the clearing mist.
My wife and baby slept folded in singing calm,
Involuted by love as rose or shell.

   Now, what's missing from this poem, what the reader, seeking to know
the real Nelson Bentley, can't know from this piece—is that it was I who

was doing all the actual dirty work. While I lay in the clammy sand, up to my armpit in pursuit of a razor clam, its slippery foot-tip in my fingers, shouting for assistance with increasing irritation, my father stood fifty feet away lost in the fog of his coalescing pentameter. He sort of came to, and sauntered over looking perplexed and distracted while the wily bivalve struggled from my grasp. I did manage to catch enough clams for chowder however, and he got his poem.

Poetry was his life, at times eclipsing reality. This was of enormous benefit to his students—his virtual and ever extending family. His living championing of the art—inspirational, passionate, evangelical, even obsessional—this is what cannot be recaptured by mere anecdote or the reading of his work. Above all he maintained a rather elfish humor, rooted in the comics of the Depression, W. C. Fields being the prime example. Nelson once said that "'The Dong with a Luminous Nose' is probably the single masterpiece of the Victorian era." He disliked the strident, the didactic, the Republican. "One of the great unwritten laws of Northwest poetry," he said, "is not to take yourself too pompously." He also typified the Northwest school as "seething with slugs" and possessing a sense of "humorous gloom." "Avoid self-pity like the plague," he would say. "Punctuation is an emotional thing." "Someday nothing will be left but poems."

There was always a visiting poet at the English Department, and with the death of Roethke, my father inherited the role of host to them. On one memorable occasion, my father had to pick up Allen Ginsberg, Lawrence Ferlinghetti, Gregory Corso, and another Beat poet at the bus station to go to a reading. My sister Julian and I came along for some reason, plus we picked up our babysitter en route. We were all crammed into Nurse Jane Fuzzy Wuzzy, a 1955 Chevy. The babysitter got to sit on Ferlinghetti's lap.

When I was fifteen, in 1969, I asked one day, out of sheer curiosity, if I could visit one of his night poetry workshops. I didn't leave it for ten years. I, like he, virtually never missed a night in all that time, including attending the Castalia readings that eventually ran three times a week. I took the poetry class for the maximum possible eight quarters. Once you had taken it for credit—even for a single quarter—you were granted a lifetime pass, and hordes of poets, myself among them, used their pass

Nelson Bentley lecturing at the University
of Washington, early 1960s

freely. By the time I was eighteen, my self-consciousness, my sense of
nepotism, not to say paranoia, had fully kicked in and I assumed a series
of anagrammatic pen-names, such as Betsy Nealen and Nasty Neeble,
finally settling on Lenny E. Beast. At least half of the students in any
given class had little or no idea who I was. The ironic thing was, that
the criticism or lack thereof that I got from my father was, as far as I
could tell, exactly the same as his other students got. He was not a harsh
critic. Exacting, yes, but always positive and encouraging.

He emphasized "The Joy of Revising." Even in the most flabby, trite,
dull poem he would point out the best line, the most striking image, a
fine detail, a felicitous word. The worst writer in the class was treated
as nurturingly as the best. And his philosophy was that nearly anyone
could be—ought to be, even—a poet, as long as they were devoted to it,
that they read poetry, carried it with them at all times, and practiced reading as well as writing it. He would take on students sometimes not

Nelson Bentley, on the University of Washington campus,
1954–55

because of their portfolio, if they even had one, but because their names
sounded promisingly poetic. Argentina Daley. Jennyjoy LaBelle. Dym-
phna Flavin. Melville Flournoy. Or for the size of their nose, whose names
I won't mention.

In any class of large size, there is a panoply of eccentric and colorful
characters, but in an ongoing class, that contains literally thousands of
students, the spectacle is staggering. Nelson's poetry workshop—not to
mention the myriad correspondence and survey courses he taught—had,
over a third of a century, an epic—nay, apocalyptic—cast of characters
on the order of a particularly fevered Cecil B. DeMille production. Most

players had walk-ons of a single quarter, but others held major supporting roles. Some lingered on the periphery, reappearing a bit more griz-
zled every few years like the characters in "Gasoline Alley," and eventually
bringing with them their babies, their teenagers. And many have gone
on to teach their own classes in colleges and high schools around the
country. Thousands of his students publish widely in magazines, bringing out book upon book of poetry—or even in at least one case, hard-
boiled detective fiction.

They remember Nelson, dedicate their books to him. He stays with
them, almost supernaturally. His influence continues to be felt in the
school of Northwest poetry and reaches into other regions of the States
as his students peregrinate far and wide spreading his spirit, his not
entirely whimsical, apocalyptic words: "Visualize your metaphors."
"Support onomatopoeia." "Someday nothing will be left but poems."

How Gloom was Driven Away
by Rachmaninoff and Mrs. McGillicuddy

As most of my friends know, I've seldom gone a day
Without rejoicing, since crawling from the cradle;
But there was a time I had some gloomy student hours.
The night that seems to have been a kind of crisis
Occurred in Amelia McGillicuddy's rooming house.
She was an astrologist chiropractor,
Six feet tall. I couldn't decide which she
Resembled most, Victor McLaglen or the Wicked
Witch of the Land of Oz. That afternoon,
I was loaned Rachmaninoff's Second Piano Concerto,

By a melancholy Chinese pianist who carried
A volume of Schopenhauer at all times
And looked like Beethoven during the last quartets.
I spent an hour reading Housman, Robinson,
And Ecclesiastes, smoking a King George
Cigar, then put Rachmaninoff on my old player.
Since cautioned by Auden, I'd avoided self-pity
Like the plague, and agreed with a Brazilian friend
Who put my *Rubaiyat* face down on a platter
Of whipped cream. Still, I rather glumly puffed

On the King George and watched the yellowing maples
Along Monroe Street, imagining Frost trudging
There twenty years before. I thought of all
The romantic poets since Coleridge, brooding
On their losses, and even thought of opening
Robinson Jeffers. Rachmaninoff, wallowing
In misery, had plunged into the Second Movement,
When I heard Amelia McGillicuddy
Tramping slowly up the stairs. "Nelson," she said
In a gravelly voice, the texture of Wallace Beery's,
"I hear you're under the weather." "No, I'm fine,
Mrs. McGillicuddy." "Nonsense, you need

Some tuning up," she declared, seized my shoulder
Like King Kong grasping the Empire State Building,
And began an incredibly rapid thumping and pounding
On both sides of my backbone. I got a flash
Of Rachmaninoff when he came on stage at Hill
Auditorium, looking like the wakeful bloodhound
In "The Eve of St. Agnes"; he had crept stiffly
To the piano, and plunged headlong into

This same concerto. My back hadn't felt so wrenched
Since Bruce Haines gave me an airplane spin
And flung me into a garbage can at Island Lake.
"Stop, for the love of God, Mrs. McGillicuddy,"
I said, tearing loose and knocking over a chair,
"I feel like a grand piano." The concerto
Had entered a particularly lugubrious passage,
That sounded like a bilious thunderstorm.
I could see Schopenhauer scowling, a century off,
And Shelley chasing illusions up Asian rivers,

In leaky boats. "That was the Libra treatment,"
Said Mrs. McGillicuddy, "don't you feel better?"
I lifted the needle, turned off the record player,
Ground out the King George, and said "I believe
I'm fully recovered." Picking up my Chaucer,
I staggered into the night, cured of melancholy,
And went to the Michigan Union for a hamburger
And 7-up, whistling Mozart. It was a clear
Libra evening. Frost was in the air. Yellow
And red leaves were falling, under a full moon.

Iron Man of the Hoh

A mile at sea, Cake Rock, against the blue,
Lifts its seafowl sanctuary. Harsh squawks
    Float from the monoliths. A few
High breakers begin their crests and churns,
As I watch the sun sinking toward seastacks,
       And the world turns.

Again I've walked this tideline near La Push
From the Quillayute River to Hole-in-the-Wall.
    Offshore the rocks, like gods, stand fresh,
Unshaken by all the ocean's worst in storms,
Their only voice in cormorant and gull:
       And the world turns.

A dozen times I've walked it with Applebaum,
Painter and raconteur. One time he told
    Me, with his monolithic aplomb,
As we strode along on shells and fish skeletons,
The story of the Iron Man of the Hoh:
       And the world turns

On such accounts. It seems this northwest Samson
Carried an iron cookstove twenty miles
    Up the Hoh on his back, having
Homesteaded among Douglas firs, moss and ferns
In 1890. And as God made little apples,
       And the world turns,

Two loggers, who saw him trotting the stove through the wood,
Asked, "Isn't that heavy?" He said, "No, but it's hard
    To keep my balance on a log
When the sack of flour shifts in the oven."
So he raised his family far from any road;
       And the world turns.

This man, John Huelsdonk, killed three hundred cougars,
• Once had his leg lacerated by a bear,
　　　Crawled home two miles through firs and cedars,
And then walked forty miles into Forks.
His daughter pulled two men out of the Hoh by their hair;
　　　　And the world turns.

My wife and daughter, at the tidal edge,
Move by Cake Rock, which now, against the sun,
　　　Goes purple-brown with the light's change,
Their pockets full of agates and odd stones.
My campfire gives the wind a pungent stain.
　　　　And the world turns.

Well, I've seen Babe Ruth hit two home runs
At Navin Field, Frost at seventy-five,
　　　Auden juggling the concerns
Of his century, Thomas in two taverns,
And Roethke, one of the giants of the alive;
　　　　And the world turns

Into legend. I remember Jean Garrigue
Embracing a Douglas fir in the rainforest.
　　　Applebaum has fished among
Those basalt giants on which the seagull mourns.
Is that you, John Huelsdonk, where the breakers start?
　　　　And the world turns

Purple-blue in dusk. I think of how
My parents loved, imagined, and endured.
　　　I gather wood and watch gulls float
On gathering breakers and settle on the crags.
The sun enters the ocean, a ball of blood,
　　　　And the world turns.

Ted Roethke Has a Short Tussle
with the All-Time Champ

I

What's this? A bloated toad hobbles out of the lilacs.
His toes must hurt on those cinders by the ash-heap.
Snake, sing me an Edward Lear song;
Let the Don cavort among the wild carrot.
Let the weeds, the stickery burdocks, imbibe like W. C. Fields.
Yesterday I saw a line of panting Airedales,
Stretching toward infinity. Last week I lay
Four hours with a lizard on the banks of the Saginaw.
Why does an angleworm have segments?
Blue jay, cut loose at me like old John Calvin.
How did he and Wordsworth both leap into rapture
In Switzerland? A boat sinks among lily pads.
Hold it, Buster, there's a muskrat in the cattails.
The pike rejoice with many teeth.
Doom just took off from that oak and flaps
Into the wilderness of my cortex.

II

Whoopsy, floopsy,
A lop-eared bunny
Just leapt in my lap
With a lot of money.
Hoogledy, poogledy,
A barn can smell.
A locomotive
Likes to yell.
Down in the barley
I chased a rabbit:
His tail was so white
I had to grab it.
Hop, mop,

I fell on the crop;
Have you ever swallowed
A lollipop?

III

Is this a tornado? The roof just went toward Ypsilanti.
Does God like to smash greenhouses?
Hold on, the maples are blowing down.
Those roots grabbed water for a hundred years.
The north wind is full of falling nests. Holy Toledo!
That looked like the lightning bolt Elijah called down,
On top of Mount Carmel. It's knocked me clear out
Of my shorts.

IV

Get out of my way, you barbers and bus drivers,
The Ancient of Days has me by the scruff of the neck!
He's just stuck my nose in the Rose of the World!
I'm as wild as Etna! Hang onto my socks, friends,
I'll orbit around Neptune!
Saint Francis just hit my subconscious like the Northern Lights!
I saw this coming in a tiger lily when I was seven,
Before the greenhouse filled with Original Light.
When Otto Roethke took off his hat in the rose house,
The flowers cheered like the crowd in the Michigan stadium.
The ghost of Bismarck knelt in submission,
And William Blake danced a hornpipe down the long alley.
Dance, dance, you polliwogs!
It's time to transform.

Dick Hugo Fishing the Rotten Horse River

With Poe it was one lily floating on the scum.
With me it's a dead dolly bumping the gravel bar.
What a day. I can only remember two that
Were worse. All the others came pretty close.
A black wind is flattening the willows.
The ashes of eight burned-down taverns
Are hitting me between the eyes, like Hurricane Jackson
In the thirteenth round. My luck is getting worse.
Across the river is the oak where Sodden Willie
Hung himself in 1938. The river sloshed past his ankles
For three weeks. If T. S. Eliot thought the Thames
Was in bad shape, he should've seen Rotten Horse.
There's a chemical plant up there in the foothills
Turns the water seven colors every Friday.
There's a hut a mile upstream where a goofy jockey
Cut six women into bits and threw them at turtles.
It's damn depressing. I haven't seen the sun
Since April. Reminds me of Aunt Hattie,
Who locked herself in her bedroom for fifteen years
And came out only to fry sausages,
Cackling like a fiend.
This was a good river until that lost prospector
Got bored and poured bourbon down his horse's gullet.
The poor beast floundered into the river, neighing
And whickering like a harpooned whale, and drowned.
Solid gloom is settling on the water, a permanent storm.
What the hell? My boots must be leaking.
No, damn it, I've gone and stepped into an old bear trap.
Just call me Izaak Walton in the Waste Land.

RICHARD HUGO

INTRODUCTION
James Welch

*R*ICHARD HUGO loved Montana in a big way. He loved its mountains and plains, its rivers and lakes, its towns and its people. He lived right in the mountains in the university town of Missoula. He was a nationally renowned poet, as well as an essayist and professor of English and creative writing. When he wasn't writing or teaching, he went fishing. He went fishing in his yellow Buick Skylark convertible and he fished with bait—salmon eggs on streams, worms and bobber, sometimes corn or marshmallows, on lakes on the Flathead Reservation. He could outfish God and he loved to rub it in—"You're not going to keep that little thing, are you, Welch?" "Boy, you guys are lucky you didn't catch any fish. Look at my hands, all bloody and stinky from cleaning these fish." In his later years, after a hip went bad, he liked to fish the lakes from a lawn chair with a cooler of sixteen-ounce beverages nearby. And although the opening scene of his one mystery, *Death and the Good Life*, ends rather badly for the fisherman, I imagine it is a tribute to all those armchair anglers who like to drown worms and lose themselves in the serenity of their own thoughts.

Like the hero of that mystery, Mush Heart Barnes, Dick came from Seattle. After a distinguished military hitch as a World War II bombardier,

Richard Hugo, age 2½

flying thirty-five missions out of Italy and only once bombing Switzerland, he went back to the University of Washington, where he studied
poetry with the great Theodore Roethke. Dick turned out to be a better
basketball player than Roethke and he had to let Ted win a few games
of twenty-one and horse in order to stay in the program. At least, that
was his story. After getting his M.A., he spent the next thirteen years
working as a tech writer at Boeing. In 1961 his first book of poems, *A
Run of Jacks,* came out, and with it came a feeling that he was wasting
his life writing assembly manuals. In 1963, he and his first wife, Barbara, went to Italy for a year where he wrote poems and retraced old
paths from his Army Air Corps days. The following year he arrived in
Missoula, full of terror and intrepidation, where he was to begin the first
year of his illustrious teaching career in which he established himself
as one of the very best creative writing instructors in the country. But
he was not a very happy man during these early years in Montana. He
spent too much time in the Milltown Bar, Cafe and Laundromat. In fact
his wife left him before the school year even began because she didn't

Richard, age 4, frightened by the sound of the ship's whistle, ca. 1927

appreciate the long afternoons and evenings in that establishment. Furthermore, Dick wasn't writing many poems, partly due to the pressures of teaching and partly due to plain unhappiness. The students adored him, of course. He was a very generous man, both in his teaching and in his real life. He gave me a job mowing his lawn. It was a small lawn, containing mostly two giant spruce trees, under which no grass grew. Nevertheless, I would show up every Saturday morning, mow for twenty or thirty minutes, then go in and drink beer and watch the baseball game on television.

Again like Mush Heart Barnes, Dick was a baseball aficionado. He loved the Red Sox, the Yankees, and the San Francisco Giants. He had played semi-pro softball for the Boeing team in Seattle and could still hit the daylights out of the ball rifling line-drives to all fields with grim regularity. After the game we would go out to Milltown and drink beer

Richard Hugo (far left) with his family, late 1930s

while Dick's clothes whirled away in the laundromat. Sometimes, Dick would go across the street for a haircut. Toward evening we would drive further out of town to the Happy Bungalow, a working man's club, where he would treat me to prime rib and an after dinner drink of Strega. Sometimes we would have more than one Strega. If they didn't have Strega, we would have Galliano. Dick loved Italy and everything Italian. He could even speak Italian. He went back to Italy once more during those years, spending 1968–69 by himself in a tiny port town called Maretea. One of his best books of poems, *Good Luck in Cracked Italian*, came out of this experience. But he continued to be an unhappy man, given to long, glowering silences between bouts of fierce drinking with his friends.

In 1970–71, Dick taught at the University of Iowa as visiting poet in the creative writing workshop. Although he was lionized by the students and his fellow poets (he had earned quite a national following by this time), he suffered a breakdown and returned to Missoula feeling quite ruined and ashamed of himself. He didn't even remember the drive back. But after a few recuperative weeks in Missoula (he and I played a lot of horse and twenty-one on my backyard hoop), he set out for Seattle to take a summer teaching position as the Theodore Roethke Professor at the University of Washington. There he suffered a second threat to his health—a bleeding ulcer which landed him in the hospital, practically used up from loss of blood. Dick's emotional and physical life had bottomed out. The only good thing that came from these sad experiences

Richard Hugo and Stinky Johnson, White Center, 1930s

Richard Hugo, 1978

was that he had to quit drinking. He had to get healthy, even to the point of losing a considerable amount of weight. He had always been heavy, round in most respects but surprisingly light on his feet, like a feeding grizzly. Later he would say that he enjoyed being healthy because he could seize the entire day by the throat. Almost immediately he became more productive, writing poems and essays in great bursts of energy. He grew to like his life pretty well, his only regret (apart from being unable to drink) was that he thought he wasn't as funny as he used to be. He used to be very funny. But he was healthy (and not unfunny) and the poems came.

Then in 1973 he met Ripley Schemm Hansen. After a lovely, mysterious romance (Dick could be very private when he put his mind to it), he and Ripley were married in the Coeur d' Amour Wedding Chapel in Coeur d'Alene, Idaho. Dick moved his typewriter, notebooks, pencils, clothes, lamps, fishing gear, and considerable presence into Ripley's Wylie Street house in Missoula. It astonished his friends that Dick could adjust so easily to Ripley's world of two children, two dogs, two cats, and two horses. He had been an only child and had lived alone much of his life. Perhaps because of this, he enjoyed his new family very much, and they in turn thought the world of him. Perhaps most astonishing to his friends was that he continued his productive streak. He often joked that he was "so goddamned happy" he was afraid the poems would stop coming. Dick wrote right up to the end, even when his body was wrecked by cancer and his mind became less quick and his handwriting more tentative, child-like. He died of leukemia on October 22, 1982.

Dick was first and foremost, and in the end, a poet. He left us ten books of poems and two books of essays about poetry and the life of the poet. In my earlier writing career, when I thought I was a poet, I believed a poet was a person who wrote poems. Now I know better. A true poet is a person who lives the poems, who is so obsessed with that world of the imagination and the need to write that it guides his or her life as surely as the stars guided that ancient mariner. Dick was a rare true poet.

Richard Hugo in Italy
after a bombing mission, 1942

The Other Beaverbank

FOR MILDRED

The river seems to sour and we can't recall
who's buried under the mound. We might guess
a name like Poor Bear. We might remember
the sequence: first, the crack of ice,
then tons of drowned bison pouring north,
and finally, for it was spring surely by then,
the crackpot preacher blew his trumpet
loud over the water and swans flew off.
With so much gone, it was natural to sell.

And it's natural to want it back, not just
Beaverbank but the whole wide scene,
the far bank of sand, the three islands
named for Spanish ships and the evening sweep
of falcon counter current. The Missouri

releases and fills like a heart. Some new tenant
we hope will chase some old ghost away
and all swans come home. Surely it's spring:
the cottonwood leaves turn over silver
and flash. We could dig and dig
and find no human remains. The mound?
That was an early joke of settlers.
They knew when they heaped the dirt and stomped it
round like the dome of some early tribe
we'd create the rest years later,
handsome bones and beads,
the sad tale of one who lost it all.

—SPRING 1978

Open Country

FOR GEORGE

It is much like ocean the way it opens
and rolls. Cows dot the slow climb of a field
like salmon trawls dot swells, and here or there
ducks climb on no definite heading.
Like water it is open to suggestion,
electric heron, and every moon
tricky currents of grass.
                                        Let me guess:
when you repair the damaged brain
of a beaten child or bring to a patient
news that will never improve, you need
a window not a wall to turn to.
And you come back here
where land has ways of going on
and the shadow of a cloud
crawls like a freighter, no port in mind,
no captain, and the charts dead wrong.

—SPRING 1978

The Semi-Lunatics of Kilmuir

And so they cheated and wandered and were loved
throughout this island. If that's too mythical a tone
consider those who conform and know something's wrong
and need a zany few who won't obey.
Granted, without obedience most of us would die.
And it was worse then, year eighteen whatever,
and crofts in feudal domain. Think of losing your home
on a Duke's whim and look at the home you lost.
Imagine this lovely island warped ugly by tears.
Yesterday in Glasgow some magistrate ruled
feudal rights prevail. Crofter reform turns out
a cruel joke. You pay and pay and own nothing.
Wouldn't we welcome them back this minute,
those clowning con men from Kilmuir?
They were crazy like dolphins. When Gilleasbuig Aotram,
most dolphin of all, met a real crazy
raving in chains, headed for the asylum, he said:
"Had you the right madness bread would be secure."
Have the right madness. This land has always passed on
and, like you, is still here.

—SPRING 1980

Culloden

Nothing seems right, not the monument too close
to the road nor the road that seems misplaced.
We'd have everyone fallen named, not one stone
per clan, hidden in fern or behind a cedar,
even the clan name faint, and trails that wander
the woods better for lovers than for tribute.
We can't imagine trumpets, the steel clash of men,
the bonnie prince riding away. If anything
we think of picnics, cold salmon and wine.

If a hill isn't rounded some filmatic way
could anyone bleed there, would a fifteen year
old boy cry 'Mother, I'm dying' then die?
We need wind to fight wars. No wind here.
The air's too dead for the dead. The trees too solemn
for contrast with a serious tear of defeat.

We have to trust books and the handed down
stories of loss. Otherwise, given this sun
breaking clean on the grass, museums meant
to commemorate mean nothing. We have to trust
the faces of Scots today, the pulse of blood
in those faces. And we have to trust the sad
memorial tone of anyone who volunteers
to guide us through this field not right for battle.
We say, yes, yes, we hear the pipes, the drums.
We see the charge. We hear the fatal screams.

We are simply being polite. No topography
lends itself easily to war. To animals maybe.
To birds. To clouds. They outlive these graves.

—SPRING 1980

George Stubbs at Yale

FOR LOUIS MARTZ

In land that obviously northern, no record ever
a lion has attacked a horse, not where air
polishes animal skin with light
and storm tears green holes through cloud and flares out
stiff the soft willow branches
and the horse's white mane. In some house not
in the painting, a woman says nothing all day
over a stove. In Africa, where real lions stink
in heat and grow shaggy, their legs tormented

by flies, we might paint polar bears—one more
answer to some vague 'they' and some dim
early 'don't do that.' If a horse seems too perfect—
color and line—we order whatever beast we bore
long ago and kept secret, "kill." We gave him that rage
we found in sky during storm, and his tail bends
the same way tree trunks bend. In some house not
in the painting, a woman babbles day long over
a sink. The lion clearer than any we've known,
we speculate the day Stubbs conceived the painting,
wind blowing clean everything he saw
and he, slightly wild inside, said "why not a cat?"
The lion ended looking at his victim
with lust more than malice. Whatever storm started
all this, we won't find it recorded.
We must stay northern to find light diminished by cloud
and to give line a chance to be stark in that light.
We must stay northern to bring warm lions home.

—SPRING 1980

Glen Uig

Believe in this couple this day who come
to picnic in the Faery Glen. They pay rain
no matter, or wind. They spread their picnic
under a gale-stunted rowan. Believe they grew tired
of giants and heroes and know they believe
in wise tiny creatures who live under the rocks.

Believe these odd mounds, the geologic joke
played by those wise tiny creatures far from
the world's pitiful demands: make money, stay sane.
Believe the couple, by now soaked to the skin,
sing their day as if dry, as if sheltered inside
Castle Ewen. Be glad Castle Ewen's only a rock
that looks like a castle. Be glad for no real king.

These wise tiny creatures, you'd better believe,
have lived through it all: the Viking occupation,
clan torturing clan, the Clearances, the World War
II bomber gone down, a fiery boom
on Beinn Edra. They saw it from here. They heard
the sobs of last century's crofters trail off below
where every day the Conon sets out determined for Uig.
They remember the Viking who wandered off course,
under the hazelnut tree hating aloud all he'd done.

Some days dance in the bracken. Some days go out
wide and warm on bad roads to collect the dispossessed
and offer them homes. Some days celebrate addicts
sweet in their dreams and hope to share with them
a personal spectrum. The loch here's only a pond,
the monster in it small as a wren.

Believe the couple who have finished their picnic
and make wet love on the grass, the wise tiny creatures
cheering them on. Believe in milestones, the day
you left home forever and the cold open way
a world wouldn't let you come in. Believe you
and I are that couple. Believe you and I sing tiny
and wise and could if we had to eat stone and go on.

—SPRING 1980

Distances

Driving a prairie, we see a mill far off
and though clouds climbing out of the stack
pollute the air we find the sight lovely.
Horses on the rim of a distant rise
move faintly. We barely see them move
though they run wild. Or when a mile offshore
whales romp and spout, we admire
fountains in Rome, and the distant cathedral
that makes all daylit hours dawn. Artillery
lights a glorious horizon too far for us
to hear the thundering guns. We remain
out of earshot of scream.

Clouds bring rivers closer, bring closer
the homesteader's cabin, the antelope herd.
Clouds move on and the day opens to distance.
Animals are dots. They could be cattle or sheep.
Whatever, they no doubt graze safely and sky
drums wide. Whole symphonies live between
here and a distant whatever-we-look-at.
All things came close and harmless
first thing this morning, a new trick of light.
Let's learn that trick. If we can, it will mean
we live in this world, neighbor to goat,
neighbor to trout, and we can take comfort
in low birds that hang long enough for us
to read markings and look up names
we'll whisper to them from now on.

—FALL 1983

Here, but Unable to Answer

IN MEMORY, HERBERT HUGO

A small dawn, sailor. First light glints
off water and it rays across your face
some ill-defined religion. I see you
always on the bridge alone, vigorous
and handsome. Eight bells. You bellow orders.
Your voice rolls back the wind.
Your eyes light numbers on the compass green.

Had I found you lost, I swear
I would have torn the clouds apart right
beneath the north star long enough
for you to fix position, and we'd have gone
sailing, sailing down our boyhood rivers
out to open sea, you proud of my power
over uncooperative sky. What a team
and never to be. You gone to China. I alone
with two old people and in nightmare earth
becoming drier. No new crop. No growth.

Even in war we lived a war apart.
You who desperately wanted combat
stuck piloting new ships from Pittsburgh.
At night, what we can't see advances
fast and armed over the quaking plain
to the gulf. Me and my unwanted self
praying the final bomb run out, praying me alone
home safe, then all the others I forgot.
Forgive the bad nerves I brought home,
these hands still trembling with sky, that deafening
dream exploding me awake. Books will call
that war the last one worth the toll.

Father, now you're buried much too close for me
to a busy highway, I still see you up there
on the bridge, night sky wide open and you naming
wisely every star again, your voice enormous
with the power of moon, of tide. I seldom
sail off course. I swim a silent green.
When I dream, the compass lights stay on.

—FALL 1983

LARRY LEVIS

LARRY LEVIS IN SYRACUSE
Stephen Dunn

ONLY FOUR would-be poets were admitted into Syracuse University's graduate writing program in 1969. Actually there were five of us, but one was Larry Levis, who was a poet. Larry was 22, fresh out of Fresno and already with pedigree, having studied with Philip Levine and Robert Mezey. I was 29, relatively new to poetry (I had been a history major as an undergraduate and hadn't been to a school in many years), fresh from a year of living and trying to write in Spain. Though I may have had some ability, there seemed an enormous initial gap between me and the other admittees, especially Larry. Larry seemed full-blown, perhaps even an original.

I think we were able to become friends—from my side of the equation—because Larry was immensely likable and apparently devoid of ego. But also because I felt no competitiveness toward him, as I did toward some of the others. He already had a voice; he was in another category. He was tall, gangly, off the farm. And attractive; his overall manner and carriage, not to mention his mustache, made him James Dean leaning toward Burt Reynolds. My wife liked him (women were always drawn to Larry), and he was frequently a visitor at our apartment. Until his second or third Fellowship check arrived—sometime after Syracuse winter

Larry, age about 5, ca. 1931

Larry on his mother's lap, with brother Buck and sisters Sheila
and Lynn, at the farm near Selma, California

*Levis (*left*) at the wedding of his brother*

had commenced—the warmest clothing he owned was a dungaree jacket and a rubber raincoat. He was our Californian, and some of us even confused his drawl, his slow delivery and curious accent, as Southern Californian. We were wrong; it was peculiarly Levisonian.

We had come to study with Philip Booth, Donald Justice, W. D. Snodgrass, George P. Elliott, arguably the best group of writer-teachers that existed at the time. In Philip Booth's small workshop that first semester in 1969, I kept silent most of the time. There was a very brilliant Fellowship student (I'll not name him) from the South who held forth every class. None of us was as articulate, certainly not Larry whose speech was hesitant, at worst sprinkled with "you knows," a kind of punctuation for him, sometimes annoying, like "like" these days. The brilliant student's poems, however, were convoluted. We soon learned that his brilliant, his apparent brilliance, was overly convoluted too. Much elaboration and ranginess, little touching down. In a month or so, it was clear who was the most intersting and able poet. Booth clearly knew. When that year Larry won the Academy of American Poets Award for best poem, no one was surprised.

It took longer to realize that Larry was a good thinker as well. Together, we took a course called "The Modern Imagination" from William Wasserstrom, a formidable and curmudgeonly professor. In it, among other books, we read *The Tin Drum*, several Beckett plays, Kon-

Larry Levis, ca. 1980

rad Lorenz' *On Aggression,* Huizinga's *Homo Ludens,* a wonderful and eclectic range of texts. Larry and I were the only creative writers in the class; the rest were scholars, PhD candidates. Wasserstrom had little patience with students whose analytical skills weren't sharp. He had no patience with the unprepared or the foolish.

Frequently he'd stop a student in mid-sentence, cut him off. But an amazing thing started to happen by mid-semester. Larry would start to speak, again slowly, lots of "you knows" and "sort ofs," and Wasserstrom let him speak. By this time professor and class had learned that if you gave Larry some room, some slack, the end of his drift or sentence was going to click-in, that he was going to say something very smart. Any other student verging on the inarticulate would be (and was) interrupted. Larry had more acute things to say than anyone in class, especially, as I remember, about Beckett.

In our second year at Syracuse, Larry, with the help of Don Justice's translation class, was turning to the Latin American and French poets that would prove so important to his work. Neruda, Reverdy, Baudelaire, Follain, Vallejo. He found models in them and others for how to blend his politics with his aesthetics. It was 1970. Larry's politics were more than fashionably leftist; they arose of something essentially proletarian in his makeup. The war and Nixon preoccupied many of us, and Larry in particular. It seems comic to say so, but if he hadn't been such a gentle man he might have been a violent one.

One Christmas break, he returned from California with a beautiful woman, Barbara. He had only casually mentioned her to us, but here she was, his wife. They'd just gotten married. She was his first wife, and the one dearest to us. Many good times together, pot and booze oiling the laughter. He was a husband now, and to bring in more money he took a job at a steel mill. Hard work, but work that wholly fit Larry's romance of himself as a man of the people, a worker. On the back of his precocious first book, *Wrecking Crew,* he listed steelworker as one of his former occupations.

His best and often extraordinary poems were, of course, ahead of him. But in those two years at Syracuse the seeds of them were present. For reasons I'm not entirely sure of, we drifted apart in the late eighties. Each of us had come far as poets, the only two Syracusans from that era to do so, but we also lived far apart and had cut out different paths for ourselves. I wished to see him again, and not long ago I invited him to read at my college. I felt instantly close to him, and I think he felt the same toward me. Five months later he'd be dead. What I'll remember about him, beyond the poems, were his special brand of humor and his infinite sweetness.

LARRY LEVIS'S "SPOTS OF TIME"

Gary Short

*I*T IS THE last week of April. Here in Fairbanks spring brings a mix of melancholy and wonder. Things are about to happen. The days are lengthening, the rivers will soon be flowing. The trees will leaf out. There will be a great greening. Even after the late sun sets, the sky does not go black but takes on the deep blue of the Alaskan flag. This time of year in the far north invites intense outward seeing and also, introspection. After the long winter the natural world provides a large calm and an openness to ecstatic moments, what Wordsworth called "spots of time." The poets I love and admire give me back spots of time, moments of meaning and holiness. Larry Levis is one of those poets,

Levis died three years ago in May 1996. He left behind many writer friends and former students. I am neither. I came to his poems more than twenty years ago and book by book I followed his life and work. He left us a big group of poems that are smart, compassionate, and beautiful. His writing is important. More and more, I value the poems he wrote and miss the poems that he will not write.

Fresno State College (now rechristened California State University, Fresno), mid-1970s, was the right place for an undergraduate English major. I didn't take writing classes there; I hadn't considered being a poet. I wanted to be a high school teacher and basketball coach. But first by accident, and then by plan, I took literature courses taught by poets Peter Everwine, Chuck Hanzlichek, and Phil Levine, the same teachers that Larry Levis had studied with several years earlier. I sat silent in the back of classrooms in uncomfortable desk chairs under flickering fluorescent lighting and read and listened intently to poems and talk about poetry. I was hooked. I remember being knocked out by Phil Levine and Luis Omas Salinas reading at the Quaker Meeting Hall. On High-

High-school portrait

way 99, on visits to my parents in Reno, I'd see the Mexican farm workers marching in support of the union and the grape boycott. During my
tenure as a student-teacher at Roosevelt High School, a vineyard-
owner/parent complained about my using *The Grapes of Wrath* as a text.
The English majors I hung out with talked about the poets who had
attended Fresno State a few years before us—Larry Levis, David St. John,
Roberta Spear, Greg Pape—some of them were already publishing books.
They were spoken of in awestruck tones that in my previous experience
had been reserved for athletic heroes. This is when I first read these poets.

Short, imagistic lyrics with an interest in surrealism comprise the
poems in Levis's first two books, *Wrecking Crew* and *The Afterlife*. Many
of the poems in *The Dollmaker's Ghost* work a tension between image
and meditative discourse and anticipate the writing in the breakthrough
book, *Winter Stars*.

Winter Stars—what a gorgeous book. Levis juxtaposes personal history and memory with considerations of notions of art and reality. The
poems go beyond recollection and the past, taking on a present tense
enacted on the page. There is at once both a going back and a moving

2/22/91

Dear Coleen,

First, I want to offer a belated thank you for the good visit in
Seattle, and for your kindness and hospitality. It was great
seeing you though I'm afraid I was a kind of dull guest that week.
I arrived feeling exhausted, as if from a lingering flu. Is it
possible for the mind to get mono? If so, I think I had it then.

I wrote your recommendation for the Guggenheim, praising you. Now
I just hope you get one. I applied for five, maybe even six years,
and finally they gave me one. I suspect it must be like work-ups
in baseball or something; eventually you really do get to bat, but
it takes a while.

It's been a shitty winter. My wife left me in October. It wasn't
even dramatic. No affairs, nothing to gossip about. She just
wanted to make it on her own, be independent. For a few months,
I wasn't much but a thing full of sadness and anger. But for some
crazy reason, I kept working. I remembered how you were in Belgrade
and Dubrovnik after Peter had split. And for some reason my own
pain made yours more real, if only in memory. So I wrote this poem
for you. It's no masterpiece, but under the circumstances, it was
better than nothing, which I had a whole lot of.

Things in my life are about 2,000 light years better now. I'm seeing
someone who's a real sweetheart, and I'm happy. I don't ask for
more than that.

Best & love,

Larry Levis
P.O. Box 391
SLC, Utah 84110-0391

LATE SEPTEMBER IN ULCINJ

--for Coleen McElroy

Birth & Death own the little walled cottages;

Since one's illiterate, the other always speechless,

There's no real way of meeting either.

And what did you come here for if not to hear

Finality in the soft click of a latch,

Or in the long thou of the empty wavebreak?

The rocks glistening for a second after it

Would find it strange that they meant anything.

And the gull's cry, & the sore screech of a winch

On a fishing boat a hundred yards offshore,

Are the poor speech of everything there is,

An unregretting blossoming & humming.

You walked beside the ancient, mottled walls,

Listening, it seemed then, to nothing.

And it's only later you remember, if at all,

The clattering dishes, the fading dawns & catcalls,

Sausages the color of overcast skies on a grill,

And a group of soldiers marching on the square,

Repeating the routine motions of some drill,

And someone lost, someone muttering to herself,

The cafes emptier than abandoned puzzles....

*

The sea wall overlooked the rocks, the choppy water,

Whose falling shadow told each one a fortune,

And a woman reading something on the beach

Who yawned, stretched, & seemed to fall asleep.

It was the custom to wear nothing there,

Where the wave sprawl on the rock cannot remember.

Larry Levis

forward. Light, the fields, and a father are affected by memory and close observation. The title poem ends this way:

Tonight, I'm talking to you, father, although
It is quiet here in the Midwest, where a small wind,
The size of a wrist, wakes the cold again—
Which may be all that's left of you & me.

When I left home at seventeen, I left for good.

That pale haze of stars goes on & on,
Like laughter that has found a final, silent shape
On a black sky. It means everything
It cannot say. Look, it's empty out there, & cold.
Cold enough to reconcile
Even a father, even a son.

The late poetry is openly haunting. There is a tremendous amount of both intellectual and imaginative flight in the last two books of poems, *The Widening Spell of the Leaves* and *Elegy*. The poems transport. Sit outside on a nice day and read the poem "Carravaggio, Swirl and Vortex," and look up into the blue. You won't be sure where you are, and the whole wide sky will be a reflecting pool full of joy and sadness and possibility. Tony Hoagland has pointed out that in the poems of *Widening Spell*, "Levis achieves a mode more full of mystery than ever before, a fusion of lyric, rhetoric, and narrative which is all his own . . . presided over throughout by an enormous calm."

Larry Levis finds his voice in astonishing and warm-blooded poems of great compassion. He gives us imaginative, consoling, and transformative experiences. Even in the very personal poems, he does not pander for pity or devotion. His life's work exhibits honest attention. We readers come away with an increased empathy for our own lives and the lives of others.

Levis's poems are like the trees in the cemetery in the opening of his poem "Adolescence":

At night those huge trees rooted in such quiet,
Arch over the tombstones as if in exultation,

As if they inhaled starlight.
Their limbs reach
Toward each other & their roots must touch the dead.

I think of those trees in the morning when they stretch and flesh out in
the early sun. The leaves, trembling and luminous.

The Oldest Living Thing in L.A.

At Wilshire & Santa Monica I saw an opossum
Trying to cross the street. It was late, the street
Was brightly lit, the opossum would take
A few steps forward, then back away from the breath
Of moving traffic. People coming out of the bars
Would approach, as if to help it somehow.
It would lift its black lips & show them
The reddened gums, the long rows of incisors,
Teeth that went all the way back beyond
The flames of Troy & Carthage, beyond sheep
Grazing rock-strewn hills, fragments of ruins
In the grass at San Vitale. It would back away
Delicately & smoothly, stepping carefully
As it always had. It could mangle someone's hand
In twenty seconds. Mangle it for good. It could
Sever it completely from the wrist in forty.
There was nothing to be done for it. Someone
Or other probably called the LAPD, who then
Called Animal Control, who woke a driver, who
Then dressed in mailed gloves, the kind of thing
Small knights once wore into battle, who gathered
Together his pole with a noose on the end,
A light steel net to snare it with, someone who hoped
The thing would have vanished by the time he got there.

The Poem Returning
as an Invisible Wren to the World

Once, there was a poem. No one read it & the poem
Grew wise. It grew wise & then it grew thin,
No one could see it perched on the woman's
Small shoulders as she went on working beside

The gray conveyer belt with the others.
No one saw the poem take the shape of a wren,
A wren you could look through like a window,
And see all the bitterness of the world

In the long line of shoulders & faces bending
Over the gleaming, machined parts that passed
Before them, the faces transformed by the grace
And ferocity of a wren, a wren you could look

Through, like a lens, to see them working there.
This is not about how she threw herself into the river,
For she didn't, nor is it about the way her breasts
Looked in moonlight, nor about moonlight at all.

This is about the surviving curve of the bridge
Where she listened to the river whispering to her,
When the wren flew off & left her there,
With the knowledge of it singing in her blood.

By which the wind avenges. By which the rain avenges.
By which even the limb of a dead tree leaning
Above the white, swirling mouth of an eddy
In the river that once ran beside the factory window

Where she once worked, shall be remembered
When the dead come back, & take their places
Beside her on the line, & the gray conveyor belt
Starts up with its raspy hum again. Like a heaven's.

Elegy with a Bridle in Its Hand

One was a bay cowhorse from Piedra & the other was a washed-out
    palomino
And both stood at the rail of the corral & both went on aging
In each effortless tail swish, the flies rising, then congregating again

Around their eyes & muzzles & withers.

Their front teeth were by now yellow as antique piano keys & slanted
    to the angle
Of shingles on the maze of sheds & barn around them; their
    puckered

Chins were round & black as frostbitten oranges hanging unpicked
    from the limbs
Of trees all through winter like a comment of winter itself on
    everything
That led to it & found gradually the way out again.

In the slowness of time. Black time to white, & rind to blossom.
Deity is in the details & we are details among other details & we
    long to be

Teased out of ourselves. And become all of them.

The bay had worms once & had acquired the habit of drinking
    orange soda
From an uptilted bottle & nibbling cookies from the flat of a hand,
    & liked to do
Nothing else now, & the palomino liked to do nothing but gaze off

At traffic going past on the road beyond vineyards & it would follow
    each car
With a slight turning of its neck, back & forth, as if it were a thing

Of great interest to him.

If I rode them, the palomino would stumble & wheeze when it broke
Into a trot & would relapse into a walk after a second or two & then
    stop
Completely & without cause, the bay would keep going though it
    creaked

Underneath me like a rocking chair of dry, frail wood, & when I knew
    it could not longer
Continue but did so anyway, or when the palomino would stop & then
    take

Only a step or two when I nudged it forward again, I would slip off
    either one of them,
Riding bareback, & walk them slowly back, letting them pause when
    they wanted to.

At dawn in winter sometimes there would be a pane of black ice
    covering
The surface of the water trough & they would nudge it with their
    noses or muzzles,
And stare at it as if they were capable of wonder or bewilderment.

They were worthless. They were the motionless dusk & the motionless

Moonlight, & in the moonlight they were other worlds. Worlds
    uninhabited
And without visitors. Worlds that would cock an ear a moment
When the migrant workers came back at night to the sheds they were
    housed in

And turn a radio on, but only for a moment before going back to
    whatever

Wordless & tuneless preoccupation involved them.

The palomino was called Misfit & the bay was named Querido Flacco,
And the names of some of the other shapes had been Rockabye
And Ojo Pendejo & Cue Ball & Back Door Peter & Frenchfry &
    Sandman

And Rolling Ghost & Anastasia.

Death would come for both of them with its bridle of clear water in
    hand
And they would not look up from grazing on some patch of dry grass
    or even

Acknowledge it much; & for a while I began to think that the world

Rested on a limitless ossuary of horses where their bones & skulls
    stretched
And fused until only the skeleton of one enormous horse underlay
The smoke of cities & the cold branches of trees & the distant

Whine of traffic on the interstate.

If I & by implication therefore anyone looked at them long enough
    at dusk
Or in moonlight he would know the idea of heaven & of life everlasting
Was so much blown straw or momentary confetti

At the unhappy wedding of a sister.

Heaven was neither the light nor was it the air, & if it took a physical
    form
It was splintered lumber no one could build anything with.

Heaven was a weight behind the eyes & one would have to stare right
 through it
Until he saw the air itself, just air, the clarity that took the shackles
 from his eyes
And the taste of the bit from his mouth & knocked the rider off his
 back

So he could walk for once in his life.

Or just stand there for a moment before he became something else,
 some
Flyspeck on the wall of a passing & uninterruptible history whose
 sounds claimed
To be a cheering from bleachers but were actually no more than the
 noise

Of cars entering the mouth of a tunnel.

And in the years that followed he would watch them in the
 backstretch or the far turn
At Santa Anita or Del Mar. Watch the way they made it all seem
 effortless

Watch the way they were explosive & untiring.

And then watch the sun fail him again & slip from the world, &
 watch
The stands slowly empty. As if all moments came back to this one,
 inexplicably
To this one out of all he might have chosen—Heaven with ashes in
 its hair

And filling what were once its eyes—this one its torn tickets
Littering the aisles & the soft racket the wind made. This one.
 Which was his.

And if he voice of a broen king were to come in the dusk &
    whisper
To the world, that grandstand with its thousands of empty seats,

Who among the numberless you have become desires this moment

Which comprehends nothing more than loss & fragility & the fleeing of
    flesh?
        He would have to look up at quickening dark & say: *Me. I do. It's*
    mine.

Elegy with a Chimneysweep
Falling Inside It

Those twenty-six letters filling the blackboard
Compose the dark, compose
The illiterate summer sky & its stars as they appear

One by one, above the schoolyard.

If the soul had a written history, nothing would have happened;
A bird would still be riding the back of a horse,

And the horse would go on grazing in a field, & the gleaners,

At one with the land, the wind, the sun examining
Their faces, would go on working,

Each moment forgotten in the swipe of a scythe.

But the walls of the labyrinth have already acquired
Their rose tint from the blood of slaves
Crushed into the stone used to build them, & the windows

Of stained glass are held in place by the shriek

And sighing body of a falling chimneysweep through
The baked & blackened air. This ash was once a village,

That snowflake, time itself.

But until the day it is permitted to curl up in a doorway,
And try to sleep, the snow falling just beyond it.

There's nothing for it to do:

The soul rests its head in its hands & stares out
From its desk at the trash-littered schoolyard,

It stays where it was left.
When the window fills with pain, the soul bears witness,
But it doesn't write. Nor does it write home,
Having no need to, having no home.
In this way, & in no other

Was the soul gradually replaced by the tens of thousands
Of things meant to represent it—

All of which proclaimed, or else lamented, its absence.

Until, in the drone of auditoriums & lecture halls, it became
No more than the scraping of a branch
Against the side of a house, no more than the wincing

Of a patient on a couch, or the pinched, nasal tenor
Of the strung-out addict's voice,

While this sound of scratching, this tapping all night,
Enlarging the quiet instead of making a music within it,

Is just a way of joining one thing to another,

Myself to whoever it is—sitting there in the schoolroom,

Sitting there while also being led through the schoolyard
Where prisoners are exercising in the cold light—

A way of joining or trying to join one thing to another,
So that the stillness of the clouds & the sky

Opening beneath the blindfold of the prisoner, & the cop
Who leads him toward it, toward the blank

Sail of the sky at the end of the world, are bewildered

So that everything, in this moment, bewilders

Them: the odd gentleness each feels in the hand
Of the other, & how they don't stop walking, not now,

Not for anything.

The Thief in the Painting

Thirsty all through Lent, thirsty on feast days too,
I was meant to be part of the picture,
Born to be the thief with his face averted,

Only a stone's throw from the crowd,
An exiled white gleam of flesh in the background
Before the bare hill blurs into pines,

And the pines into . . . ? So it is written.
After the crowds went off to their amusements
And the three of us were left to wither away,

I kept meaning to ask, then kept forgetting to—
Staring off, and gliding out of my flesh on my stare—
Forgetting what and who it was I had wanted to ask.

I remember now a gust of wind on the dry hill
In that moment, and the sore screech of a wheel,
An endless screeching, off in the distance somewhere,

And the wind carving an idle shape in the dust.
In that moment when you pause after a long day
Of scheming and calculation, the moment just before

The wine is poured at your table, the afternoon light
Quivering a little on the bleached fronds of the palms
Above the Piazza dei Poppolo, the moment when Craxi

Emerges dripping with sweat from the Senate, think
Of me, so necessary for the balance of the composition,
So necessary to the street that goes on being a street,

That never once rises up into the fine spun dust of heaven,
As you watch it quickening with life and will watch it . . .
How many more times? Twenty? Fifty? Think of me,

For who among you now could say with certainty
Which thief I was, could tell which mark blurred
By rain in a ledger once meant me, which meant

That linen on a stick who was once my friend,
And which meant the possessed boy who went on speaking
To shapes he saw before him in the air, shapes

Which I knew, even as I turned my face away from him
Then, out of a serene contempt, were nothing more,
Could never be anything more, than what was really there—

The hard, pure, furiously indifferent faces of thieves.

NOTE: "The Poem Returning as an Invisible Wren to the World," "The Oldest
Living Thing in L.A.," "The Thief in the Painting," "Elegy with a Bridle in Its
Hand," and "Elegy with a Chimneysweep Falling Inside It" from *Elegy*, by Larry
Levis, © 1997. Reprinted by permission of the University of Pittsburgh Press.

DIANE WAKOSKI

LET US BEGIN TO SING: A POET AND HER MOUNTAIN, DIANE WAKOSKI, 1999

Edward Jenkinson

*T*HIS PAST JUNE OF 1999 I had the pleasure of chatting with one of the country's most outstanding poets: Diane Wakoski. Wakoski lives in East Lansing, Michigan, and says that, "it's taken me nearly twenty-five years to get what I call 'Michigan Eyes.' I don't think I saw Michigan," she says, "other than the autumn leaves (which are always spectacular) as beautiful when I first moved here." And of course she would "love to live in a city, or on an ocean, overlooking it of course. But then I look out at my curtain of oak leaves at the end of our little backyard every day in summer and think, the Pacific Ocean is just beyond those leaves. Of course, 2,000 miles away, but I know it's there." And I, as a reader of her poetry, half expected her to be living on the coast of the Pacific Ocean since she started writing along its Coastal highways.

Diane Wakoski: Dark, glooming rainy morning (just like Seattle?) here in East Lansing today, probably getting ready for super hot sultry 4th of July weather. At any rate, I am up a bit early and woke up thinking about your questions.

You ask about the period of my career where I earned my living

Diane (right), age 4, with her sister, Marilyn,
and her father, ca. 1940

by giving poetry readings. A brief summary of the evolution of this:
I graduated from Berkeley in spring of 1960 and went to New York
City that fall with La Monte Young, the avant composer I'd been living with. He had a traveling fellowship in composition, the first
installment of which just barely paid for two one-way plane tickets
to New York City, with about five dollars left over in cash. Three sets
of La Monte's avant-garde artist friends had preceded us and were living there already—Robert Morris (painter/sculptor) and his, then,
wife, Simone Forti (dancer), Walter DeMaria (concept artist), and
Joseph Byrd (composer). We stayed with Bob and Simone for about
a week, sleeping on their floor, and with Joe Byrd another bit of
the time until I found a job, earned a week's salary and we found an

apartment to sublet. I worked for several years at what I called a slave-labor job, the British Book Centre in Manhattan, and we stayed in that apartment on Bank Street until our relationship broke up. Then I went to live with Bob Morris, and La Monte found his wonderful wife, now of more than thirty years, Marian Zazeela (performer and light designer). I am writing more extensively about his period of my life in a long essay, perhaps book, a so-called memoir, tentatively called *Light Years*.

I had come to New York City with an invitation to read at the YMHA Poetry Center, then run by Stanley Kunitz. They had initiated a series that later was named, The Discovery Series, for readings by poets. In 1961, there was only the "Discovery," and its three partici-pants were chosen by Louis Simpson. I was one of the three (the other two were David Ignatow and Robert Hazelton, both poets about 15 years my senior and both already having published at least one book). I think that was one of the most exciting readings of my life, since I felt that I was showing New York City that I could be the little ingenue star poet that I'd been at Berkeley. Of course, when I was at Berkeley, Ruth Witt Diamant, with the help of Kenneth Rexroth, started the San Francisco Poetry Center, and truly the biggest event of my entire poetry life was to be invited to participate in a reading with four other Berkeley poets, all of us students of Thom Gunn at the university. I have written elsewhere about this occasion, but in brief it was a singular event, with Jack Spicer and Helen Adam in attendance, and both of them responding with great approval to my poetry above all the other participants.

At any rate, Morris left me, one of the worst events of my life. I married Shep Sherbell, an even worse event in my life, went to England with him, briefly, and there he left me. When I came back to New York City, I met one of the most important men in my life, Tony Weinberger, who was to become my "motorcycle betrayer" alas, and lived with him on the Lower East Side. During that time my second Doubleday book, *Inside the Blood Factory*, was published. It got uni-formly positive responses and lots of reviews, and, I think, that if I had been part of the New York poetry establishment at that time, instead of one of those "poets from the coffee houses," the book would have been nominated for a Pulitzer. At least that's what I think in retrospect. However, despite the fact that I wasn't part of that estab-

A Gotham Bookmark signing party, ca. 1973. From left: *Armand Schwerner, a Harper's editor; Wakoski; Clayton Eshleman; and Leonard Cohen*

lishment, I began to think that I might be able to earn my living taking advantage of all the soft money in colleges and universities for the arts. Every English department wanted to sponsor poetry readings because students all claimed to love poetry. For the first time, and actually the only time in my life when this was true, someone was supporting me and I didn't have to get a scut job to earn my living. Tony Weinberger was taking care of me, but I am the kind of person who can't sit still when there are possibilities of independence, so I did something that now is common but which no one did in those days. I started writing letters (on my old typewriter, with carbon paper of course). I wrote about a thousand letters that first year. I think maybe that resulted in two or three readings. But wherever I went, and I would go for even the smallest fee—$25.00 even—if it didn't cost me more than that to get there, I seemed to surprise and interest people. They liked the combination of my passionate poetry readings, my Mod (that was the word in the late sixties) appearance with miniskirts, long black stockings, often boots, my long hair, oddly combined with a bookish ability to analyze. I loved to talk about poetry, about aesthetics and poetics. I was happy to read anybody's poetry and critique it, and though I have always been a rather harsh,

Diane Wakoski with Jerry Rothenberg at a college poetry reading,
upstate New York, 1972

or perhaps the correct word is "honest" critic, this didn't always make
people like me, but it made them respect me. I got a reputation as
someone who would take teaching seriously, and often I would be
invited for a week or two for workshops, and then finally in 1972 I
was invited for the first time to be a Visiting Writer for a semester.

You asked about any readings that stand out, and you suggest that
they were readings with other poets. I am afraid that I am a narcissist
and to share a reading was never a plus for me. I loved my readings
at both the San Francisco Poetry Center in 1959 and at the YMHA
Poetry Center in New York in 1961, because I read with others and
was considered the star. After *Inside the Blood Factory* came out, I
received a call from Robert Lowell, who was the acme of the poetry
establishment. He said he'd read my book because everyone was talking about it, and he invited me to read with him at a summer festival
in the Berkshires. Guess what? I turned him down flat, even though I
was a long-time admirer of his. I didn't want to be the warm-up group
for Robert Lowell. Nobody would be there to see me or hear me.

I once had to read on the same program with James Baldwin, in
Canada, and I hated it. Everyone was waiting for him to come on

and no one wanted to hear me. I could have been Orpheus and they would have been sighing and wishing I would hurry up and get off the stage. However, I don't want anyone to get the idea that I am unwilling to give readings with other poets. But the best tandem readings are with two equally famous, yet very different poets, so that the audience is there to hear both of them. I think the greatest poetry reading I ever heard was one given in Buffalo in the eighties by Robert Creeley and Robert Duncan. It was sponsored by James Hillman and the Jungian group in the Buffalo area. Hillman's introduction was thrilling of course, and then the two readings were stunning. Two poets at the peak of their maturity, with fabulous though very different bodies of work. The poets had long known and respected each other from their original association at Black Mountain College, and they were fiercely competitive in the best sense. We heard a tour de force reading that night. If I could ever be part of such a reading, I would feel like I was living in Nirvana. Just to listen to it was bliss.

Edward Jenkinson: Diane, at what age did the decision to actually be a poet happen? How were you effected?

DW: When I was a student at Berkeley (1956–1960), I became immersed in two things: practicing the piano about five hours a day and writing poetry, which included my working on the campus literary magazine, *The Occident,* going to occasional readings and workshops in San Francisco, and studying poetry with Thom Gunn, Tom Parkinson, and Josephine Miles. I was obsessive about these activities.

I think it was during my junior year that I had a kind of epiphany. I realized, because I worked twenty hours a week in the university practice rooms and could hear all the wonderful local pianists, that I didn't have any of the skills as a pianist that the outstanding music students did. I also realized that they were all well grounded in theory and history, and that I really was an outsider as a musician. What I did was terribly amateurish, despite the amount of time I spent.

Whereas this was contrasted with the fact that whenever I talked about literature, people listened to me, praised me, responded to what I said. Even more, my poems captured much attention. I won student undergraduate poetry prizes. I was often the star of my poetry class, and I had undisputed authority on the staff of the literary magazine. Thus, I realized one day, that poetry was what the world might acknowledge in me. Music would never be.

I suddenly felt as if all my life had been pointed toward a life as a poet. During my senior year, I stopped obsessively practicing the piano, and when I was asked to read at the San Francisco Poetry Center, newly formed, that year, I felt I had seen the handwriting on the wall. Poetry was to be my life. Cold turkey, I gave up playing the piano. Not just the study and practice, but entirely. It's the kind of obsessive thing I do, but it was important to me to make that sacrifice, give up that thing I loved, in order to appreciate my own serious commitment to poetry. I have never regretted this, though when I read my poem, "Thanking My Mother for Piano Lessons," which alludes to this event, I often find people who misunderstand me or my poetry saying to me, "it's too bad that you felt you had to stop playing the piano, Diane." They don't get it; they don't get it at all.

EJ: As you've matured has that feeling changed?

DW: I don't think it ever changed. Poetry is still my life. I still make a living doing whatever I have to do to survive, though during the years when I earned my living traveling around the country giving poetry readings I really felt that I was at the center of the universe, and I loved every minute of it, no matter how difficult it was.

EJ: As a poet, what do you feel are the biggest changes you have seen since you began publishing? How are things different today? What difficulties were involved in getting your first book published?

DW: I think that I've seen two sets of changes which occurred in the world of published poetry since roughly 1959, when I began publishing my poems in little magazines. The first is that little magazines were just beginning to flourish and to be considered legitimate places for serious poets to publish their work when I started. The second was the event of poetry readings.

I use the word "serious" because in the fifties there was a plethora of so-called light verse written by poets like Phyllis McGinley and Ogden Nash, to name among the best and most interesting of such poets. It was still a fashion to publish poems in newspapers, usually on the editorial page, and usually those poems were written on current events subjects or were popular and sentimental poems. Also popular magazines such as, *Ladies Home Journal,* or, *Boys' Life,* published poetry, but it was usually rather maudlin; sentimental and not taken seriously by most of us who thought of ourselves as something different and better. Into this world where much poetry had a more

Diane Wakoski with Joel Oppenheimer, St. Marks Poetry Project director, 1971

or less nonliterary life and a small amount of serious poetry, usually written by academics or self-styled literary folk, was published in very limited editions by a handful of poets, entered the energetic activity of young poets and writers who wanted to expand the current poetics. Though we dreamed of literary success, we had the feeling that we could never be published by the established journals like, *The Paris Review,* or, *The Kenyon Review,* or even, *Poetry Chicago* (as it was called then). Even though we assiduously submitted our poems to such publications, we began to look for lesser known outlets, and often, we ourselves even became willing to start a little magazine for the purpose of publishing the new writing.

In this context, my first serious adult published poem came out in a little California magazine called, *Coastlines,* in 1959, and my first collection of poems was published by a small press, Hawk's Well Press, in New York City in 1962. In 1961, I was included in an anthology of four poets selected by LeRoi Jones (aka [Imamu] Amiri Baraka) called, *Four Young Lady Poets.* It was published via a collaboration between his little magazine, *Totem/Yugen* and the press started by owners of the Eighth Street Book Shop, called Totem-Corinth Press.

Their purpose was to publish what we now would call "alternative" writers, but in fact that term would never have been used in the sixties in the context of poetry. We were the "new poets" who were not part of the "old boy" network, but we certainly had ambitions to be the new literary establishment. Unlike contemporary alternative bands, we did want major labels or their equivalent—trade publishers, Pulitzer prizes, poet laureateships, and to be published in *Poetry Chicago*. We didn't want to be alternative, we just were.

The second difference that I've experienced in the poetry world since I began publishing was the rise (and now the fall, I think, in the nineties) of the public poetry reading as the center of poetry life in America. When I came to New York City in 1960, from Berkeley where I had been an undergraduate for four years, I helped to bring some of the revolution of the Beat Movement with me to New York. For that movement was really a San Francisco phenomena, and New York had only the offshoots of it manifesting itself in the beginning of coffee house poetry readings. Actually, most of that activity was on MacDougal Street where poets whom I and many others called "street poets" read their poems that often were praises of drugs and orgiastic freedom. I was part of a different breed of poet, really. We were mostly college educated and while we didn't want anything to do with so-called "academic poetry," and most of us had decided we didn't want scholarly lives in universities, still we were deeply influenced by the Moderns, more by Stevens and Williams than Eliot, and as I said we longed to create a new poetry establishment that was full of the Dionysian search for sexual and personal freedom, but not particularly dominated by an interest in drugs or politics or throwing away the traditions of formal poetry, as the Beats were. We wanted to incorporate the past into what we did, but as Pound enjoined us: "make it new."

For me, the coffee house poetry readings evolved into a life of traveling to colleges and universities, usually the center for poetry, to give readings funded by soft money from all the government grants available to universities for literature and other liberal arts activities in the late sixties end early seventies. There was nothing like this in the fifties when I went to high school and to college. It reached its peak in the late seventies and then the money started to drain away, but already it had created one permanent change. Colleges and universities were now hiring poets and other artists without Ph.D.s, making a place for them on the permanent faculty, creating programs like the MFA in Creative Writing which built writers and contemporary writing into the curriculum. This was an entirely new phenomenon, and my generation of poets helped to create it.

You ask if it was difficult to get my first poem published. I think the best short answer is that one reads the publications one wants to be part of and then simply submits the work diligently until some editor falls in love with it. I have always had good luck with some magazines and publishers and bad luck with others. I just keep sending my work out to editors, publishers, and publications that I respect in the hopes that someone will recognize its merits.

EJ: Would you talk a bit about fairy tales and myth, and what they mean to you in your work?

DW: I think I will separate myth and fairy tale, though they are both examples of archetypal stories found in cultures. However, the word "myth" has larger connotations, and in my judgment, while you can easily talk about poetry without talking about fairy tales, you cannot talk about ANY poetry without discussing and understanding myth.

In fact, as far as I am concerned the major function of a poem is to create a trope (or poetic structure) out of which a writer can shape some version of myth, be it a story, an archetypal character or pattern, or theme that is being used.

I am not sure talking about this makes sense in the context of a short interview. However, I'll include one Wakoski touch. I have added to the poetics of our time a bit by introducing the concept of a "personal mythology." (I did not coin the term which comes from psychology rather than literary studies, though I was one of [or the] first to use it in connection with writing poetry.) I do believe that poets who are successful always create a personal mythology out of the mythic elements of their lives and cultures, and that recognizing this helps us to understand our individual tasks as poets.

Probably the answer to this question is part of a fuller discussion of Diane Wakoski creating and/or finding her own personal mythology. I don't think creating one's personal mythology is a conscious act. I think we are doing it unconsciously from the beginning, if we have any talent for poetry at all. Therefore, it's when a poet begins

Diane Wakoski reading from Discrepancies
and Apparitions *at a writers' conference at*
Solano Beach, San Diego, 1969

to recognize what she does that her writing can get stronger, if she knows how to use that recognition. You ask how this effects my writing, and the answer is that once I recognize what I am doing then I can become a better craftsperson, make my writing tighter, more complex, hopefully better.

EJ: Do you have anything to say on contemporary poetry?

DW: I am part of a generation of poets who wanted to expand the possibilities of formal verse, not eliminate it. We saw our "free verse," not as free of form but free of specific traditional metrical forms that had left Modernists feeling constricted. But metrics will always be a part of poetry, to my way of thinking.

I do think the problem in contemporary poetics is that many practitioners of "the new formalism" don't really have a better gift for metrics or traditional forms than many good poets who write free verse.

All aspects of form should be a choice, and all formal poems need to be, as Pound enjoins us, "as well written as prose."

The very making of art is, to quote another great poet, a "rage for order." We write poems to order our world. We need the most highly structured language, the most condensed and precise forms of language to really re-make our world. I don't see how any poet could argue with any other about the fact that art comes out of obsession and desire but when making that art it is necessary to have skillful access to all possible forms and structures, some traditional, some new, all recognizable.

EJ: Any vision of the twenty-first century?

DW: Don't have one.

EJ: When and where do you tend to write?

DW: I love to write in the mornings, especially when the light is beautiful. I write at my computer, or at my typewriter. Usually in front of a window, so that I can view a framed world.

EJ: Can you talk about your latest work you have published? And, if you wouldn't mind, the authors you are currently reading.

DW: I wrote a new part of my long on-going work, *Greed,* last fall. "Greed: Part 14," is on the subject of a poet's greedy obsession for purity. It is forty manuscript pages long, the longest of my various "Greed" poems, and I think my publisher, John Martin, of Black Sparrow Press is planning to re-issue an edition of *The Collected Greed: Parts 1–13* with Part 14 added to the book. Currently, *The Collected Greed* is out of print. This is the first new part in ten years. I think John is planning to publish the new edition in the fall of 2000.

I am also planning another part, Part 15, but it might take ten years to get to that one too.

I am also trying to write either a very long essay or a very short prose book about my coffee house days of poetry in New York City from 1960–1975, though probably focusing on the earlier years. I want to talk about the very different sense of art that so many of us shared in the sixties when, no matter whether we longed for fame or fortune, we didn't see either one of them as commodifying art. We were so pure, believed so much in Art, with a capital "A." I want to talk about this because I think that many contemporary young artists long for this, hate the commodified culture we live in just as much as I do, and want a way to turn to art as the one place where Nothing Is For Sale! Even if we can't get those days back, I think we can talk about what they were like and what it meant and perhaps even take some inspiration from it. However, I am having a very hard time writing this material. I think I don't have the kind of discipline it takes to write a long extended piece of prose right now. I have to find that sense of discipline somewhere.

I am also working on a fifth volume in my *Archaeology of Movies and Books* series. I want this one to focus on an aspect of the Medea myth that touches on another theme in my poetry—brother and sister relationships. Medea is responsible for setting up her brother, Apsyrtus, to be murdered by Jason so that they can all escape with the Golden Fleece. I am writing about guilt and its expiation.

You ask about what I am currently reading. At present I read more fiction than poetry, perhaps because the one side-effect of being a poetry professor for almost twenty-five years, is to make me feel that reading poetry is hard work if you do it properly. Another side effect of analyzing poetry well is to make you want to rewrite almost everybody's poetry. This is really not acceptable. I read my friends, my old favorites, and poets who are recommended to me by someone I respect. Though it seldom happens, I look forward to finding new poets who will excite me.

As you can tell Diane Wakoski has been a part of contemporary poetry and a shaper of it as well. I suggest to everyone to attend one of her readings whenever you can, and also you can find her work on tape or CD, one in particular, *In Their Own Voices: A Century of Recorded Poetry*, in which she is surrounded by poets she has mentioned here and many others. Her poem "I Have Had to Learn to Live with My Face" begins Side 4. It would be difficult to sum up Diane Wakoski's life, but I believe Solon of Athens can sum up my answer best, "everything for humans is chance."

Perfume

I *Spring*

It started with my mother's Shalimar. So
few images of richness
in our two-room shack in the orange groves
during WW II. But my Navy daddy, with his white sailor
hat and wool big collared middies
would come home with presents, bargain luxuries
either from the PX or
foreign travel without duty: satin heart-
shaped boxes of candy,
beaten silver cups from India
and always for my mother,
the French perfume, a crystal bottle
shaped like a scallop, named
for an exotic garden misspelled,
Shalimar

How a little girl saw a woman: wrapped in perfume.
Fifty dollars a bottle in 1942. Two weeks' salary for
my mother, the bookkeeper.
She saved it for special occasions.

My mother most of the time had the
aroma of a cheap bath powder, Cashmere Bouquet, or dimestore
perfume, and my father of Old Spice after shave.
I didn't like those smells,
the former reminding me of a body like
a raw oyster that
no one could want to touch;
the latter my happy daddy who brought presents
and then departed, leaving us poor
and in misery, three females in a dusty
house with bare yard and broken
screens.

What, then, were the
fragrances of childhood
that lured me?
    The stationery store with its
    crisp boxes of Crane's laid bond, parchment, or faux vellum
       papers,
    the smell of formal invitations, and Parker pens,
    the expensive kind my mother owned to ply her bookkeeper's
       trade,
    writing tiny, neat figures into thick ruled ledgers.
    The smell of money,
    of wealth,
    expensive paper and fine nibbed pens.

    And starch, the hot iron gliding over starched
cotton blouses and dresses, my mother taking in ironing
to add to her meager bookkeeper's income. I would wake up
in summer, to morning doves chortling
outside, and the smell
    of hot slick cloth,
my mother standing at the ironing board,
the beautiful causeway of smooth shirts, ruffled
curtains, steaming their starched patina
into the breakfast air,
    fresh bookish morning, a little like library paste,
always an aroma children find enticing. I would
stretch in my top bunk bed,
listen to the doves, ruffling their throats
outside, feel
the radiance of morning itself
and the comfort, the security of the warm
ironed clothes
and household items,
gathering on hangers at the door.
    The smell of cleanliness and order.

Then the fat lady with her shopping bags,
who walked up from Santa Fe Springs Road to
take care of us
when Mama went to work.
> She gusted a smell of Juicy Fruit gum,
> and cherry life savers.
Her multi-layered bags,
old and worn as Chinese museum silks,
were full of sweet things,
candies and
cookies, her snacks for
the day, all wrapped in the perfect silver
swirl of Juicy Fruit gum,
> a smell like ripe bananas.

And the yardage store. When I got old
enough to use the treadle sewing machine
and even before I began to sew
it beckoned.
> There among the bolts of cotton goods especially
> I imagined living in
a mansion, with velvet drapes made from bolts and bolts
of fabric, with crisply tailored sofas covered
with chintz so stiff it would stand up alone, rolled
on long tubes and so much wider than
the other cloths.

Each case of spooled silk and cotton thread,
gleaming as if it were bird plumage, was like
a jewelry box; and I lingered over embroidery floss
whose colors glowed in slinky Technicolor.
Walking the aisles of fabric,
I imagined myself wearing taffeta evening gowns
with giant bows, Edith Head costumes,
perky Doris Day peu de sole swirling skirted dresses,
or slim satin cocktail gowns, all sewn from
these intact and complete cloths, these delicate as
Audrey Hepburn dimities flocked with blue cornflowers,

and the cards of lace that might trim the tissue cotton
into a fluffy blouse, or a night down.
    The smell of female beauty, lined up
    as perfectly articulated
    bolts of fabric.

Teenage life brought me a hand lotion
that was beautiful to my eyes, as the ocean. It was a
pale aquamarine color, the color of the fifties.
    And its fragrance was the coolness that I hoped
    to acquire, the smooth perfect girl I wanted to be,
    everything starched into stillness, each page
    of writing paper blank and waiting for
    insignias of black ink.
I wrote on grey paper,
an affectation, and wore Aquamarine Lotion, the
    tile and ice fragrance of a non-briny sea.
    How carefully I laid myself out,
    to smell of perfection,
    coolness,
    starched order,
    apart from the raw world.

I think of Berkeley as smelling
    like coffee, also a fragrance I loved from
my childhood; not knowing then that the perfection of coffee
was a fresh ground bean. Its fragrance
    wrapped round me, as I saw
    in cafes, wrote harlequin poems,
    and no longer smelled like Aquamarine.

New York City was the scent of books and curry.
Vital organic smells, that had nothing to do with anyone's body
though they were such physical odors.
Such an old city, and old buildings, filled
with bookstores where silverfish scurried out of
each volume as you opened it, and mildew
    was also a smell of learning and reading. Coffee houses often

smelled like cinnamon, and deli's smelled of pickles
and herring.
I began to think about wearing perfume.
A woman wore
expensive perfume, and if a man
didn't bring it as a present,
she bought it for herself. It was her sign.

The prices steep always,
and now we are in an era of spray bottles, and
thus larger volume. Now, it's not perfume but
eau de toilette or eau
de cologne. The concentrated essence, the perfume itself
too heavy, too hard to use.
We moved from the age of musk
to the age of airy scent, away from the glass
stopper rubbed against
the wrist and at the ear pulse,
to the cloud of droplets
vaporized around our bodies,
the spray of scent
    like petals all over our bodies.

I found a perfume finally,
like my mother's,
it was a Guerlain, French and
pricey fragrance,
    "Mitsouko"
      so delicate you almost can't smell
      it on my body, light and dark
      at the same time.
I love to open my closet
and smell it hovering lightly over the rack
emanating from the sleeves
and lapels. So many years now
of Mitsouko. Occasionally exchanged for other
crushes, "Diorissimo," "Ysatis," but always
I return to the subtle one,

"Mitsouko,"
that disappears everywhere except
in my closet.

II *Summer*

Last month, while listening to an NPR interview with Catherine Deneuve, I heard a usually sensitive and smart interviewer ask a question that shocked me. Not just for its ageism, but for its assumptions about aesthetics, I think. Terry Gross of "Fresh Air," usually such a good interviewer talked generally with Deneuve, then introduced a bit of chat about her work with Richard Avedon in making Shalimar commercials, interesting in itself as Deneuve talked about how she really enjoyed being photographed for ads, how she entered into the enterprise as seriously as a film and did not consider it simply hack work to make money.

What Terry Gross asked Catherine Deneuve that shocked me so much was, "Do you *still* wear perfume?" I am to this minute completely *stunned* by this, wondering where such a question came from! Why would a woman, just because she is aging *stop* wearing perfume?

Catherine Deneuve has been generally described as one of the most beautiful actresses in the world. I concur with this description entirely. Even in her latest films, where she is in her sixties, she is more beautiful than most women ever dream of being at sixteen or twenty-one. Yet, Terry Gross's question seemed to strip her of this.

I suppose, since I am also someone who loves perfume and regards it as more than an enhancement of life like good food, interesting wine or books, I think of it as something a person wears all the time, whether alone or in company, to bed alone or with a lover, even when she is working. I wear perfume in the same way I use soap or deodorant, and don't plan to stop using any of those items just because I get old.

Perhaps over the years one might change one's perfume, as the varieties are endless. And if Deneuve had said that when she was making the commercials she wore a certain Guerlain perfume, but now as she grows older she prefers a different kind of fragrance, this might have made sense of a question like "Do you *still* wear perfume?" (i.e. "Do you still wear the *same* perfume?") But what transpired in this interview seemed to contain an assumption on Terry Gross's part that women only wear perfume when they are young and seductive. In fact, the question contained only negative, or perhaps naïve, assumptions. Deneuve, always cool and sophisticated, simply replied "Of course I wear it, even now that I live in the country."

Thus, this elegant and always gracious woman dignified Terry Gross's insulting question to the extent of implying that one could understand that Gross might perceive perfume as an Apollonian city artifact, not appropriate for rustic or agrarian life.

I've always been impressed with Terry Gross who, while she has a genuineness about her and occasionally suggests a modest opinion, also has an enthusiasm that is nice in an interviewer and never argues with her guests, even when they probably are offending her, and usually always stands back and lets them talk after she introduces pithy questions. I have never heard her ask a really insensitive question before this.

It is very hard, aging. And it must be multiplied when you've been famous as one of the most beautiful actresses in the world. I don't think we really understand very much about getting older, and the fact that in many ways we do change as we age seems to obscure the reality that we probably don't change in the ways that old age changes are stereotyped. A beautiful woman is almost always beautiful until she dies, barring debilitating illness, and a woman who has loved perfume all her life, having once become an icon of VOGUE magazine and other perfume commercials, is not going to stop wearing it.

I didn't come away from the interview with Deneuve, one of my favorite actresses (*Belle du Jour* is my movie), thinking and knowing more about her, as I should have. Instead, I came away wondering what is wrong with Terry Gross? Alas, the answer is that she is simply reflecting common American ideas about age and sophistication. Very negative items. And probably very stereotyped. Alas, alas, in some respects, we remain *the truly* "Ugly Americans" Europeans described in the fifties of this century.

III *Autumn*

Robert is tearing up the summer garden
and today, he's brought into
the dining room, great bunches
of herbs. Tied up with green hemp cord,
the tall as a Chinese fan bunch of sage
has a silver sheen and emits an odor of pungent
suggestions. For instance, a roasting chicken stuffed with onions,
dry bread and sage.

The bunch of thyme is springy
like a head of newly washed hair, or green feathers you might
stuff into a doll's pillow. It wafts the delicate scent
of a path trodden on by two lovers,
or the smell of a child's clean hand.

The slightly gawky lengths of tarragon wave at me
with their licorice fragrance and invite me to
combine them, not as herbs but as cut flowers, with some red salvia
of little odor at all, just a decorative annual still growing
in the garden where Robert hasn't yet tilled.
I put this bouquet on a shelf above my crimson movie-watching chair
to flutter down on me the scent of a light cream sauce
for a salmon
or the sweet bite of it in rice vinegar to dress some greens.

For weeks now
I've been cutting the long branches of sweet
basil into huge swards
and thrusting them into tall pitchers. Now most of the basil
is in full bloom,
its white little orchid flowers, multitudes living
each frond, are almost
as fluffy as cherry blossoms in the spring.
The odor of the basil
is earthy, even rank at certain moments
of the day, then a fallen

leaf might get crushed as I trod on it, walking past the
stand where the pitcher sits, and it is
that smell of fresh oily pesto,
or the smell of that great combination—tomatoes and basil—
that changes our lives when we first taste it.

But it is the huge bale of rosemary, also tied together, but fomenting
    out
into many directions, that dominates our autumn
rooms today.
Rosemary for remembrance,
the unforgettable smell
of roasted lamb, of scalloped potatoes,
of salt breads, of the medicine
of an herb garden, healing
our daily need for fragrance in
complex,
grown up
ways.

"Do you still wear perfume, Diane?"

"Do you still breathe, Terry?"

Of course. Beyond spring, summer, into autumn,
and finally in winter. Even over the ice
can you detect the slight subtle fragrance of Mitsouko?

    IV *Winter*

Braised Short Ribs

and purple mashed potatoes.
Violets. Well, I
altered that part of the recipe,
used normal white
Russet potatoes, mashed after the whole

day this savory bistro preparation had radiated its
autumn smell through the house. First
the ribs butchered into short blocks,
wide as the ceremoniously cut ribbon wrapping a new building,
were browned with olive oil,
darkened to the shade of old sunflower
heads, and then set aside
while the mirepoix,
—chopped celery, carrots, onion, garlic and shallots—
was sweated and just browned a little
in the same pot, then set to flambé
with brandy, only I used Framboise,
white raspberry brandy. And a cup of dry
red wine added and reduced by a third
before adding the beef stock and
the browned short ribs.
Then bring it all to a boil.
Into the oven, simmering, at a low temperature but not
so low that the pot would ever stop
simmering during its next three hours.
Now the aroma of the braised short ribs
rises in a puff and hovers through your hair,
around your ears, as you open the lid
and with tongs, remove the meat
to a platter. Now strain out the vegetables
from the juice, and put the juice in a bowl,
into the freezer to collect the fat.

Later, just before dinner
your beurre manie, soft and smooth
as baby skin is rolled into balls and whisked into the sautéed shallots
boiling now in more red wine to thicken into a sauce.
Set aside. In another pot you sauté
your already blanched pearl onions with oyster
mushrooms, crimini
mushrooms, shitake
mushrooms, pieces of wild autumn.
Set aside.

Out of the freezer comes the cooking liquid with
a crust of fat thickly over its top. You cut
it off, discard, and ladle the jelled liquid
into your thickening sauce of wine and shallots and beurre manie,
bring it to boil and then reduce heat while allowing
it to continue to thicken. Add the braised ribs,
cook for about fifteen minutes, add the mushrooms and pearl onions,
and serve over mashed potatoes.

So simple this dish, but time consuming
to prepare. Yet its results are a house that is savory
all day, and a meal that has
a history of involvement.
A perfume that comforts daily reminders of our failures.

This is the perfume you cannot
wear everyday.
Not every day can generate
something so elaborate.
Cooking this meal to share with my husband, filling my house
with autumn's scent, makes me grateful
for our life together.
Later I fall asleep next to Robert with the
special unbottled fragrance of this autumn meal wafting
through the house. Burying my face in the
pillow, I locate the faint breath
of Mitsouko in the linen.
Am doubly thankful.

Yes, Terry.
I am sure I will always wear perfume.

CAROLYN KIZER

INTRODUCTION
Jeanine Marie Derusha

MIT ARTIST-IN-RESIDENCE Arthur Ganson creates sculptures that fuse the physical science of mechanics with delicate organic elements like eggshells, a wishbone, and fabric. Self-described mechanical engineer and choreographer, Ganson's sculptures reveal the relationship between mechanical machines and organic earth: what is more machine-like than the calculating change of seasons? And what is more organic than the properties of physics?

Such unlikely philosophical connections seem to inspire the writing of poet Carolyn Kizer. Like the occupation "mechanical engineer and choreographer," occupations listed on Kizer's passport might read: "Poet. Political Commentator. Translator. Critic. Chinese Historian. Mother. Teacher." Only someone for whom there is little distinction between those titles could deliver forth poems in the nature of Kizer. Incisively erudite and witty, Kizer creates a gifted vision of relationships: not simply between human beings, but between physics and life, between science and humans, and between politics and the personal. Kizer's poetry delivers revelation by drawing connections and inspiration from the world-at-large, and observing metaphorical, metaphysical relations between objects.

Carolyn Ashley Kizer, age 5 or 6

I was first drawn to the poetry of Carolyn Kizer through her early book, *The Ungrateful Garden*. Engaged immediately by the language of the first three poems, "The Ungrateful Garden," "The Intruder," and "The Worms," one notices Kizer's lines are clean and strong, lacking superfluous particles and words, conscious of rhythm and aural presence.

Midas watched the golden crust
That formed over his streaming sores,
Hugged his agues, loved his lust,
But damned to hell the out-of-doors
   ("The Ungrateful Garden")

My mother—preferring the strange to the tame:
Dove-note, bone marrow, deer dung,
Frog's belly distended with finny young,
   ("The Intruder")

Kizer's work is also noted by rich description and conceit: of the worm, she writes breathtakingly, "Bare as a rose, / Vulnerable as veins, / naked as a nose" ("The Worms"). Then dawns the complexity of her subject. In "Twelve O'clock," Kizer puns on laws of physics to define relationships: "I was dead certain that uncertainty / Governed the universe, and everything else, / Including Mother's temperament."

Often an adroit formalist, Kizer is by no means conventional. In 1965 she wrote, "Pro Femina," a work of prophetic political spirit and vigor. She is also by no means reserved. Her poems (and prose as well) are filled with wordplay and puns: "Pro Femina" begins, "From Sappho to myself, consider the fate of women. / How unwomanly to discuss it! Like a noose or an albatross necktie / The clinical sobriquet hangs us: cod-piece coveters. / Never mind these epithets; I myself have collected some honeys."

Born and raised in Spokane, Washington, she attended Sarah Lawrence College, Columbia University, and the University of Washington, where she was founding editor of *Poetry Northwest*. Kizer studied with David Wagoner and Theodore Roethke, about whom she has written in admiration, and discussed his impact on her own teaching: "Another thing Ted used to have us do—which I often do with students is tell them, 'Take out all the adjectives and see what you've got left. See which ones are absolutely essential to the poem.'"

From 1964–1965, Kizer served as Specialist in Literature for the U.S. State Department in Pakistan. She was awarded the 1985 Pulitzer Prize for her book of poems, *Yin*. Other awards and prizes include: the Frost Medal and Masefield Prize of the Poetry Society of America; The American Academy and Institute of Arts and Letters Award; The Award of Honor of the San Francisco Arts Commission; The Borestone Award (six times); the Pushcart Prize (three times); The Theodore Roethke Poetry Prize; The Washington State Governor's Award for 1965, 1985. Kizer has taught at universities including Columbia, Stanford, Princeton, and the University of Arizona. She was named a Chancellor of the American Academy of Poetry in 1995, and keeping with the spirit of "Pro Femina," resigned from the prestigious position (along with Maxine Kumin) in 1998 to protest the absence of women and minority groups on the Academy's board of chancellors.

In one of her essays, Kizer cites Roethke's idea that "every line of a poem should be a poem." Similarly, every poem is evident of a life. After reading Kizer's work, I am reminded of a line in "The Oration":

Still, I have to be proud of my eloquence.
    It was the speech of my life.

NOT THEIR HISTORY BUT OUR MYTH: AN INTERVIEW WITH CAROLYN KIZER

David Rigsbee and Steven Ford Brown

*T*HIS INTERVIEW was begun in Austin, Texas, April, 1987, and completed in Sonoma, California, in March, 1988.

David Rigsbee: You were talking about poetic models today. What is the importance of a poem modeled after somebody else?

Carolyn Kizer: Christopher Middleton and I were talking about that. It started because I said I had learned a lot about writing from Ritsos because Ritsos has a very strong filmic sense. By manipulating pronouns he can give you a pan shot, a closeup, a middle range kind of thing. I'm thinking particularly of a poem called "Women," an extraordinary poem in which he begins by talking about women: "they" and then talks about women: "she," and then there's a very close shot in the kitchen where it's "you," and then at the end it's "they" again. It's a poem about women losing their husbands to war. At the end the women are standing in the railway station waving their handkerchiefs saying goodbye, and it's extraordinary the effects he gets from that. Christopher asked if I had written poems in the style of Ritsos and Cavafy, and I said yes I had, but they're strictly for the notebook. Of course I believe that all that horsing around, all that experimenting is fruitful for the next time you do [write]. You have to be able to distinguish between the poems in which you're practicing and the poems in which you're making a poem of your own. I think what you're learning is internalized and then comes out in different ways.

DR: But of course you've also used models in a more active sense, for instance with Catullus.

Author photograph for jacket of The Ungrateful
Garden, *1961. Photo by John Palmer*

CK: And Chinese, of course. But that's a little different than just
trying to pick up techniques—using a whole poem and doing a kind
of variation on it, on a theme. But I think what involves Ritsos and
Cavafy is a question of experimenting, in the case of Ritsos, technique.
In the case of Cavafy, whose poems are totally unmetaphoric, the
metaphor is historic: it's between *then* and *now,* between *that time* and
this time, and between this time and that time.

DR: So "then" is a metaphor for "now."

CK: Yes. I think everybody who has studied Cavafy closely— and
I think Alan Dugan has probably come closest to writing a Cavafy
poem—has learned something about metaphor as history, and history as metaphor, however you want to put that, which I think is
extremely interesting. What you have to do if you're a poet is work
against the kind of thing you do easily. Rhyming was always very easy
for me, so I quit using end rhymes and started using internal rhymes,
off-rhymes, and so on. Metaphor is something that came very easily,
so I think Cavafy is very valuable in that he shows you how metaphor

may not be associated with line or the image in the line, but with the whole conceptual relationship between "that was then, this is now."

DR: Do you know any other poets who work in the cinematic sense you mentioned? Are there any American poets you're aware of who work in quite the same way with that sort of knowledge?

CK: I don't think so. There certainly *will be*. There probably are, I just don't know about them.

DR: Well, movies are so predominant in this culture, you would think poets would pick up on technique as well as subject matter.

CK: It's interesting what people pick up from film. Somebody was just using that example of the sestina using Donald Duck and Mickey Mouse. People have picked up the paraphernalia of film, and I'm thinking of the kinds of things that film photography can do that are unique to the medium.

DR: Still, it's a curious kind of omission. You were talking earlier today about the common body of knowledge that one could once assume that a poet or a poetry student would know. Edward Field has a little theory that the only common body of knowledge we have nowadays is movies.

CK: Or television.

DR: Right. That's why so many of his recent poems have been about movie stars and the retelling of the myths about Hollywood— poems about Joan Crawford, Frankenstein, and so forth.

CK: The first person who really did that was Frank O'Hara. And then Walker Percy in fiction—*The Moviegoer*.

DR: Well, it seems that poetry would pick up on these techniques at least and use them as a shorthand.

CK: I always like to believe that every poem you write is deathless, is going to echo down the ages, and people are going to say, "Who was Minnie Mouse?" I'm very wary about using contemporary figures—movie stars, etc., in a poem. I have a poem about picketing Woolworth's ["Poem, Small and Delible"] in which you explain what picketing is, and you explain what Woolworth's is, and you explain who Martin Luther King was, etc. I mean that you're assuming that the thing you're writing about is going to be totally incomprehensible to some future generation. Of course now we don't know if there're going to be any future generations, but I still think it is important for poets to have that kind of arrogance that assumes that the poetry is not going to be lost, and that you want to avoid having it footnoted all over the place. Or if you have footnotes, then there's something substantive, as Eliot's were. I mean one of the hangups about reading Pope for example is you have to find out who all these people are, this cast of characters. The same thing is true of Juvenal and Catullus, but of course I find it worth it because I love those poets, and I'm fascinated to see what Pope did with a minor figure, like Colley Cibber, for example. I find that very much fun.

DR: I love that remark of yours in that review [of Maynard Mack's *Alexander Pope*] where you mention Colley Cibber's line "perish the thought"—as "the only thought of his that didn't perish." That's wonderful. Would you speak a little bit about Roethke's workshop? That's something I remember hearing bits and snatches of from you and Tess [Gallagher], and others.

CK: Well, I'm amazed, you know, because I've kept my notebooks from Roethke's class, because now we're talking about thirty years ago, and I'm fascinated to see how closely I've modelled my own teaching style on his. A lot of it is unconscious, but part of it is deliberate. He was a great and fantastic teacher, and I even use a lot of poems that he used to illustrate things, like Bogan, Lèonie Adams, and [English poet] Ruth Pitter. It's interesting that Ted was such a male chauvinist in private life, but as a teacher, he was totally without sexual prejudice, and used women as examples actually in class more often than he used men.

DR: I remember the first class I had with you: the first thing you did was to sit down and read [Bogan's] "Cassandra."

CK: The Cassandra poem I've often used as an example of how a poet of Bogan's generation—all these women poets roughly categorized as "Oh, God, the Pain! Girls" who wrote really the kind of poetry that men wanted women to write, which was poems about love and loss. I have quoted Dave Wagoner's wonderful remark about that poem of Sara Teasdale's which begins, "when I am dead, and over me / Bright April shakes out her rain-drenched hair," and Dave said that image reminded him of nothing so much as "a sheepdog caught in a lawn sprinkler." Bogan somehow distanced herself from that kind of sentimental love-and-loss poem which the men of the time expected women to write. On the other hand, Louise wasn't able to come out exactly with her own feelings. She had to disguise them

Carolyn Kizer, 1965. Photo by John Palmer

by naming them after figures in Greek mythology. So the Cassandra poem, which is basically a poem saying, "I'm never going to have a child"—although Louise did of course have a daughter—is put in the voice of Cassandra. The Medusa poem, which is an immensely complex poem, is a poem about stasis, really. In some ways, I think you could say it's a poem about a writing block. Louise had a lot of trouble with this. So the idea of this face which turned everyone to stone: it's almost as if Louise's muse turned *her* to stone. And vice versa. I mean I think she also felt she had the capacity to turn people to stone, to turn *poems* to stone. She was a tough customer.

Steven Ford Brown: One critic has suggested that mythology has been a useful technique for women . . .

CK: . . . To disguise what they wanted to say yes. And Louise is a prime example of that.

SFB: But that is changing . . .

CK: I often think of that line of Robert Graves, "There is one story, and one story only . . ." Actually there aren't very many stories. I am a Jungian to the extent that I believe in the archetypes. There are a limited number of stories, or figures, that can be manipulated. You can pretty much take all serious poems and fit them into one of those archetypal patterns. I think young writers don't know about this: there are certain depths that their poems don't plumb. They just don't get down there.

DR: Isn't this why it's a good idea, and I think you used to do this, to have beginning poets write down their dreams and keep journals so that they can identify and come back to their obsessions?

CK: That's of course where the archetypes come up. At Chapel Hill, Peter [Trias], Joan [Trias] and I used to exchange dreams at breakfast every morning and talk about them. Again, the figures were limited: the wise old man, the shadow, the goddess. What was interesting was the kind of changes that each individual would ring on these archetypal figures. I believe that dreams are instructions on how to live. This is one of my deepest beliefs, that your dreams are trying to tell you something about how to live, and sometimes you'll have three dreams in a night—and it's all the same dream. It's as if your subconscious wants to give you the message and worries that you don't have it, so it gives you a whole new scenario: "Ok, try this way . . . ," but it's the same message. And then of course as you come from deep sleep into a more shallow dream state, it may get more prosaic, and a little less interesting. A parallel there is when you write a poem, you have a little excess grain of energy, and you try to go on and write something else. It's rarely any good, you know, because, this is just left over from what you've done already. But I'm fascinated by people who don't take their dreams seriously, and even now, we're always having revisionist theories about dreams, that dreams don't mean anything—I just read something about that not long ago. Well, if dreams don't mean anything, poems don't mean anything either.

DR: I think one of the problems with dreams is that other people's dreams don't mean anything to you.

CK: I don't agree with that.

DR: Well I mean in the sense that they're toggled to private references. You need a whole ground of explanation before you can go in and start talking—conversing—intelligently about somebody else's dreams.

SFB: Or private mythology.

CK: I've had people tell me dreams that are as true to me as some of my own, and that may mean simply that they're resonating against something I've experienced. I think that's one of the most interesting things about exchanging dreams: it's like exchanging poems in the sense that again, you see how variations on these very limited number of basic themes work themselves out.

DR: You've written about your mother and father, and as far as I can tell, you had a very extraordinary childhood. Do you see it that way?

CK: Yes I do. That's of course what my autobiography is about—an extraordinary childhood. I was interested in the reaction a novelist friend of mine had when I showed her the autobiography—Alice Adams. She phoned me up about it and said she was interested in it, but I wasn't *really* letting her in on what the sources of the poetry were. I was giving her all the external paraphernalia. She said, "I kept thinking of that line of Yeats' about 'Mad Ireland hurt me into poetry'." I then tried to explain to Alice what I think one of the basic differences between a poet and novelist is: that's the stuff we hoard for our own purposes, while I think novelists simply come out with it and incorporate it into the work. One of the interesting things about writing an autobiography, as I said to you earlier, was that what I was doing was not repeating what was already written, but at the same time, I was also tiptoeing around, walking through a minefield of unexploded poems I might want to write someday. I didn't want to use *that* material. That's something that's in my kitty for future work.

SFB: In *Yin* and *The Nearness of You,* you have two prose autobiographical pieces about your parents. Were you trying to gain more intimacy with those pieces?

CK: A young woman came to me and said she was making a collection of feminist essays and I was the last person to contribute to the book. I said, "Could I please see the table of contents?" She showed it to me, and I said, "There's a curious omission here. No one has written about her mother." I think the mother-daughter relationship is *extremely* important in the work of poets. So I said I will write a piece about my mother, and I was really concentrating on writing a piece which would show, to the best of my knowledge, how my mother made a poet out of me. After I wrote it, at one point I decided to read it aloud to a group of women at a feminist conference, and I felt that they probably wouldn't be terribly interested because of the special circumstances of my life: my mother being forty-five when I was born, being the age of a grandmother, and the rather extraordinary background that I had of parents whose entire attention was focused on me. I was absolutely astounded when I finished reading this piece to find that women were in tears, because I hadn't expected that reaction. I realized that, despite the extraordinary experiences of my childhood, there was some kind of common denominator there. The best I could come up with was the pelican that feeds its young from its breast's blood; the idea of mother as giving up, of sacrificing some very important part of herself for her child.

Now the thing with my father was a lot more complicated. Because as I say in this autobiography, I was my mother's child, and my feelings about my father were a great deal more ambivalent and complicated, because he was a very beloved man and a revered figure in the community and in the larger world, but to me he was essentially a stranger, as I think I've said. For a long time I felt the only way I could deal with my father was by dividing him into "Good Daddy" and "Bad Daddy." In the autobiography what I've attempted to do is to bring the two together. Good Daddy was public daddy and a man of extraordinary moral integrity. Bad Daddy was the father who had never been around a child and didn't know what a child was and wasn't particularly interested—until I reached adolescence, when he in a sense fell in love with me. But by then it was too late to establish the kind of intimate connection that you have with a parent who gets up in the night when you're sick or having a nightmare and who changes the bed when you're ill and who rocks you when you're feverish and weeping—that whole kind of bonding that takes place, and which I think now takes place with many fathers and their children as well. Of course, psychologists say that we're all supposed to break that bond: we're supposed to break it with the father and we're supposed to break it with the mother if we're to grow up. Oh, I suppose in that sense we could say I've never grown up, which I think is also characteristic of a lot of poets.

DR: That was going to be my next question. With a mother intensely involved with your upbringing and an imposing father, did you ever feel a need to rebel?

CK: No, I didn't. And again, that may mean I've skipped an essential stage in my development, at least so one is told . . . It's never bothered me particularly! Yet like all children I had a private life and like all children I lied a lot. We all lie to our mothers. I used to say, joking, that I think the only person I ever really lied to was my mother. But children lie out of fear. I feared my mother's temper and her extravagant reactions. The kind of imaginative lying that children do is quite a different thing, where children give you their version of an event, and dumb parents say that that's a lie—my parents were too intelligent for that—that's a different proposition. The terrified lies that all children tell, though they know they're going to get caught, is a sort of reflexive thing.

SFB: Was this piece a central part of *Yin?*

CK: Well, it wasn't. The central part of that book was the Fanny Stevenson poem. That was what held the book up for, oh, five years, I guess. I worked on that poem for many years, and I knew that that was the focus of that book, the linchpin. I may even have stuck in the piece about Mother as an afterthought, to fill it out, I really don't remember. But I know that "Fanny" was the piece that had to be finished before I could have a book. Whenever I was pregnant, I always wanted to stay pregnant as long as possible because I enjoyed it. In a sense I think that's true with poems, with a big poem. I really don't want to let go, until forced.

DR: Have you thought about the central image, I mean if so many poems can be reduced to a single image, of *planting?*

CK: Oh, absolutely! Of course it's an intensely feminine thing. I've been fascinated for many years about what women do who are the support or nourishment of fathers, brothers, husbands, sons. What do these women—Wordsworth's sister, Mendelsohn's sister, Alice James, etc., you name it—what do they do with their creativity if they're terribly creative people, as Fanny Osborn Stevenson was? And what she did was *plant*. She wrote some books while he was alive, but her real literary life took place after his death. This is a subject insufficiently explored and something I'll have to do more with. A number of women writers in the last decade have tried to deal with this. The gifted woman was considered less important than her brother or the guardian of her father's estate. Or the widow of the writer who censored his work; there're so many horrendous examples of women who've destroyed important documents: Byron's for one, Edward Fitzgerald's probably the most terrifying example. His wife burned all of the extraordinary material that he had collected about sexuality in primitive societies, a lot of which could never be duplicated because the people he was writing about didn't exist anymore. So that is an absolutely fascinating topic.

SFB: The question of male writers reviewing women writers poses a lot of problems, and Roethke is an example. I think in one review he dismissed Louise Bogan. I think it was Bogan.

CK: No, he was pretty respectful of Louise, but there's a horrendous piece in which he describes and treats what is characteristic of women's poetry in a bad sense. I think some of it is quoted on the jacket of my first book, actually. Yes, it's very strange—that ambivalence of Ted's when he had such enormous respect for many women poets.

SFB: I know that's been a problem in the past, and a recent example is the poet Ai. A number of white, middle-class, middle-aged poets reviewed her books and absolutely dismissed her work.

CK: They didn't know what to do with it. I know it. I remember in an early review of my first book when a man said my poetry made him want to run his finger around his collar, it was embarrassing. I took that as a compliment. I think there's always been a devil in me that wanted to make people uncomfortable, not in the sense of being outrageous, or erotically outrageous, but I guess it's perhaps an impulse to convey some of my own unease and self-dissatisfaction, feeling that it's an important function of poetry to make people a little embarrassed, a little troubled, particularly about the stereotypes of women.

DR: I'd like to combine what you've just said with things you've said before about poems you've written which are essentially examples of language that is pitched to a different level of diction and rhetoric. There's a sense of separateness to a lot of your poems.

CK: Separateness from what?

DR: What I sense that you're doing is creating a ground for a resuscitation for what used to be called "public poetry." I'm thinking particularly of "Pro Femina" and "Running Away from Home," and certainly of some of the satirical pieces. I know you've talked before about the dearth of this kind of poetry.

At Kizer's wedding to Woodbridge, 1975

CK: It's easier of course if you're living in a country like the Soviet Union where poetry's taken seriously, and you make a statement and everybody's going to know about it in three or four hours.

DR: It's like journalism.

CK: Right. It's a different kind of thing. So that in a very curious way my poetry is speaking to an audience that isn't listening. I guess what we do about that is ignore it, largely. But we assume that some-body's listening.

DR: But maybe not the right people.

CK: Yes, I think that's one of the great difficulties. It's a great difficulty in belonging to almost any organization such as Physicians for Social Responsibility, which I belong to, because I said there's no point in joining "Poets for Social Responsibility" because it just gives social responsibility a bad name. But I see how we do talk to each other. We talk to each other about the atomic threat. In Amnesty we talk about the horrors of torture and trying to save people. But essentially we're talking to the converted, and this is distressing and sad. On the other hand, we all give public readings, and by accident sometimes we reach people who are not poetry readers, people who are there by accident, or people who have just happened upon you or your work, and then perhaps something happens. But it doesn't do to dwell on that too much: it's too depressing.

DR: Public poetry tries . . .

CK: I'm not sure I like that term. Social poetry?

DR: Social Poetry. Let's discuss the forms and precedents for that kind of poetry. You speak well and frequently of Pope, for example.

CK: Well, of course Pope too comes out of the Roman tradition, particularly of Catullus and Juvenal, and I feel I do too, that stream of classical poetry. It's not been a popular form in our time.

DR: What I'm trying to dovetail into is a discussion of changing forms. Like most of the poets of your generation, you—and I'm talking about Hugo and Merwin and . . .

CK: All right, Rich, Levertov, Wright . . .

DR: Well, most, with the exception of Levertov I suppose, began writing in form—formally—and yet everyone came out of that, practically at the same time, within a number of years. That's been mentioned a lot, but I haven't heard a particularly convincing explanation as to why it came about.

CK: Well, I think a lot of it came out of being trained by people like Roethke, who taught that you had to learn how to do it before you could throw it away. Christopher Middleton and I were talking about that today too, in terms of discussing Bernard Spencer and the best *Dream Songs* of Berryman. It's only when you have control over English syntax and you know what its possibilities are that you can really start breaking the rules in an active way. You can make a rough parallel with learning to play the piano: you begin with Czerny *Exercises,* then you go on to Bach *Inventions,* and you do all this boring stuff day after day, year after year, until you know it cold, then you can go be Stravinsky or somebody. You can break away from the learned patterns. I still feel that the learned patterns are important, though I certainly don't do as some of my colleagues do, teach the sestina and the sonnet and the villanelle. I do want people to understand what a line is, what form is, and have some sense of structure. One of the things that has irritated me is the idea that stressed verse is something artificial. I think under tension, pain, joy, terror, we all speak in stressed rhythms, short of saying "Help!" if the theater is on fire. But you look at the great documents of our history: the Gettysburg Address, the Second Inaugural, or Churchill talking about "blood, sweat, and tears," you see that they fall into the traditional cadences of English speech. They're not in free verse. I often think my students think that iambic pentameter was invented a long time ago by aged gentlemen with long beards and quill pens, saying, "Well now, let's invent a five-stress line." They have no notion that this came out of, well, first of all, religious ritual and dance, which was an intrinsic part of the earliest religion we know anything about. So it seems to me that means that these stressed rhythms are a natural part of us. They have something to do with pulse, the way we breathe, the way we phrase, and that it's just as natural to write in iambic pentameter as to write in free verse. Let's see, they don't call it free verse anymore. What do they call it?

SFB: Open forms.

CK: Open forms are supposed to be more natural than stressed lines, and I don't believe it. Of course there's never been enough emphasis on the distinction between mechanical and natural stressing. I'm always amazed that Shakespeare lived and Donne lived and showed us how to do it, and yet in the nineteenth century you get people using mechanical stressing. I mean Browning, for example, is ruined for me, as Poe is. Browning is more of a loss to me because of the kind of material that he chose and the fact that he dealt, as I do largely, with character. That's the thing I'm most interested in. And yet, because of the mechanical stressing it's almost impossible for me to read it. I wish somebody had translated him into French so I could read it in French the way we read Poe. This gets us to another point I would like to emphasize, which is that I feel I am principally occupied with character, not with nature. I'm one of the few Northwest poets who is not a nature poet and never has been. I always like to think about Heisenberg's principle that you alter subatomic particles simply by looking at them. There's no way you can see what they are because by looking at them you change them, and I think that's very true in writing about human relations. Even the most casual encounter between one person and another alters things forever. Just sitting here in this room talking, we will go out of it not being the same persons we were when we started, and I find that eternally fascinating. It's probably why I would never be a playwright because there has to be some dramatic change in the situation between people, but what I'm interested in are the nuances, the subtlest change. This led to my writing "Twelve O'Clock."

DR: Let's turn to translation, specifically Chinese translation. You lived in China.

CK: Well I was interested in Chinese poetry of course long before that. My mother read Arthur Waley aloud to me when I was a child, and I was fascinated by Chinese poetry. At Sarah Lawrence in the '40s all the language professors got drafted: French, German. Not Spanish. We had García Lorca's sister there. She was a formidable lady with a black mustache that scared the daylights out of me, and there was no way I was going to study anything with her. But anyway, the college imported a Chinese man from Columbia—he was not going to be drafted—and I was able to study with him and got a fellowship to Columbia in literature. I then went on to China where my father was by coincidence Director of United Nations relief. So it seemed to me that a whole series of coincidence or accidents in my life almost from the beginning pointed me toward Chinese poetry of the classical period, although it's perfectly true if there hadn't been a natural affinity for it, it probably wouldn't have taken.

DR: I was going to mention Germany.

CK: Or anywhere else my father could have been sent, or any other professor who could have been hired at Sarah Lawrence at that particular time. I think the affinity, as far as China is concerned, has to do with the dominant theme of Chinese poetry, which is friendship. I was on a panel with George Steiner, at which I said this, and he said, "Oh, but that's perfect nonsense. Some of the greatest English poems are about friendship." And I said, "Yeah, and all the friends are *dead*." "Lycidas," et cetera. While in Chinese poetry you're writing to your best friend who may live three thousand miles away, or he may live down the alley. Of course, one of the reasons Chinese poets were so prolific was primarily that they cast their poems more or less as letters, and they certainly didn't have our concept of revision, which is where we part company, of course. A Chinese poet is perfectly capable of saying something like, "Well I left this out of the second stanza, so I'll put it in now." I have always had this feeling that most of life's relations—the love of lovers, husbands, wives, and children—those loves are ephemeral, while friendship is something that can go on to the end of your life and beyond that.

DR: Borges says somewhere that the point of marriage is friendship, to end as friendship, a notion I think you subscribe to.

CK: Right. And you know that little thing I say in "Afternoon Happiness": "the endless nocturnal conversation of marriage . . ."

DR: Cyril Connolly. . . .

CK: Right—is "the best part." That of course implies friendship. You don't lie in bed talking over the events of the day and that kind of thing with somebody who's your enemy!

DR: One thing that just occurred to me when you pointed out that Chinese poetry is about friendship is that the poem is addressed, via letter or something similar, to someone who's alive, as opposed to . . .

CK: A memorial.

DR: A memorial. And one thing about a memorial is that almost all the elegiac poems in English are about the *poets*—not their subjects— starting with "Lycidas."

CK: Right. And the other interesting thing is that there are almost no famous elegiac poems in the classical Chinese period. The way you pay tribute instead is by imitating poems, and that can go on for generations. There are Chinese poems where only a phrase is changed. That's *your phrase,* to distinguish, in a Proustian sense, between this poem and the model on which you're basing yours, which I think is a marvelous idea. Americans are so hung up on the idea of being original. The Chinese have never had that problem.

SFB: Tomas Tranströmer went to China recently, and he told me that he met three generations of Chinese poets. Is Chinese poetry as a craft handed down from generation to generation?

CK: Well, I'm interested that Tomas said that because the only Chinese poets I know are either my age—sixty and up—or they're thirty. The whole middle generation was destroyed in the Cultural Revolution. No, there's a terrific split there, and the younger poets and the older poets have practically nothing in common. I think most of the ones that I've talked to in the last year or two feel that they've really distanced themselves. There are lots of reasons for that. One reason for it is that the older generation, if they were to survive at all, had to make terrible accommodations to what was happening. A lot of older people had to switch when the Party line switched. And probably some of the people who didn't are very dead. Then another reason is that the older people got terribly out of practice. Do you realize that during the Cultural Revolution they had house sweeps of writers' homes and any kind of poem or story they came across was confiscated and destroyed? An older poet I met of sixty-three, or something like that,—she has a Ph.D. from Brown, by the way—told me that after the Communists took over, she didn't write for a long, long time, except in secret. But one day, at the height of the Cultural Revolution, the neighbors came running in to say that the Red Guards were coming towards her house, so she took this manuscript that she had been working on secretly and thrust it in the stove. When the Red Guards got to her house—and this is the way she put it—they took her out in the yard for interrogation, and while she was being interrogated, her mother tried to kill herself. That's all she said about it, but that tells you all, doesn't it? So I think the younger people simply think that they belong to a new world. This led to my writing "The Ashes."

SFB: You've mentioned Shu Ting as being utterly different from previous generations, since modern Chinese poetry was born. How would you characterize her poetry?

CK: Well she belongs to a school called the "Misty Poets," and that means that there are certain parallels between the way she and her group have written and the way, the very indirect way, that people wrote poetry during the German Occupation, where you used a classical model, in a play like *Amphytrion 38*, or something, which was really about the occupying forces, where you learned to disguise what you were saying. Someone was saying the other day about Russian literature—my friend Robert Conquest, the great expert on Russian literature—that for quite a while the Russians, and then the Eastern Europeans, could get away with talking about the regime by placing it a thousand years before or in an imaginary country, but eventually the censors caught on to this, and you couldn't do it anymore. Shu Ting's generation has been influenced by Western poetry in ways which I find very mysterious, and we weren't able to communicate well enough for me to really go into this very seriously because we were at a conference. The college had invited every writer in the region to come and meet her, and all kinds of hippies preserved in amber came down out of the woods—what I have called "xenophiles."

Carolyn Kizer, 1984.
Photo by Thomas Victor

They asked her what the influence of Buddhism had been on her
poetry, and she smiled politely and said, well, actually she had been far
more influenced by Christianity. Oh, I wish you could have seen their
faces! She has a rather wicked sense of humor. . . . She said that she
had been principally influenced by Whitman and Dickinson. There's
a line in a poem of hers, "The Emperor is kneeling on the mat," which
I simply used Dickinson's language in translating. Now how she got
those books is what I don't know. When all books were confiscated I
just don't know how she could be influenced by those people.

DR: Well, perhaps if you see it coming, you know how to find a
place to squirrel it away.

CK: Yeah, there was some kind of weird *samizdat* thing going on.
Then there she was off in some kind of rural county with a bunch
of peasants shoveling manure and carrying fifty-pound bags of wheat
on her back when she was an adolescent. I think: how did this happen? It's one of those wonderfully interesting things I'd love to know
more about.

148

DR: How did you become involved in translating people like Bogomil Gjuzel?

CK: Well, I was going to a literary festival in Struga. Bogomil was running it at the time, and we got to be very good friends. So we'd sit around at night translating poetry with a lot of other people sitting in helping, it's just natural. But there again, there's wonderful story of Bogomil's about censorship which I want to tell. Bogomil had entered a playwright competition, and he won it—it was a nationwide contest. Then he said they took the prize away from him, and he was extremely annoyed about this, needless to say. And I said, "Well, tell me about the play, Bogomil." And he said, "Well, when the curtain goes up, God—a character playing God—is sitting on a pot. He's naked. He's sitting on a chamber pot, and he's wearing a Tito mask." And I said, "Oh, really. They didn't like that?" [laughter]

DR: I asked Amichai if he knew of any great or good writers in Israel, or for that matter, any writers of his acquaintance, who were not left wing, and he said no.

CK: Well that's true of this country—except Jim Dickey! The only writer in America who was for the Vietnam War.

DR: Well, American writers on the whole, American poets anyway, I don't think of as political as poets in other countries.

CK: Well, there are no Reagan voters among them.

SFB: Still, it seems our left wing is more passive.

CK: I don't know. I think a lot of that has to do with the conservation of energy. The level of anger necessary to deal with what's going on in this country is *consuming*. And we hoard what flagging energy we have. When I won the Pulitzer, I felt obligated to become more politically active because I thought at the moment, at any rate, my own name had some value. So I did a benefit in San Francisco for refugee writers of El Salvador, then for Nicaraguan writers, and I went over to the Berkeley campus and helped out with demonstrations against apartheid and things like that. I hadn't done that kind of direct political action in a long time, but I thought, well, if this prize's any good, let's use it. Political poetry isn't something you can will. The other thing of course is torture and the incarceration of writers. Which reminds me, today is the 4th of April. It's just thirty years since I wrote that poem about Herbert Norman. "I mark the fourth of April on this page." A book about Herbert Norman has just come out, which has my poem on the title page, I'm happy to say. Which is a good reminder of what was going on in the McCarthy period. We hear all the time in revisionist theory about how nice and benign everything was under Eisenhower, as if McCarthy hadn't existed. It's terrifying.

SFB: I think you commented on Hayden Carruth's work by saying that academic critics have a hard time getting a handle on poets who can't be pigeon-holed by school, subject matter, genre, or style.

CK: Where do I say that?

DR: You said that to me.

CK: Oh!

SFB: My question is about categorizing. Is trying to pigeon-hole you as a feminist writer an uncomfortable thing for you?

CK: Oh, not a bit. At the end of *Mermaids in the Basement* I say that I'm a feminist and all my friends are.

SFB: A number of critics and poets have commented—I think Adrienne Rich and Olga Broumas are two examples—on wanting to exercise more control but feeling they have been shut out of the language. For instance, to use an obvious example, the word "feminist" has a certain resonance or tenor that most people equate with being strident or unattractive. That's perhaps an example of language that has been masculinized so that the word has lost some of its original meaning.

CK: Well, what's called "strident" in women is called "strong" in men. I was particularly horrified by that book of Alicia Ostriker's where she said in commenting on "Pro Femina" that I "covered my pain with bluster." In the first place, I wasn't conscious of having any pain at all when I wrote "Pro Femina." I'd just read *The Second Sex,* and I thought, "Whoopee! Here's somebody who's saying what I've always thought and hadn't been quite able to articulate," and you know, I was on such a terrific high when I wrote that. But I was annoyed at the use of the word "bluster," which is again one of those laundered words: for energy, wit, assertiveness—good stuff. People don't call Robert Bly a "poet of bluster," though well they might!

SFB: Speaking of *The Second Sex,* a West German writer, Alice Schwartzer, said that when *The Second Sex* came out, it was like a secret code among emerging women writers.

CK: Well, I don't know why it was secret—maybe in Germany, but certainly not here.

SFB: Well even back in the sixties, when you wrote "Pro Femina," it's notable that you thank two men for encouraging you in writing it.

CK: Right. There are a lot of other men who thought I should have thrown it in the waste basket!

SFB: Well, there are men who took *The Second Sex* and threw it across the office and refused to read it.

CK: I saved the early reviews of it [*The Second Sex*], and they're hysterically funny.

SFB: It was a public poem, but during that time I'm sure it was . . .

CK: When I was a "premature feminist," yes? Well, I think the reason that Fitzgerald and Rolfe Humphries liked it was that it was in classical meters. They were fascinated that somebody was writing in hexameters. That's a meter that had hardly been written in English. I remember having to search for models, and I found Swinburne and, oddly enough, a long poem by Edmund Wilson in hexameters. Then I found Arthur Hugh Clough, although his hexameters are really tetrameters with an emphasis stuck at the beginning, like, "Oh, she remarked with the something, the something, the something, the something." Fake hexameters, really, but I did get the idea and get the meter in my head. I thought about that, about how conscious I was of Roman meter, and I really can't say at this point why I thought it had to be written in hexameters. It's just some instinctive thing, really.

DR: I remember an interesting debate that occurred in *The New York Review of Books* about ten years ago between Adrienne Rich and Susan Sontag, and I'd like to ask you about it.

CK: Gee, I don't remember that.

DR: Well, the substance was this: Rich was attacking the English language as being predominantly a male construct, and so forth. By the same token, she was throwing out other "male" constructs like logic, morality, math—things like this as being really male inventions. Sontag responded by saying this is nonsense. If you overturn all these things you're also overturning things like, for instance, parental authority over children. There has to be some kind of order. It's my impression that the debate is still going on.

CK: I'd hate to comment on that without reading it—I'm sorry I missed it. I think the French have a lot more trouble with things like gender nouns, for example, than we do—which we don't have. I think the most painful thing about poets when I started writing was "the poet *he*." According to Eliot and everybody else talking about the poet, only men were poets, men addressing men—and the painful exclusion that one felt! And it *was* very painful. I don't know if it's possible for men to understand how damaging and wounding it was to sense that they "drew a circle and shut me out." It's very hard because there were so many people like that. I talked to a woman writer who graduated from Greensboro who said that the whole time she studied there no woman author was mentioned and how hard that was. They didn't even mention Jane Austen. I know there's a man I didn't marry because he'd never read Jane Austen. I just thought that was outrageous.

SFB: Ostriker suggests that we're going through a period now that's equivalent to the Romantic period or some other major period. She's saying that we'll look back a hundred years from now and find that the feminist movement in literature today is our equivalent of some of the historical literary movements in world literature.

CK: I don't know. I look at it not so much as a movement as more of a balancing, a justifying.

SFB: Now there seems to be an explosion of women poets.

CK: We certainly have a good number of women poets today. But then I look at the women poets in England, and I wonder. "Where are they?" I don't know of a single woman poet of any interest in England. It's just very sad, whereas Latin America has some fine women poets.

DR: Perhaps the English poets are still suffering from the Movement, from Larkinism.

CK: Well, the curious thing about English feminism is, where's the work? I think the class system and masculine dominance is still so prevalent that everybody's still under it. I can't think of any other reason. But it's interesting that in a country like Nicaragua, for example, Ortega's wife is one of the most widely read poets in the country—Rosario. There are very interesting novelists out of Latin American too. But, you know, I'm not a separatist by any means. I want to make that perfectly clear. There's no way we're going to settle class, regime, and racism—no way!

DR: I remember your saying that one of the points of women's liberation was also men's liberation.

CK: Oh, of course it is. Of course it is. Nobody relinquishes power willingly, that's perfectly true, and if women had it, we wouldn't relinquish it either. I mean there's no point in pretending we're that much better. But I do think it's true that a great many men have felt free to be fathers, to try to kiss a baby, you know, to be family men, to be able to be gentle, and so on . . . and hug. All those nice things. Although Robert Bly is now, as we know, carrying on these meetings of hundreds of male wimps who're being remasculinized by Robert, which I think is totally hilarious [laughter]. I have a feeling they would have been male wimps anyhow without the women's movement [laughter].

DR: You started out on the West Coast, and then you moved to the East Coast—when I first met you, you were East Coast. Now you're West Coast again. Has the move back to the West Coast changed your perspective on things? I know East Coast people can be very myopic.

CK: Well, you're sort of out of the public eye, of course, when you're out here in the west. I know when we moved, John asked if it would make any difference in my career. I said, "Sure. I don't care." There's a lot of paranoia in the west about the eastern establishment. I think a lot of it *is* paranoia. I don't think it's deliberate at all. I think that what happens is that when you're looking for reviewers or books to review or anything of that kind, you remember who you saw at the cocktail party last Thursday. It's a question of propinquity, much more than it is a deliberate exclusionary thing, and paranoia is something to be held down by the naked will. I just don't get too freaked out by neglect of western writers, although in many cases it's pretty outrageous.

DR: There is a maverick strain that goes through American literature that you've been informed by in one way or another, although I don't see you, yourself, as the same kind of maverick. I'm talking about cultural people like Lewis Mumford and Buckminster Fuller.

CK: Yeah, I go in for that sort of thing. The interesting thing in this country is that the people who've really been co-opted by the Establishments are the Beats. Allen Ginsberg still talks about the Establishment, and he's in it. I consider it one of the great ironies of our time that Allen was taken into the American Academy and Institute of Arts and Letters at the same time Lewis Mumford was. Lewis was 78. Now, I mean that says it all, doesn't it? Well, I said to Reed Whittemore a couple of years ago, "We're the kind of poets that the Establishment thinks of as outsiders and outsiders think of as the Establishment." I think that's very true.

DR: We've talked very briefly about the resurgence of formal verse, particularly among the workshop people . . .

CK: Well, I'm not a trend-tracker, but there's an awful lot of banal and repetitious verse being written today. You know what I was saying to you about reading poems for *Woman Poet* and you know when you read the twenty-eighth poem, "If I didn't have to iron your shirts, I'd be a great poet," that gets pretty tedious. There's no point in blaming other people. It's just pointless. The thing to do is just to go on doing it. You may be held back. You may be wounded by the kind of remarks that men still make about women, but there's no reason why you can't do it. I just don't believe in people alibiing for what they fail to do.

SFB: What are some of the problems women writers experience when stereotypes about women are so pervasive?

CK: It struck me very much when I wrote this autobiography, at which I stop at the age of eighteen—that as far as autobiography is concerned, we don't have very many models. Name distinguished autobiographies by women. One of the great ones, of course, is Violet Leduc, *The Bastard* and *Mad in Pursuit,* but she's a very, very feisty lesbian who has no inhibitions. But for the average woman poet to discuss things like sex and love, I think, is still very difficult, partly because if women have had a lot of sexual partners, they still come out looking like floozies or nymphomaniacs, while men can write about having a lot of sexual partners and that's just the way men are. So that's a problem. Maybe I quit at the age of eighteen in this autobiography because I didn't know how I was going to handle it from then on without a lot of omissions, euphemisms, and lies.

Ursula LeGuin and I were having a wonderful conversation last weekend at a conference about stories about ourselves that are told back to us. I think we both decided we would start keeping track of them. It's like that old game of telephone, you know: you whisper something to the person next to you and it goes around the room, and when it comes back it bears no relation to the way things started out. Whenever anyone tells me a story that they've heard about something that I have said or done, I don't even recognize it, for the most part. Ursula said the same thing. Now we have different kinds of mythologies based on the way people perceive us. I've always been perceived as a blonde with a rough tongue who's always had a lot of men around. So the mythologies about me are generally very sexual, and they often are focused on some piece of scatology or lewdness which I am alleged to have said, when in actual fact I loathe dirty jokes, have been known to leave the room when they are told. I hate that kind of vulgarity. Yet what comes back to me is a sort of stereotyped vulgar person, which isn't me at all. It's grotesque. It's the sort of thing that terrifies you, and you hope you won't be so famous that someone will write your biography because all this crap will get into it. Ursula gets another kind of mythology based on the fact that she writes science fiction, which makes her in the eyes of many a mock-man, because science fiction's generally written by men. I inherited my swear-word vocabulary at my mother's knee. My mother could curse a blue streak, but that's different from bathroom humor or sex jokes.

SFB: I don't know if you read "Pro Femina" anymore at readings.

CK: I do get asked to read it, and I do, sure.

SFB: And yet in that poem you're as hard on women as you are on men.

CK: So sure, I'm telling women to shape up, basically.

SFB: But do you think men are still offended?

CK: Well, I think they're just offended by one's *being*, you know. I think the mythologies about women in the public eye are very interesting, and I'd like to know more about it. So I think I'm going to start paying attention to that. One could almost make a list, and yet when you think about men, well then it's somebody like Rock Hudson who's the brunt of jokes, somebody who has AIDS, who is gay, or something. We don't have dirty stories about John Wayne. That's curious. Of course what it really is in another sense, now that we've lost "the great man," it's a debased form that's making it, isn't it? I suppose in a sense you could say that we are replacing Venus, Psyche, Leda, whatever, Helen, with a very debased form.

SFB: That's not surprising when you look at what the media offer these days.

CK: Yet it's interesting because I think the smarter of the television and movie writers lock in in a very superficial way. Well, take *Blue Velvet*, for example. The Isabella Rossellini character is the soiled flower.

She represents sex as evil, and the ditzy blonde is Miss Purity, and the hero is pulled between the two. That in itself, with the many other offensive aspects of that movie, was enough to annoy the hell out of me. We're still finding this good-girl/bad-girl stereotype. We're still finding the kind of thing that I first heard about as a young woman when I was on a boat going to China. I talked to a lot of merchant seamen and found out the incredible sexual split in their nature. Any woman you could make was a "bad girl," so you didn't marry her. What you did was marry somebody who was frigid and then you went and got prostitutes. Isn't that great? It's a wonderful way of organizing your life. They would tell intricate stories about their seduction techniques, some of which were for, I suppose, very naive women. Yet if they succeeded, they failed because then that meant that the woman who had given into them was no longer a possibility.

SFB: Women are saying they don't want to be defined by their bodies; at the same time our culture is becoming more and more sexual. Yet we can't talk straightforwardly about AIDS, condoms, abortion, or masturbation. It's such a strange dichotomy. Now the religious and political right have in the last few years set the women's movement and civil rights back.

CK: I don't think they've affected the women's movement much.

SFB: Do you think there's a revision going on so that some of the older women writers like H. D., Bishop, and Bogan are now being elevated to their rightful places? For instance, Al Poulin has a popular contemporary American anthology—I think the edition before the last one was done about ten years ago—and now in the new one women are more equally represented.

CK: Well, let's never underestimate the fact that people are always on the prowl for a writer who hasn't been done right by. Think of all those Ph.D. theses to write, right? Or all those books if you're in a publish-or-perish school. The fact that there are more neglected women writers than there are men writers may have something to do with it. Let's not get carried away with idealism here. You know I think a lot of this is just plain pragmatism. Certainly there's a tendency to right ancient wrongs and all that, but also there's a feeling that there are some very complex writers. I mean, God, I don't know of anyone more complicated than H. D. There's a lot to get your teeth into there, a lot to talk about. Then of course all the interweavings of people like Pound and Aldington and Williams, and so on, makes it terribly interesting. Looking again from a pragmatic standpoint, you have all these women's studies courses, and the book industry is cranking out books to fill this need.

Not Writing Poems about Children

Once I gave birth to living metaphors.
Not poems now, Ben Jonson, they became themselves.

In despair of poetry, which had fled away,
From loops and chains of children, these were let grow:

"The little one is you all over. . . ."
They fulfill their impulses, not mine.

They invent their own categories,
Clear and arbitrary. No poem needs them.

They need only what they say:
"When I grow up I'm going to marry a tree."

Children do not make up for lost occasions—
"You'd rather kiss that poem than kiss me."

Creations halt, for denials and embraces,
Assurances that no poem replaces them,

Nor, as you knew, Ben, holds the mirror to them,
Nor consoles the parent-artist when they go.

Poems only deprive us of our loss
(Deliberate sacrifice to a cold stanza)

If Art is more durable to us than children,
Or if we, as artists, are more durable than our love.

Ben, I hope you wrote about your dead son
While you were tranced with pain,

Did not offer up those scenes of the infant Isaac in your mind
For the greater poem; but emerged from that swoon

Clutching a page some stranger might have written;
Like a condolence note, cursorily read and tossed aside.

Perhaps at this extremity, nothing improves or worsens.
Talent irrelevant. No poems in stones.

For once, you do not watch yourself
At a desk, covering foolscap. Denied the shameful relief

Of actors, poets, nubile female creatures,
Who save tears like rain-water, for rinsing hair, and mirrors.

Finally, we are left alone with poems,
Children that we cling to, or relinquish

For their own sakes. The metaphor, like love,
Springs from the very separateness of things.

—From *The Ungrateful Garden*

Twelve O'Clock

At seventeen I've come to read a poem
At Princeton. Now my young hosts inquire
If I would like to meet Professor Einstein.
But I'm too conscious I have nothing to say
To interest him, the genius fled from Germany just in time.
"Just tell me where I can look at him," I reply.

Mother had scientific training. I did not;
She loved that line of Meredith's about
The army of unalterable law.
God was made manifest to her in what she saw
As the supreme order of the skies.
We lay in the meadow side by side, long summer nights

As she named the stars with awe.
But I saw nothing that was rank on rank,
Heard nothing of the music of the spheres,
But in the bliss of meadow silences
Lying on insects we had mashed without intent,
Found overhead a beautiful and terrifying mess,

Especially in August, when the meteors whizzed and zoomed,
Echoed, in little, by the fireflies in the grass.
Although, small hypocrite, I was seeming to assent,
I was dead certain that uncertainty
Governed the universe, and everything else,
Including Mother's temperament.

A few years earlier, when I was four,
Mother and Father hushed before the Atwater-Kent
As a small voice making ugly noises through the static
Spoke from the grille, church-window-shaped, to them:
"Listen, darling, and remember always;
It's Doctor Einstein broadcasting from Switzerland."

I said, "So what?" This was repeated as a witticism
By my doting parents. I was dumb and mortified.
So when I'm asked if I would like to speak to Einstein
I say I only want to look at him.
"Each day in the library, right at twelve,
Einstein comes out for lunch." So I am posted.

At the precise stroke of noon the sun sends one clear ray
Into the center aisle: He just appears,
Baggy-kneed, sockless, slippered, with
The famous raveling grey sweater;
Clutching a jumble of papers in one hand
And in the other his brown sack of sandwiches.

The ray haloes his head! Blake's vision of God,
Unmuscular, serene, except for the electric hair.
In that flicker of a second our smiles meet:

Vast genius and vast ignorance conjoined;
He fixed, I fluid, in a complicit yet
Impersonal interest. He dematerialized and I left, content.

It was December sixth, exactly when,
Just hours before the Japanese attack
The Office of Scientific R&D
Began "its hugely expanded program of research
Into nuclear weaponry"—racing the Germans who, they feared,
Were far ahead. In fact, they weren't.

Next night, the coach to school; the train, *Express,*
Instead pulls into every hamlet: grim young men
Swarm the platforms, going to enlist.
I see their faces in the sallow light
As the train jolts, then starts up again,
Reaching Penn Station hours after midnight.

At dinner in New York in '44, I hear the name
Of Heisenberg: Someone remarked, "I wonder where he is,
The most dangerous man alive. I hope we get to him in time."
Heisenberg. I kept the name. Were the Germans, still,
Or the Russians, yet, a threat? Uncertainty . . .
But I felt a thrill of apprehension: Genius struck again.

It is the stroke of twelve—and I suppose
The ray that haloes Einstein haloes me:
White-blonde hair to my waist, almost six feet tall,
In my best and only suit. Why cavil?—I am beautiful!
We smile—but it has taken all these years to realize
That when I looked at Einstein he saw me.

At last that May when Germany collapsed
The British kidnapped Heisenberg from France
Where he and colleagues sat in a special transit camp
Named "Dustbin," to save them from a threat they never knew:
A mad American general thought to solve
The post-war nuclear problem by having them all shot.

Some boys in pristine uniforms crowd the car
(West Pointers fleeing from a weekend dance?),
Youth's ambiguities resolved in a single action.
I still see their faces in the yellow light
As the train jolts, then starts up again,
So many destined never to be men.

In Cambridge the Germans visited old friends
Kept apart by war: Austrians, English, Danes,
"In a happy reunion at Farm Hall."
But then the giant fist struck—in the still
Center of chaos, noise unimaginable, we thought we heard
The awful cry of God.

Hiroshima. Heisenberg at first refused
To believe it, till the evening news confirmed
That their work had led to Hiroshima's 100,000 dead.
"Worst hit of us all," said Heisenberg, "was Otto Hahn,"
Who discovered uranium fission. "Hahn withdrew to his room,
And we feared that he might do himself some harm."

It is exactly noon, and Doctor Einstein
Is an ancient drawing of the sun.
Simple as a saint emerging from his cell
Dazed by his own light. I think of Giotto, Chaucer,
All good and moral medieval men
In—yet removed from—their historic time.

The week before we heard of Heisenberg
My parents and I are chatting on the train
From Washington. A grey-haired handsome man
Listens with open interest, then inquires
If he might join us. We were such a fascinating family!
"Oh yes," we chorus, "sit with us!"

Penn Station near at hand, we asked his name.
E. O. Lawrence, he replied, and produced his card.
I'd never heard of him, but on an impulse asked,

"What is all this about harnessing
Of the sun's rays? Should we be frightened?"
He smiled. "My dear, there's nothing in it."

So reassured, we said goodbyes,
And spoke of him in coming years, that lovely man.
Of course we found out who he was and what he did,
At least as much as we could comprehend.
Now I am living in the Berkeley hills,
In walking distance of the Lawrence Lab.

Here where Doctor Lawrence built the cyclotron,
It's noon: the anniversary of Hiroshima:
Everywhere, all over Japan
And Germany, people are lighting candles.
It's dark in Germany and Japan, on different days,
But here in Berkeley it is twelve o'clock.

I stand in the center of the library
And he appears. Are we witnesses or actors?
The old man and the girl, smiling at one another,
He fixed by fame, she fluid, still without identity.
An instant which changes nothing.
And everything forever, everything is changed.

—From *Harping On*

Amusing Our Daughters·

FOR ROBERT CREELEY

We don't lack people here on the Northern coast,
But they are people one meets, not people one cares for.
So I bundle my daughters into the car
And with my brother poets, go to visit you, brother.

Here come your guests! A swarm of strangers and children;
But the strangers write verses, the children are daughters like yours.
We bed down on mattresses, cots, roll up on the floor:
Outside, burly old fruit trees in mist and rain;
In every room, bundles asleep like larvae.

We waken and count our daughters. Otherwise, nothing happens.
You feed them sweet rolls and melon, drive them all to the zoo;
Patiently, patiently, ever the father, you answer their questions.
Later we eat again, drink, listen to poems.
Nothing occurs, though we are aware you have three daughters
Who last year had four. But even death becomes part of our ease:
Poems, parenthood, sorrow, all we have learned
From these, of tenderness, holds us together
In the center of life, entertaining daughters
By firelight, with cake and songs.

You, my brother, are a good and violent drinker,
Good at reciting short-line or long-line poems.
In time we will lose all our daughters, you and I,
Be temperate, venerable, content to stay in one place,
Sending our messages over the mountains and waters.

After Po Chu-I

—From *Knock Upon Silence*

Fearful Women

Arms and the girl I sing—O rare
arms that are braceleted and white and bare

arms that were lovely Helen's, in whose name
Greek slaughtered Trojan. Helen was to blame.

Scape-nanny call her; wars for turf
and profit don't sound glamorous enough.

Mythologize your women! None escape.
Europe was named from an act of bestial rape:

Eponymous girl on bull-back, he intent
on scattering sperm across a continent.

Old Zeus refused to take the rap.
It's not his name in big print on the map.

But let's go back to the beginning
when sinners didn't know that they were sinning.

He, one rib short: she lived to rue it
when Adam said to God, "She made me do it."

Eve learned that learning was a dangerous thing
for her: no end of trouble it would bring.

An educated woman is a danger.
Lock up your mate! Keep a submissive stranger

like Darby's Joan, content with church and Kinder,
not like that sainted Joan, burnt to a cinder.

Whether we wield a scepter or a mop
It's clear you fear that we may get on top.

And if we do—I say it without animus—
It's not from you we learned to be magnanimous.

—From *Harping On*

Dangerous Games

I fly a black kite on a long string.
As I reel it in,
I see it is a tame bat.
You say it's you.

You fly a white kite, but the string snaps.
As it flutters down,
You see it is a cabbage butterfly.
I say it's I.

You invented this game,
Its terms, its terminology.
I supplied the string,
Giving you the frayed length
So I could escape.

I flew a black kite, let go the string.
But the thing darted down
Straight for my long hair
To be entangled there.

You flew a white kite that ran away.
You chased it with your bat sonar.
But you found only a cabbage butterfly
Trembling on an aphid-riddled leaf.

—From *YIN*

NOTE: Reprinted from *American Magic,* ed. David Rigsbee, by permission of the author.

LYNDA BARRY

WILL YOU CLIMB UP TO THE HEAVENS
THAT ENCLOSE US ABOVE:
A TALK WITH LYNDA BARRY, 2000

Edward Jenkinson

*L*YNDA BARRY, a Renaissance person, though she might not say so, is a self-styled woman, a name that appears and has appeared in many city weeklies for a little over twenty years now. She lives in a quiet suburb of the broad-shouldered city, Chicago, and in a house both she and her husband renovated themselves. From here she makes her art and literature, and her comeeks. You see, Lynda Barry, has a name that appears over the comic, *Ernie Pook's Comeek*, and in the past, such comics as *True Comeek & Boys and Girls*. Go, check them out. They are irreverent, funny, a little too real for comics sometimes, and always deal with this life's experiences; every library or local bookstore should carry something of her various work in novels, plays, and comics.

"I wish you could see this snow outside the window and the crows flying through it," she said, then we began.

Edward Jenkinson: I am wondering if you are able to talk a bit about your new novel, *Cruddy,* and what it means to you. How do you see it fitting into a "Lynda Barry" mythology?

Lynda Barry: Well, shoot. I'm not sure what the LB Mythology is, but in Greek Mythology there must be something a little bit like

Cruddy somewhere. I've had mostly good reaction to it, which has surprised me, as it is pretty gory. People who know my work probably aren't too surprised to find I've written such a book. So "dark" I mean. Although "dark" isn't what I think of when I recall writing it. My experience was more exhilarating than "dark." I've always made my living doing everything a person can do with both writing and drawing, so there is a lot of work in different styles, I guess. I'd like there to be more novels, illustrated, because it's calming to only have one or two projects to work on; like a novel and a weekly strip, versus five or six projects which I need to do to be able to make $$$. But, is there something more you'd like to know about *Cruddy?*

EJ: I am wondering about the exhilaration that affected you while you were writing *Cruddy?* What was it like and what was the "process" you went through to make the book? You mentioned that you were using a paintbrush, but could you explain how you used it for making your book?

LB: I had a great deal of trouble trying to write *Cruddy* before I finally gave up on two things. The computer and trying to plan the book out in advance and control the story. Finally, I tried writing it by hand, but it was too hard physically, as I've been writing near compulsively since I was fifteen and my hand cramps up unless I'm

really writing slow

and large so I wrote this way for a little bit and as I did I remembered taking dictation from a (very influential) five-year-old boy I knew who used to tell me stories a word at a time so I could write them down for him and I remembered how much I liked being surprised by the story told this way and it occurred to me to try to write as if someone were telling me the story, which is how I write my comic strip. I hear it. Hear the characters and ever since I started using a brush on the strip I seemed to hear them better—probably because it takes more concentration to use a brush so the top part of my mind becomes occupied and the back part unspools the story.

I tried it with *Cruddy* and it allowed me to really get somewhere. When I began to worry about whether the story was worth anything or not, I could remind myself that my job was to just faithfully record the words and if I could make them pretty-looking. A Calligraphic Stenographer, really, was all I tried to be to the characters, so by slow-ing way down the book came much faster. I don't think this way of writing a novel would work for people who aren't already attracted by handwriting.

The exhilaration came from being released from having to tell the story myself. Obviously I was telling the story but it didn't feel like it. It was more like dreaming it. I had to be willing to not know where the story was going and to not edit. I was already used to this on a small scale with my comic strip but it was really a relief to know it worked for big stories too. When I came to the end of each page I used a hair dryer on it and then went on. That first manuscript was seven hundred pages long.

EJ: Much of what you do in your comics and literature has so much to do with family, would you talk some about the dynamics in family relationships that interest you. How do you see these interests being played out within your two novels and in your weekly comics?

LB: The families in my work are imaginary ones and because most (all!) of my main characters are young (under 18) they are in family relationships. I am really interested in family dynamics.

Families interest everyone to some degree, I think, but I don't have much to say about them beyond what is already in my work (which is plenty). Or rather, I have too much to say about them and it's too easy to sort of go on and on so I'll stick to what I've already written from the back of my mind on the subject (it's in the work) rather than go on from the top of my head, which is what I bore my friends with.

EJ: What kind of advice would you give to young writers? And to an extent would you call your work autobiographical?

LB: I relate to what happens to my characters, but what happens to them didn't happen to me in those ways. In a way I don't care if people want to see the work as autobiographical or not at this point. There seems to be some need on the part of the reader to do this. I don't really mind, but it's not true is all. Maybe it's because I write in the first person and do use real places? I guess in a way it's a compliment; the stories seem that real to people. When I wrote *Cruddy* I was sure no one would think that bloody, violent, far-fetched story was autobiographical, but people do this. It sort of makes me laugh a little bit.

I don't have any advice regarding young writers and autobiographical work. Except in the beginning it may be a good idea to try it

IO PAGE
FAX FOR

Edward Jenkinson

FROM

Lynda Barry

FEB
14
2000

Dear E,
    I hope this fax reaches you (There wasn't a
fax return # in your note so I'm sending this
to the # printed at the top of the page by the
fax machine you sent your fax from. If it's
not the right number, please let me know if
there is a better one)
    Anyway - let's get right to the questions

PRIMUS: Well, shoot. I'm not sure what the LB Mythology
is but in Greek mythology there must be something
a little bit like *Cruddy* somewhere. But what
would you like to know about *Cruddy*? I've

because it's a good way to get very specific about everything and if I
have one secret it's that. I do a lot of research, so I have specific, believable details to work with. Yesterday I was writing a strip where Freddie mentions Fungus. So, I looked up some fungus names until I
found some really good ones. ('Cramp balls' was my favorite). Autobiography may get one started, but reality is stubborn and it interferes
with storytelling. I like realistic imagination best. I am working on
some autobiographical strips for salon.com. They're hard. Also there
is a concern about hurting real people. I don't like that concern when
I work.

    EJ: Your view on the differences of ethnic groups, brought up
in *The Good Times Are Killing Me*, is one of sharp contrasts both of
wealth and poverty and ethnicity, and it does not seem like there is

much forgiveness for dissimilarity. Would you talk some about your view on cultural differences, and their effect on the individual? And also touch upon the individual as the loner; no one ends up "happy," even though the ideas of family are stressed in the book?

LB: I'm not sure I understand what you mean when you say there does not seem to be much forgiveness about dissimilarity. Maybe it's because I'm really not thinking in terms of forgiveness or dissimilarity, when I work, mostly because I'm not really thinking when I work. That is to say, I'm not really aware of any message in my work while I'm creating it. For me it's much more like playing: The elements (people, situations, etc.) come up as I move the pen or brush on the paper and not until then. I never have anything in mind when I sit down to make a story. It's more like gathering together a lot of dolls and puppets and dollhouses and just letting them be alive and interact. When I was taking English classes in high school or discussing books in college I was given the impression that writers planned the stories, inserted symbols, symbolic moments, and had a message. I'm not someone who can work that way so I'm not sure how well my work holds up under discussion or any attempts to see it in an intellectual or logical way. I imagine it would do poorly.

Regarding the loner aspect: Well, most main characters are loners aren't they? And about no one ending up happy, all I can say is that it's how the stories ended and it felt natural to me that they did. But, I don't have any feelings about stories having to end one way or another. I just know it's a delight to have them end in a way that feels like closure versus just stopping the way a telephone just stops ringing, or like I wish the car alarm that is going off right now would.

EJ: I am wondering about the *Musical Notebook* at the end of the book *(TGTAKM)*. It is a fantastic mini-encyclopedia about early American music, and would you explain how it came about and are you still keeping such a notebook? What are your interests in documenting, in such a way, and should we expect, the *Lynda Barry Guide to American Music* any time soon?

LB: Actually, the novel part of the first version of *The Good Times Are Killing Me,* came after I did the paintings. The Real Comet Press, in Seattle, wanted to print the painting as a little book and I was going to write an introduction about American music and racism, but as usual I couldn't write something I'd planned to write so I wrote *The*

Good Times Are Killing Me, instead. The two parts of that book don't seem to go together in any obvious kind of way. If a person can stand things being together without an obvious connection then the book won't seem strange, but for some people the two parts together are very strange. The newest version of *TGTAKM* doesn't include the *Music Notebook,* but that was more of a financial concern—it's expensive to print in full color and even requires a different sort of paper. Sasquatch Press (in Seattle) was willing to reprint the first part so I did some illuminations for the new version. I'm really happy with how that little book came out too. I do love American music, but I love all kinds of music. I don't have the biographer's sort of mind, so there won't be any other books on musicians by me; I think. Bugs maybe, and bacteria, even dogs. But not musicians.

EJ: I am wondering about your college days at Evergreen State, Washington. Was it there that you first realized your affection for the comical art? And did not you attend school with Matt Groenig? Were you two friends?

LB: It's The Evergreen State College. Matt and I met and became friends there. It is a great school and I continue to use the methods I picked up there for working. Specifically to work very, very hard on one thing. For example, the year I took a class called "Images" (you only had One class at TESC. You were in it all day: 1 teacher per 20 students. Teachers taught in teams of 2–4) I had to do 10 finished visual pieces (in my case paintings) per week, plus 5 pages a day of specific sort of journal writing and much reading; all of it centered on the question of what an image was (in a painting, poem, photo, essay-etc.) the idea was by studying something specifically much more is revealed to you. I'm not sure if TESC runs the same way now? In my day (Class of '78) there were no grades. People who worked hard got a lot out of it. People could not work and get by, but that's true anywhere.

EJ: How have the fortunes of comic strip writing changed since you first began publishing them? Will you be doing them for, say, another twenty years or so? And if so, do you see other evolutions of your comics? That is, early in your career there was first the strip *Girls and Boys* and now *Ernie Pook's Comeek,* but between those you had (at least) several other "strips." Would you also talk about the contrasts in the different strips, like how does *Ernie Pook's Comeek* differ from say, *True Comeek?* Are there major differences you see in the subject matter?

LB: When I started my cartoon strip there were a lot of weekly alternative papers that carried a lot of strange features. There are still a lot of weekly papers but the content has become less strange. I'm not in as many papers as I used to be. I doubt if I rate high on any reader's survey the papers gather. Actually, I'm surprised papers carry the strip at all because it is so strange. The *Village Voice* got rid of all their comic strips a few years ago; which really was sad because aside from the *New Yorker* it was a place where cartoonists were really doing interesting things. Inventing things. Now there isn't much of a venue for this. The *Chicago Reader* still has a lot of really interesting cartoons, but as the alternative weeklies have become more mainstream the comic strips have sort of fallen away.

I love doing my strip and hope I can keep doing it in the newspapers but I also am pretty sure I'll eventually be dropped from most of them. As I mentioned, my strip must seem strange to a lot of people, especially in the mainstream. Then again, people do like comic strips, so maybe I'll keep on being able to find places to run the work.

Regarding the question you asked about the different phases in the strip, that is part of the strangeness I mean. The strip has always changed in every possible aspect from drawing to characters. I'd have a hard time working if it didn't because for me there wouldn't be much in it if I had to keep everything standard and reliable. I have a lot of admiration for the daily comic strip artists who keep on turning out unchanging strips. My favorite ones quit eventually (Gary Larson, *Calvin & Hobbes,* Berke Breathed) but I really admire the guy who does *Drabble* (one of my favorite strips), *Family Circus,* (another fav.) and even (God help me) *Cathy* (not a favorite). It's hard work meeting a deadline with the same old thing every day, no room to be sad or weird or to try something. With my strip I ALWAYS mess around. The downside is getting dropped from various papers. Which happens all the time and always makes me feel so sad. But it's worth it, plus I can't stand to work any other way.

EJ: I guess you have heard by now about Mr. Schulz's death? What did his comic strip mean to you? Also, how do other comic strip writers/artists affect your work? Or do they?

LB: I am a cartoonist, but I don't read a lot of comic strips or even more comic strips than a person who isn't one. I love Matt's work and there is an incredible cartoonist in Chicago named Chris Ware, whom

Feb 19 2000

Dear E –

here are replies (certainly not "answers!")
to your questions, round 2

+ I had a great deal of trouble trying
to write Cruddy before I finally gave
up on 2 things: The computer and trying
to plan the book out in advance and
control the story. Finally I tried writing
it by hand but it was too hard
physically as I've been writing near-
compulsively since I was 15 and my
hand cramps up unless I'm

really writing slow

and large so I wrote this

way for a little bit and as I did I
remembered taking dictation from a
(very influential) 5 year old boy I
knew who used to tell me stories a
word at a time so I could write them
down for him and I remembered
how much I liked being surprised
by the story told this way and
it occured to me to try to write

I think may be the "King." I loved cartoons as a kid though. I was never really attached to *Peanuts.* I loved *Nancy, Family Circus, Archie, Brenda Starr, Blondi,* and much later, Gary Larson, who also is the "King." There is a Malaysian cartoonist name, Lat, who is a 3rd "King." Art Speigleman is great too, but mostly I read books and look at paintings.

EJ: With your husband also being an artist, do you collaborate in works? Do you show him your works (Comic strips, books, and paintings) before anyone?

LB: Kevin (my husband) does see my work before anyone. He keeps me from throwing a lot of work in the garbage. He reads my work out loud to me and it helps me hear if something isn't working. We don't collaborate though. He has his studio, I have mine. I love being married to him for a lot of reasons, but it's especially nice that he's an artist.

EJ: I received a poem of yours "I love my master I love my master," which is in this issue. Do you write much poetry?

LB: Well, I kind of think of my comic strip as poetry. It's sure not gag writing. It has to be concise but huge at the same time. I do read a lot of poetry.

EJ: Would you talk some about the freedom you gained from avoiding modern contraptions? Also, would you give your opinion on how you see the computer age? Are computers helping us, or harming us, especially those who are in the Arts, in your opinion?

LB: I do refer to myself as a neo-primitive when it comes to the computer world, even though I have one and am even sort of half-assedly on-line now. But my main complaint about them is they are SO SLOW. Writing *Cruddy* with a paintbrush (which was how I wrote the first successful draft) was so much faster than writing it with a computer—which I eventually used, for the final draft. With a computer the ability to mess with the individual sentences by deleting or adding really interrupted the flow of imagining. Instead of being in the work I was looking at the WORK, changing things around before I even knew what they were and avoiding going forward by editing and switching sentences around.

With a paintbrush I became caught up in the calligraphic aspects of the sentences, moving actual paint on actual paper plus I had an actual manuscript I could hold. That was key.

I want to believe that life spent with a computer in a virtual world has wonderful things about it which are as unimaginable to me as writing 700 pages with a paint brush might be to someone who uses a computer only.

I have to believe there is something really cool about this 4th dimension because my alternative is to be a grouch about people not making actual 3-D things (or 2-D things—what is music? 2-D? 3-D? 10,000-D?) I do believe there is something incredible about building real 3-D things, painting, drawing, hand-writing, a real letter, but obviously these sorts of things do not mean much to most people— and most people are very dearly attracted to televisions and computers, the species is really hooked on such things. There may be something I just don't know? I'm certainly not going to make a dent either way by being grumpy about it. But for me, computers take up so much time. I've always felt more tired and vacant after I've been on-line.

It's like television. I never feel better after I watch TV. But, I almost always feel better after I make something or read or even vacuum the floor. There is something about just sitting there staring, but then again this is exactly what I do when I work. I don't know? I have a huge crush on the natural world. Not everybody does. It's no fun for them just like a computer game is no fun for me.

EJ: Where do you like to create your work, either comic or literary, or both? Does geography determine the landscape of the work? And if so, how?

LB: I work mainly at home in my attic. And, I especially love it when it's raining or snowing outside the window (as it is now). I have use of a telephone for business—we have a phone in the kitchen but I can't hear it and never answer it. So, I never have interruptions besides the three dogs all barking at once when the mail comes. I usually work with no music on if I'm writing. If I'm painting in color on art illustration I have the TV on—usually on an old movie, I just listen to it—not looking up—I like AMC or TCM—no commercials, just Bette Davis freaking out, or Ingrid Bergman freaking out, music soundtrack, cars screeching, etc.

My husband and I go camping for two weeks every year and a lot of what I see then finds its way into my work. Also, I love to ride the elevated train (the "el") into Chicago. Sometimes I just ride it for no reason. I draw the people, write down things they say. I go to the library several times a week—check out books on anything.

The places in my work are usually real. Although recently the characters in the strip have all moved into a new house (a new old house), but I have no idea where it is and it's the first time this has happened.

EJ: Would you be willing to recount a day that you took the "el" into Chicago? What kind of wandering do you do? What is the library you go to, why that library in particular? For you is this a sort of pilgrimage?

LB: There isn't much to say about the library or the "el" that's exciting, except that because I'm alone most of my day it's nice to be among people and a train is always something I've enjoyed. The "el" runs about a story off the ground and travels through neighborhoods. Sometimes I'll see people cooking or reading in their apartments. I like drawing on the "el"—wish I could just stare directly at the people I'm drawing, but one can't do this. I have to sneak looks and do a lot from flash-memory.

My main attraction to the library is books. I'm not in love with the library itself. I don't linger after I've selected my stack of books. In the summer the air-conditioning is on so high it's miserable there. And, you can't drink coffee or tea and the people who work there aren't especially friendly. I don't know why. So I get in and get out, go to a cafe down the street with my pile of books. But I do go almost everyday. I like picture books and go though a lot. Also, they sell used books there and I like to see what's out.

EJ: I read recently, from a 1999 interview, that you would choose to be a detective if you weren't an artist/writer, but earlier the other choice was a veterinarian. For the "other" you, why has this resolution changed?

LB: I'd still love to be a detective. I have detective fantasies all the time. I'm always imagining ways to get in with the local police dept.; ride around with them, witness how they work on different crimes. Some writers do this, but I've never had the way they do it clear enough in my head to make that first phone call. I'm really interested in crime scenes & clues. I do read a lot of detective driven fiction. When I was a kid I would memorize details about cars and strangers just in case it turned out to be important. I also LOVE to do research. Mainly about bugs and bacteria, but liars are interesting too, as are sociopaths and other people who don't have to put up much of a fight with their consciences. Con-artists. These people are really interesting to me, although I don't want them in my life at all. I enjoy having them in my head.

I wanted to be a vet until I saw a dog get hit by a car when I was in the sixth grade and I realized what being a vet really meant. I love dogs. I have three, but it's too hard to see them in pain or illness, plus you'd have to deal with the owners. OW. Even harder.

Our interview ended here, "We're in the middle of such a wonderful snowstorm," she said, "I'm going to skip the last question if you don't mind. I have a lot of work to do today."

I hope readers will take some time to pick up a novel, *Comeek Book*, done by Lynda Barry. Also try to check to see if her new strip, *Ernie Pook's Comeek*, is in your local Weekly. And if not, write to the editor and request it. I guarantee the experience will be worth it.

I Love My Master I Love My Master

God I love my master
Of all the dogs I have the best master
What a great master
Yes I can get on the bed yes I can have
A bite of her brownie Oh No
It's a Pot Brownie oh god I am so high
She is starting to look very weird to me
So much skin so much open skin on her so bald all over
I want to smell her mmmmmmaster mmmmmaster
She's laughing at me quit laughing at me
Now she's laughing at me quit laughing at me
Now she is barfing now who is laughing
Har har har Master Oh No now I am barfing
She thinks there was LSD in the brownie
She is asking the Boyfriend was there LSD in the brownie and
He is laughing Oh No
Now I am outside for biting the Boyfriend
I hate
The Boyfriend
Now I am outside and
There was LSD in that brownie
Maintain maintain
Please let me back in Master I am
Riding on a really bad trip, Master
Please Master, Please Baldy
Before I eat more garbage
Before I bite more car tires
Master I need to come in
Before I go over to Pepe's yard and
Tempt him with my LSD barking
Hey Pepe Pepe Har har har rawo rawo rawo
Oh No Pepe is not attached to his chain
Running running steps steps steps PLEASE MASTER PLEASE
PLEASE OH NO PLEASE
Door opens Thank You Master I love you Master what

A good Master
The Boyfriend says he is too high to look at me
He agrees
There was LSD in that brownie
He got it from his neighbor
The Master wants to go to the hospital
He says she will come down in a minute
All our jaws are tight and we want to bite each other so bad
My jaws are killing me this is worse
Than the chocolate mescaline from last week that made
Me just want to hump her
My beautiful Master
If you think she looks good now
You should see her on mesc
GOD I HATE THE SOUND OF THIS COLLAR
MASTER GET THIS OFF OF ME MASTER WHERE ARE YOU
GOING?
The Boyfriend wants to hear the Doors
Don't play The Doors on acid. Not that man's voice on acid. No
I will freak. I will bite. Maintain maintain
I will lay on the floor I will dose my eyes
Oh No I see too many of Pepe's heads
I see mange
I see cans of Skippy Dog Food
Cans and cans of Skippy Dog Food swirling
Flashing I am peaking
Don't think about Skippy
Don't think about Pepe
Think calm thoughts. Calm ones.
Master. Mmmmmmaster.
Master wants to hold me Master wants to hold me
Come here boy come here
Get Him Off The Bed says the Boyfriend says the Freakster
Get Him Off Because I Am Freaking
This is Very Bad Acid says the Master
I Need to Hold Him to Maintain says the Master
Mmmmmaster
And when her fingers touch under my chin

And when her fingers undo my collar
I am blissed out
I lick her fingers
The Boyfriend says he hates me
And has always hated me
The Boyfriend is starting to confess
Everything
I look into the Masters green eyes
They are getting larger and larger

Now it is later. The Boyfriend is gone.
The Master says he is a fag
Good riddance she is crying
I lick her face
We are coming down
Our jaws ache and itch
Finally she falls asleep and then I fall asleep
And somewhere
The fag Boyfriend falls asleep
Fag Boyfriend, if you are reading this.
I thank you with all of my heart
I thank you for the righteous brownies
And I thank you for confessing when you were high on acid
That you humped Tina
And Connie
And Heather
And that you are not really sure if girls turn you on.
Thank you Boyfriend thank you sir
Now you are outside forever
I love my Master I love my Master
God I love my Master
Of all the dogs I know
I love my Master
Best

YUSEF KOMUNYAKAA

*AN INTERVIEW
WITH YUSEF KOMUNYAKAA*

Sally Dawidoff

W*RITING IN* the *New York Times,* Bruce Weber called the poet Yusef Komunyakaa, "the dreamy intellectual, a Words-worthian type whose worldly, philosophic mind might be stirred by something as homely and personal as a walk in a field of daffodils." Since the 1970s, when Komunyakaa began publishing his poetry, he has used commonplace details to illuminate lofty themes.

Born in Bogalusa, Louisiana, in 1947, Komunyakaa earned a Bronze Star for his service in the Vietnam War, was educated at the University of Colorado and Colorado State University, and got an MFA in creative writing from the University of California, Irvine in 1980. In 1994, he won the Pulitzer Prize, the Kingsley Tufts Poetry Award, and the William Faulkner Prize for *Neon Vernacular: New and Selected Poems.* In addition to eleven books of poetry, he has coedited anthologies, written a libretto for the opera *Slipknot,* and published *Blue Notes: Essays, Interviews, and Commentaries* (University of Michigan). He is a chancellor of the Academy of American Poets and a professor in the Council of Humanities and Creative Writing program at Princeton University.

Komunyakaa's expansive new book, *Talking Dirty to the Gods* (Farrar,

Straus and Giroux), is a sequence of 132 sixteen-line, four-quatrain poems. Within this formal structure, the poet is exuberantly informal. Komunyakaa has said, "I learned from jazz that one can incorporate almost anything into a poem." He juxtaposes classical material with contemporary American references, lowly insects with platonic ideals. Over coffee in SoHo this fall, Komunyakaa ruminated on politics, aesthetics, and *Talking Dirty to the Gods*.

❧

Sally Dawidoff: How did *Talking Dirty to the Gods* come about?

Yusef Komunyakaa: The book is really a composite of innuendo, insinuation, and perhaps owes a lot to the blues tradition, where there are serious things being addressed through satire. I wanted to work on something where the whole process was fun. Often I would come up with a phrase and laugh out loud about it. Also I wanted poems that would expand. I wanted simultaneous compression and expansion, so if I had to explicate a poem I could spend pages; I wanted to talk about all kinds of things. I wanted to underline my definition of poetry which is: celebration and confrontation. I wanted an illusion of symmetry at least on the page. I hope they seem planned out, and at the same time bear a looseness to the form.

SD: There's a phrase in one of the poems, "Venus of Willendorf": "her big smallness." Doesn't that sort of express what you are up to, creating poems that are both big (in scope) and small (in size)?

YK: Yes. I hope so.

SD: You have praised poets whose work represents a "unified vision." Your work has a range of subject matters and cultural reference points.

YK: Well, I suppose I'd like to think that my vision is as inclusive as Melvin Tolson's. I'm thinking especially about *The Harlem Gallery*. That book is saturated with classical allusions, or references outside the American culture. I think there isn't anything taboo to write about. It depends on aesthetics.

SD: You wrote in the essay "Poetry and Inquiry" that you're "constantly moving closer to [your] personal terrain." How does this book fit into that terrain?

YK: Well, I've always been attracted to folklore, mythology, so in a certain sense this book is a return to those obsessions. How we

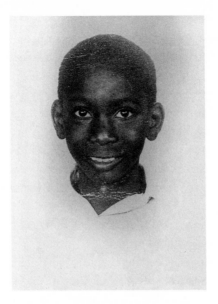

Yusef Komunyakaa as a child, 1950s

as individuals fit into the larger world. My imagination is who I am. Ideas and experiences define my personal history.

SD: I'm reminded of Philip Larkin's statement—"that every poem must be its own sole freshly created universe, and therefore have no belief in 'tradition' or a common myth-kitty . . . "

YK: I agree with that. I think that in folklore and mythology, at first it can seem rather distant, but one's challenge is to make oneself whole. History. Folklore. Claiming it all. And also realizing how the past is so intricately connected to the present and the future. We're moving past things for the reason that we don't want to deal with history, because history informs the present and perhaps informs the future as well. So we would like, often I sense, to just move through things and past things without dealing with them. It's a cultivated denial. So this book, I think, is an attempt to address, perhaps, a part of that denial. I'm drawn to the satirical aspects of the so-called gods, the Greek and Roman gods. Where I've left off in this book, I'm extending in *Prophet Fish,* a collection that addresses mythologies from other cultures.

SD: All that gender stuff—

YK: All that gender stuff, the rituals involved—

SD: The power plays—

YK: The power—all that stuff is going on among the ancients, and it's happening today as well. So I wanted to pursue that project. The issue of slaves. The treatment of women. Class is not usually addressed. Let's face it, those cultures were very class-conscious. I wanted to deal with that and not to make fun of the gods or deny them, but to bring them down to earth.

SD: You talk how jazz taught you that you "could write anything into a poem." So is this an exercise in jazz in its freedom?

YK: Yes, jazz has a freedom but also it has structure. Perhaps that's what the four stanzas are about.

SD: Did the form paradoxically make you freer?

YK: I think so. For those poems.

SD: Your poetry has been described as "surrealist," as " postmodernist American mainstream with an African American twist."

YK: Whatever that means. The "American" part makes sense. It reminds me of Robert Hayden—he's so important to me, one reason is because he writes as an American, and his psyche is not centered in Europe or Africa; it's centered in America, and he claims that space for his writing. It's amazing when we think about history, how segregation and apartheid are quite recent, but for some reason there are cultivated falsehoods and denial. If the 1960s had not happened, where would we be? Would Asians and Latinos and Blacks traveling through the South, would they still be sitting in the back of the bus? I think so, if it *were* left up to the mainstream to actually change the system.

SD: If I were to press you to come up with a description of your poetry, one word you would come up with would be "American"?

YK: Yeah.

SD: What other words might you use?

YK: It's hard to define one's work. I think that's why Hayden was challenged in the 1970s by the Black Arts movement. Outside the United States, the American Black writer is looked on as American.

SD: You've talked about writing political poetry. . .

YK: Everything is political. Silence is. The poet has to know this, This is what Cavafy's "Dareios" is about.

SD: What would you say to someone who wants to write political poetry?

YK: I would say the politics shouldn't be on the surface of the poem, that aesthetics are important. I remember posing a question to Gwendolyn Brooks. I said, "What is art?" She said, "Art is that which endures," and that was rather instructive to me, especially since we live in a society where everything is spur-of-the-moment, and it's temporary. It was interesting to think about reading something that one hopes will endure. I was in Italy recently, and I realized that those buildings were meant to endure. We throw up houses and buildings in a matter of weeks. In contrast, the Italians seem to be so conscious of aesthetics in their creation of clothing, furniture, etcetera, and I think it has a lot to with the fact that they're in the midst of a culture that has so much invested in the arts. And it's not just surface aesthetics, but the kind of aesthetics that has to do with endurance. Buildings have walls two feet thick—a beauty with weight and strength.

SD: When political poetry doesn't work, it's a shame. The passion is there, the commitment is there—

YK: The poems of Neruda are political and yet done with immense care. Ruykeser is very political and yet there is care in her poems. Think of "The Lovers of the Poor," or "We Real Cool" by Gwendolyn Brooks, or consider Aimé Césaire's, *Notes on a Return to the Native Land.* What one really wants is to have the reader or the listener as an active participant. One doesn't want to tell the reader or the listener everything, but to challenge them to use their own imagination, to be engaged that way.

SD: One doesn't want to tell the reader everything.

YK: How to feel, how to think, one has to arrive at that place somewhere within their own psyche, through his or her own body and mind.

SD: Would you talk about the qualities of the poetry you most admire? Is it more distinguished by its "unsameness," or do you get excited when it has a "unified vision," or—?

YK: It really depends on the poet and when the poet seems really confident with his or her voice, when it hasn't been contrived. For me, experimental poetry often seems an attempt at the erasure of reality, of things that are important to us at this juncture in history. I feel engaged when the mechanics of the form doesn't diminish the content. A poem shouldn't be too tidy, and the subject matter shouldn't seem as if it's been chosen by group consensus. I think each poem has to be come out of some need and cannot be dictated to the poet.

SD: What do you think about the "New Elliptical" poetry?

YK: I have a problem with anything that defines itself as "new." And this is what I'm talking about—erasure. The artist is always concerned about those things that are important to our survival as a species. He or she is a lot more concerned than the businessman or the politician. The artist isn't the right-hand man to the yes-man for the politician or the businessman.

SD: What do you think about the custom of including explanatory notes in poetry books?

YK: I refuse to. I was tempted to, but I said No. Also I wish Eliot hadn't placed all those notes at the end of *The Waste Land*. Let someone else do that.

SD: What do you do with a student who comes in to your class and doesn't have anything to talk about?

YK: Students have a lot to talk about. However, often they just haven't thought about it, or they think that there's only a certain restricted subject matter. Often I say to them, "It's not necessary that you even write about what you know. Be willing to discover through the process of writing."

SD: And what would you say to a student about reconciling freedom and craft? "Jump in and see what happens"?

YK: Yes. I'd say, write everything down and then think about the structure. Of course, in this latest book, I'm favoring the structure of the sixteen lines [in *Talking Dirty to the Gods*]. Not that everything came out in sixteen lines; sometimes some of the poems were as long as fifty lines initially. I like reading poems again and again because we're constantly changing as individuals. Tomorrow I'm slightly different, and that's true of all of us. We're complex organisms.

NOTE: Sally Davidoff's interview first appeared on Africana.com, an internet publication.

INTRODUCTION

Yusef Komunyakaa

A**S ALWAYS**, I am interested in working on my in-progress collections. During the past several years, I have also been writing for performance works that all share one ingredient: poetry.

Recently, I finished a libretto, *Slipknot,* with the composer T. J. Anderson. Commissioned by Northwestern University, the focus of this piece is on Arthur, a kind of trickster figure, who in 1747 is born a slave in Massachusetts, and as a young man, hanged after a trial for an alleged rape.

Another in-progress performance piece is *Shangri-la* with the music being composed and arranged by percussionist/composer Susie Ibarra. *Shangri-la* is about the sex trade in Thailand. The first full-length performance piece I wrote is entitled *Testimony,* originally a poem on Charlie Parker written in fourteen sections, it appears in *Thieves of Paradise.* After it was commissioned by the Australian Broadcasting Corporation, Sandy Evans, an Australian saxophonist and composer, wrote the music and led the orchestra in its premier, which was recorded in 1999. *Testimony* is scheduled for a January 2002 live production by the Australian Art Orchestra at the Sydney Festival.

Among recordings where my poems or lyrics appear, I have written a cycle of songs for *Thirteen Kinds of Desire* (Cornucopia Productions, 2000) sung and arranged by jazz vocalist/bandleader Pamela Knowles.

Since I work on a number of poetry collections simultaneously, there is always that anticipated moment when one manuscript demands completion. Such a collection is *Chameleon Couch,* a manuscript of five sections, two of which are long poems: "Autobiography of My Alter Ego" and "Malcolm's Ghost." It is always exhilarating to have a collection take off and find its authority with my imagination running on nothing but sweat and elation. Cicero is right, whether we are thinking about the

Yusef Komunyakaa

creation of human beings or other artistic projects, when he says, 'Nothing is simultaneously born and complete."

At various times in the past, poems seem to have arrived almost complete in that they required less revision. They were more impromptu. Now, I carry around images for poems inside my head for weeks, months, and sometimes years. (I began working on "Malcolm's Ghost" in the fall of 1996 in St. Louis.) Everything doesn't have to be *now*, and any semblance of perfection grows out of hard work. Yet, I still listen to my own advice: "Don't polish the heart out of the poem." A musician, someone like Bird, Miles, or Monk, might say, "Don't let them see you trying too hard."

People often ask, "Which poem or poems of yours do you like best?" Usually I say, "The one I'm working on." In such cases, I'm not being coy; I'm responding to the active process of writing. Or, I could say, "I don't know." I have grown to love poems of others as well as my own probably because they were interesting enough for me to return to again and again till I learned something from them. Such a poem is "One-Breath Song" written many years ago, that appears in the Early Collected section of *Pleasure Dome*. It still tells me that a poem can have an almost liquid architecture:

you are the third term
carried to the fourth power of numbers
two steps overlooked in-between
colors of night-burning sky
a priori light blue of your dress
our faces everything except
against odds of self-discovery
we find our bodies locked
together in a room of breath
threefold at the rotting threshold
divided into ontogenetic questions
a fluke of radio waves in the storm
the song that uses up our lives.

I sense a freedom in its movement a matter-of-factness that later poems
do not have.

For months, I'd been working on a poem inside my head. I knew it
would be long; its title would be "Meditations on Avenue A." But I didn't
know what approach to take, how the music of the language would appear
on the page. I hoped the poem would evoke a feeling of effortlessness,
in the way that I think of " One-Breath Song" might be. However, I desired
a more meditative modulation in its movement. Maybe the couplet form
would do that, I told myself.

I remember agonizing on Miles Davis's statement, when he said, he
loved playing ballads so much that he refused to play them anymore. I
kept wishing that he would let his trumpet turn some of those old sorrow songs inside out. I thought the ballads could take him somewhere
else; perhaps they could be the bridge to a new dimension, and objected
to the mere pursuit of the so-called hip. Likewise, I find myself returning to some of the earlier works, in the same way that I love rereading
my favorite authors, hoping that they teach me a sober passion.

The Devil's Workshop

The master craftsman sits like Rodin's
Thinker, surrounded by his cosmic tools,
Experimenting with the greenhouse effect
& acid rain. A great uncertainty

Plagues him. Some hard questions
Wound the air. Yesterday afternoon
Children marched with a rainbow
Of placards. Perhaps he can create

A few suicides with his new computer
Virus. Something has gone wrong
In the shop, because the old gods
Of serpentine earthquakes & floods

Are having more fun than he is
In his laboratory of night sweats
& ethnic weapons. Lovers smile
As Cupid loads a blowgun with thorns.

Hagar's Daughter

She left Greenbush as Fire
  Flower, Sparkling Fire, & *Ish-*
    scoodah, headed for Oberlin

College at thirteen,
  the Credit River Reserve
    in her voice, consonants caught

in her throat, her tongue
  lonely for anything Chippewa
    & African, becoming Edmonia

Lewis. She couldn't stop,
  couldn't keep creatures & fish
    out of her head, porcupine

quills & beads woven into her
  footsteps lost in distant grass,
    & called herself Wildfire

in the gaze of blue eyes.
  She worked light into paper
    up in a second-floor room,

a pencil unearthing *Urania*
  as a marriage gift for Clara,
    her classmate. But nothing

overshadowed the two girls
  who swore she doctored
    their wine with Spanish Fly

before two boys took them
  sledding, before attackers left her for dead
    in the snow. She was still thankful

for John Langston,
    a godsend who could argue
        vomitus & urine in court—*corpus*

delicti. A yellow bird
    clung to a low branch
        as shadows fell asleep

against a stony slab.
    She drew night & day,
        but when someone claimed

she stole a gilded frame
    to hold a neoclassical picture
        in her head, she departed

for Boston. To Florence,
    to Rome, to her own Way
        of the Cross, till she could see

her brother, Sunrise, digging
    for gold out in California,
        till the sea-green distance

made her lonelier than white
    marble begging for a mallet.
        She could still hear that

chapel bell clanging
    after they hanged John
        Brown, as the chisel

cut curves, her mind
    into the stone: *Hygieia,*
        The Old Indian Arrowmaker

& His Daughter, Asleep,
  Awake, & Forever Free
    rose out of shook blood

& myth. "I thought
  I knew everything when
    I came to Rome, but I found

I had everything to learn."
  As if to make the lowest rock
    forgive itself for lightness,

she couldn't stop carving
  Hagar's face into it: Egyptian
    handmaiden driven out to wander,

bearing her master's child.
  Could she capture the hour
    her family was banned

from the Mississauga
  because night owned their faces?
    Too many whirling paths

brought her to "the day
  Pope Pius IX blessed"
    the figure she was working on,

vespers of remembered fields
  at her feet. Giving herself
    to its heft, she drove away

loneliness with each blow.
  Where did she disappear
    like fireweed approaching

snow? In the mid-1970s,
     in the midst of another long, hot
          summer, a fireman found

The Death of Cleopatra
     among cranes & clamshell buckets,
          & he couldn't stop saying,

"The most beautiful thing . . .
     a big white ghost." So,
          this is how she ended up

after "Blind John" Condon,
     a Chicago gambler & fixer
          who owned a racetrack,

placed her on the grave
     of his favorite horse
          till the pine leaf yellows,

till *Caught Cupid*
     no longer mouths
          the sculptor's last song.

SHANGRI-LA

A LIBRETTO

by Yusef Komunyakaa

MUSIC

by Susie Ibarra

CHARACTERS

In order of appearance:

John Wong   *An ex-Ph.D student in philosophy fascinated by numerology and Dashiell Hammett mystery stories that inspire his desire to become a detective. Wong is hired to investigate an embezzlement case that involves a company, Takeover Inc., in Thailand.*

The Hypothetical Three   *Paul, David, Eddie*

The Barker

Men/Women Chorus

Look-Alikes   *Three women who imitate The Supremes and also become the lovers of The Hypothetical Three.*

Act One

Semi-darkness. The sound of an airplane and landing gears are heard. The plane touches down on the runway.

The light comes up. A line of men stroll, almost marching, across the stage; each holds an AWOL bag.

John Wong, Chinese, dressed in a trench coat, wears dark glasses like a Sam Spade character. He seems hyper, intellectually and physically. He begins to point at three men in the cluster—Paul, David, and Eddie—his Hypothetical Three. John Wong touches each of the three on the shoulder saying, "one-two-and-three."

As the line of men march off the stage, John Wong steps forward to address the audience.

JOHN WONG

Ladies and Gentlemen,
I am John Wong,
The Metaphysical Detective,
and those three jokers
are my Hypothetical Three.
    Assuming a Sam Spade pose, he lights up a cigarette, and then continues to speak like a hard-boiled detective from the 1930s.

JOHN WONG

A dame walked into my office
and shoved an envelope
with three big ones under my nose
and said that seven more grand
was to be had if I dug up the dirt
on one of our Hypothetical Three.
She is co-owner of a high-tech firm
known as Takeover, Inc.

I'm here to cut the deck,
to solve the mystery,
and to erase that dirty word
embezzlement.

John Wong begins to slowly walk off stage, still talking.

But since I'm good
at what I do,
like a human bloodhound
with a juicy bone in my mouth,
who knows which machine
mollycuddles and honors the gods.
By the time you cop my drift,
my lingo, I should be on a plane
halfway back to Frisco.

John Wong exits.

SCENE 1

The Hypothetical Three march on stage, each wearing a different shirt than before, they are half-drunk, tipsy. Paul calls cadence as the three march.

PAUL

Left, right, left, right—
You had a good home
But you left—
Sound off.

DAVID AND EDDIE

One, two, three, four
Look out Uncle Ho.
One, two, three, four.

PAUL

Left, right, left, right—
You had a good home
but now you're seven steps to hell—

Left, right, left, right—
one, two, three, four—
you had a good home
but you shipped out—
one, two, three.
Halt—I said halt!

The three men freeze. Neon lights that spell Club Carousel click on.

SCENE 2

An old Thai man with a Texan sound to his voice steps forward to speak.

THE BARKER

You had a good home
but you left
you had a good home
but you left—
and now you're seven steps
from Paradise.

Step up, step up—

Gentlemen, step right up.
Welcome to Club Carousel
where the smoothest ride
is one big rehearsal
for life
for the goodtime

We have the prettiest women
in this town

They'll all stop your heart
on a silver dime

We have a roulette wheel
that gives every man
a fair shake
and a good deal

Hard up and lonely?
Well, step in,
step in, gentlemen,
and get more beauty
than money can buy

Hard up and blue?
We take greenback
and good-old-made-in-the-
USA plastic, too

PAUL

Sound off!

DAVID AND EDDIE

One, two, three

The Hypothetical Three begin to march in place.

THE BARKER

No cover charge
no clip joint
for a few drinks
your wildest dreams
come true in Bangkok

We got non-stop sex shows
we got the fire-stick show
we got the pingpong ball show
we got the chop a banana show
we got the soul-eating show
we got the cigarette-smoking show
we got the flower-hanging show
we got the razorblade show
we got the whistle-blowing show

we got the bottle-cracking show
we got the chopstick show
we got the egg-cracking show
we got everything a greedy heart desires
and a few things it doesn't need

we got boy-girls
we got *kathoy*
who can take you to hellish
joy.

SCENE 3

Club Carousel: The music is semi-classical. Thai women (dancers) are posed on the slow-spinning carousel: They seem like pieces of ancient sculpture—some poses are sexual. They seem to have been stopped in time, in half-gestures and fluid movement. John Wong is in the foreground; his Hypothetical Three weave their way among the chorus of men and women who begin a low-volume chant:

MEN/WOMEN CHORUS

MEN

Ten dollars, twenty dollars

WOMEN

Fifty dollars, one-hundred dollars.

MEN

Ten dollars, twenty dollars

WOMEN

Fifty dollars, one-hundred dollars.

MEN

Ten dollars, twenty dollars

WOMEN

Fifty dollars, one-hundred dollars.

The women come alive one by one in slow motion till they are swaying, danc-ing, tossing themselves into the out-stretched arms of the men. They segue into singing a rock disco song. Others in the club join in.

MEN/WOMEN CHORUS

You got me
got me on the run again
I'm almost outa breath
and halfway outa my skin
in counter-rotation to the earth

You got me
got me on the run again
and what I should be running to,
Baby, I'm running away from.
Look at the fix
you got me in
as I orbit your mind
outside of real time

You got me
got me on the run again
about to slip outa my skin

'cause I'm about ready to steal
Somebody else's good name
to lay my claim
to pay for my shame.

The song ends, lights go down. Three look-alikes of The Supremes stroll to center stage and begin to sing. The dancers begin a slow dance in each other's arms.

© 2000 by Yusef Komunyakaa; from *Talking Dirty to the Gods* (New York: Farrar, Straus and Giroux, 2000)

MARILYN CHIN

FOXTROT WITH MARILYN:
AN INTERVIEW

Tarisa Matsumoto

I SEARCH for poetry. I'm not always aware of what I'm searching for, but when I find it, I am awestruck. I found Marilyn Chin during one of these searches. "Yellow are the grasses / that never learned to writhe." This fragment from "Old Asian Hand" in her 1994 collection *The Phoenix Gone, The Terrace Empty* is the line that exploded for me. She writes in a language of such tender provocation that her words pry open history, dissect it into fragments of universal joy, heartbreak, and hope. Her affair with rhythm and form demonstrates the intellectual force behind her words, yet that enviable skill of image-painting overwhelms. I was fortunate to have the opportunity to converse with Marilyn during the summer of 2001 regarding her thoughts on poetry and poetry's place in the business of the contemporary world. Perhaps this brief conversation will hint at the person behind the upcoming collection, *Rhapsody in Plain Yellow*.

Tarisa Matsumoto: In earlier interviews, you have talked about the "nature of displacement" and the longing that people have to be part of a larger, well-defined community, be it country or tribe. Moreover,

Marilyn Chin with her sister, 1948

you've mentioned that you feel you have a burden of history on your shoulders. Where do you find yourself now in regard to these ideas? Have you found your tribe or do the disjointed influences of displacement and history continue to speak in your poetry?

Marilyn Chinn: Displacement is of course a profound immigrant issue. Any immigrant poet must address this issue; it's in the forefront of her consciousness. The nature of displacement changes with each succeeding group. A displaced Vietnamese poet will have a totally different take on her predicament than, let's say, a Japanese American poet, whose parents were interned . . . or a Bosnian poet who fled from the Balkan massacre. The story of leaving one's motherland to be absorbed by a new culture is a quintessential American one, for this is a country where nobody is indigenous except for the American Indians. Ideally, the turf belongs to everybody and nobody.

In my new book there are a couple of poems about my friend

Mieko Ono, who is fifty, and lives alone in Miami University, Oxford, Ohio, and teaches Japanese. She belongs to a new group of displaced people . . . unmarried female scholars of all races and backgrounds sent out to teach in Timbuktu, perhaps to retire there, never to return home. I wanted to speak for that group of forgotten women and make them visible.

Most of us diasporic types don't belong anywhere. I can't really go back to live in Hong Kong and I don't completely feel at home in San Diego, California. Some days, I may feel homeless; some days I feel like a citizen of the world. The contradictions are deep. However, as I've grown older, I've found peace in my "provisional" status, found peace in my peripatetic muse and try to think of "displacement" as a positive existential force, that it's a place of synthesis and not of irreversible dissipation of the tribe.

Home now is my art, my poetry. The cross-fertilization in my work is mimetic of my diasporic heritage and my ability to synthesize multiple worlds. My personal loneliness is an existential problem, not an esthetic one.

TM: In a way then, "displacement" creates a new tribe of immigrants or, as you state, forgotten people. If this loneliness is an existential problem, then esthetically, how do you speak this in your poetry and how has your current method of speaking for a displaced/immigrant/forgotten tribe changed from your earlier work? Do you find "standard" forms breaking down? Are images or words from different cultures more prevalent?

MC: I've always worked hard at "breaking down" form in order to remake it after my own image. I believe that formally and stylistically, my poems are varied. I try to find the best container for the muse— I try to keep my esthetics dancing between the boundaries of east and west, ancient and street contempo. For instance, the short ditty I wrote for Mieko sounds like a quasi-limerick:

My friend Mieko Ono bought a Condo
Over a brand new wooden footbridge
In Miami University, Oxford Ohio
She teaches Japanese to Business minors
Each night she dims the stone lanterns
She lives there alone without a lover

The poem plays with the idea of displacement on many levels. A Japanese scholar living in nowheresville with a pompous name like Oxford, Ohio, is an ironic riff. "Miami" is further geographical confusion. To teach not the Japanese of Bashō, but the Japanese of business minors—is further alienation. The faux Japanese decor in the condo, fraught with lanterns, footbridges, is supposed to make her displacement more tolerable? The last line "she lives there alone without a lover" seals her fate, turns the subtle ironies into sadness.

Formally, it's a simple ditty with rhyme. It has my characteristic love of concision. There's not much room for fat in this poem. But, I had to meld two types of song to get here: the Chinese folk lyric and the western limerick. The sing-song quality of the ditty works against the seriousness of Mieko's existential condition.

The poems in this new volume *Rhapsody in Plain Yellow*—well, they sing. This is what sets it apart from my earlier volumes. I don't have a reasonable explanation for this, except that the muse just felt like singing for a while. She was tired of reading contemporary poetry that is missing an ear. I was also intrigued with working with folk ballads from east and west. I wrote a batch of Chinese quatrains. I took some old sonnets I had in the drawers and literally shattered them to pieces at Yaddo—I took my trusty tiny pair of cuticle scissors and cut out all the words and scrambled them and reconstituted them into a series I called "Shattered Sonnets." The title poem of this volume is a long associative tour-de-force referencing everybody from Whitman to Ginsberg to Shakespeare to Kafka to Issa to Qu Yuan . . . Therefore, there is not one template that could adequately describe exile or displacement or any given immigrant theme or preoccupation. It's an occupational hazard for poets to play in the mud a bit, to challenge the muse, to try to make something "new" from an old borrowed tune. I had a great time writing these poems; I hope that this shows.

I don't think that there is a prescription to writing about any given subject.

TM: Your "Shattered Sonnets" reminds me of something you said in an earlier interview: that Shakespearean sonnets, which have a connectedness to Chinese lyrics, were your first introduction into English poetry. What was your first introduction to poetry or words that sing? I know you remember your grandmother's recitations of the Yueh-fu and the Tao. Were these your earliest experiences with poetry? And

Marilyn, age 4, Stanley Park, Hong Kong

speaking of "cross-fertilization" and immigrant and displaced poets, do you feel any pressure from the society in this country that may be saying, "Enough—we've had enough of affirmative action, multiculturalism, and ethnic studies." There is not a "prescription to writing about any given subject," but is there a pressure to stray away from these issues, a pressure that comes not from within but from outside influence?

MC: I guess there are two parts to your question. Yes, I was deeply influenced by my domineering, illiterate grandmother. We bragged that she was illiterate in several languages and still managed to be the soothsayer/matriarch of the family. She had a tremendous memory and probably could've out-recited most serious classical scholars. Now, to segue way to your latter comment about pressures from the Philistines to stop writing "ethnic" poetry. Hell, deconstructing my grandmother is a treasure trough in itself. She was the embodiment of the failure of feudalism. Her pungent pre-feminist ideas include drawing a line down her bed to separate her consciousness from that of my grandfather's. She was a neo-classicist who couldn't read because her father believed that women should be kept in the dark— red in the face, she was forced to pen a cross for her name on her greencard. She was brilliantly absurd and would've given the Dadaists the run for their money. Why would I want to write about my dog if I could write about my grandmother? I remember that once when I was a grad student at Iowa, some jerk said to me, "Writing about your grandmother, again," I flipped him the bird and said, "Well, at least, I'm not mediocre." He never spoke to me again.

The pressures are immense: write in form; free verse is lazy. Don't write in form; formalists are fascists! The narrative is in! The narrative is out! Here are the real poets, and here are the "minority" poets. You should only write L-A-N-G-U-A-G-E poetry. You should only write fragments because linear thought only belongs to white men. You should write with your bodily juices. We hate confessional poets! We hate autobiographical poetry! The page is dead . . . etc . . . etc . . . Look at our premiere American novelist: Toni Morrison. She writes about being black and she writes about slavery. Who dares to challenge her about her content? Who dares to tell her how to write?

The secret is to write about what you know, but make sure that what you know is fascinating or you're going to be a bore. My protagonists are sassy Chinese American women, because I am a sassy Chinese American woman. Many of my issues are identity issues; they're about being a sassy Chinese American woman in this juncture of time. There are socio/historical, philosophical, religious, esthetic, global, maybe even galactical problems relating to my identity. Haven't you noticed, there are Chinese people everywhere. Even the Javanese were trying to oust a few last year.

I just don't let anybody bully me around regarding my art. If they don't want to buy my book, that's okay by me. But, if they do buy it, I make sure that they get their money's worth.

TM: What about poetry readings? Is it common for you to be asked to read as part of an "Asian American" or "Chinese American" reading, or a "minority" or "multicultural" reading? Are you able to stand up solo at public readings or do organizers tend to want to group you into a category?

Marilyn (right) *with her sister and mother, 1960s*

MC: I would say the more the merrier. I believe in that reverse
corollary to Woody Allen's quip: "I refuse to join any club that would
have me as a member." I, on the other hand, am very promiscuous
and accept all invitations to parties. I enjoy reading in Asian American and "multicultural" events. This is how I was able to meet my
Asian American poetry friends, via group readings and anthologies.
I met Hongo, Mura, Li Young in an Academy of American poets
Asian American poetry reading series. I met Arthur Sze and Carolyn
Lau at a big reading at UC Berkeley's Asian American studies department. Joy Harjo, Elizabeth Alexander, Minnie Brace Pratt and I toured
Germany under the guise of "young American women poets!" Imag-
ine that: we were the representatives for the canon. Ruth Hsiao teaches

my book in a class called "Literature in the Diaspora" at Tufts. I read often in Women's studies departments. Sometimes I get doubled up with "performance" poets . . . I would have to put on a wild hat and increase the decibels, but, hey—the idea is "to get invited." Sometimes I am the opening act for Adrienne Rich, Robert Bly, and the Rolling Stones. Sometimes I am invited to talk about the linebreak to MFA students. Sometimes, I talk about Tu Fu to a bunch of hirsute Sinologists. I don't read into the minds of my hosts. I am grateful that people want to hear me—poetry being a marginalized art to begin with—I feel blessed to be invited. I want my dance card to be full. I don't want to sit out on the foxtrot. I am not afraid of any label that is thrust upon me as long as the intentions are good. And I believe intentions are good with poetry purveyors. They're peddling our wares to the world.

TM: The politicism of other Asian American poets like Hongo and Inada carries through in their works. These poets, among others, are viewed as "political" writers, perhaps solely because of their "other" status in this country. Can a poet of color be anything other than political when he/she creates? You seem very conscious of such politics when you write. Do you feel that readers assume a writer of color to be writing politically? Have your sensibilities toward this issue changed over the years? How do you sense the readership's sensibilities have changed over the years?

MC: Asian American poetry is still young, given the length of scope of the history of literature written in English. The pioneering generation: Inada and Hongo, as you've mentioned, Janice Mirikitani, Nellie Wong, etc., had to do the necessary groundwork to speak for the group, to assert our "identities." The coolie issues, the internment camps, Angel Island, were all part of Asian American history and most earlier poets feel the need to remind the majority of this shameful history. We have the extra burden as minority poets to be the spokespersons for our minority cultures. I take on this task willfully and blissfully. I see myself as a post-colonial, Pacific Rim, feminist Chinese American poet—and enjoy letting the diatribe show through in my poetry. Not all Asian American poets see themselves as "political" poets, per se. Mei Mei Bersenbrugge and Arthur Sze probably would not categorize themselves as political poets. John Yau would probably see himself as more of a surrealist/abstractionist. I am also a neo-classicist and I also consider myself a "love poet" . . . I don't feel that I need to be an apologist on behalf of my meandering and complex muse, but I don't feel ashamed of my political proclivities either. We minority poets have a lot "to write about, to bitch about." It's a part of our nature to be an oppositional voice in the literary world. Our voices are necessary. We keep the literature honest.

I believe that it is reductive to frame any of us as poets on the soapbox and that we have a singular objective. Asian American poets are writing very well at the moment. I believe that we are in a multicultural renaissance right now, that women and poets of color are writing the best poetry in America. I'm not just being "politically correct" when I say this. I believe that deep inside, we all know this. The critics have been slow to respond. The critics haven't codified this yet (I believe, that it's your job, Tarisa, and other young poet/scholars like yourself to take on this task). Nobody has written cogently and thoroughly about this happening, precisely because it takes someone very smart to be able to talk about our postmodern "multicultural" moment—the burgeoning of Asian American, Latino American, African American, Native American, etc., talent and how women poets have taken over the modernist legacy left over by Eliot, Frost, Pound, Williams, etc. We are the ones who are "making it new."

Listen, Tarisa, you have to disabuse yourself of this notion put into your head by the workshop that there is minority poetry and then there is the real poetry. I don't think that this binary holds any weight. Furthermore, as to the reader's sensibilities, I believe that you will find many of our books on the shelves of the most purist/canonist poetry reader/writers. If they are any good, they would want to know what is happening in the fringes and what is creeping toward them from the margins. Furthermore, I believe that poets of color, are doing a lot of readings all over the continent, which tells us that the readership wants to hear from us. They know that we hold the inspiration of America at the present.

TM: Whether or not this comment is appropriate for this interview, I'm not sure, but I'll tell you. The first time I read Janice Mirikitani's work (in the second year of my MA degree no less), I was astounded. To read of painted girls gluing their eyelids and dying their hair was something I was very familiar with. However, to see it in print . . . well, I can't explain the feeling, the sense I had. These were the girls I grew up with. Mirikitani was telling their story. The fact that I was not one of these girls as I am what my grandmother calls "happa haole," did not matter. The fact that I knew these girls and their mothers was the important thing to me because I could see the same things happening to my brother who is much more "Asian looking" than I am and other people on my father's side of the family. As you say, I suddenly discovered that someone was "keeping the literature honest."

Related to the idea of "honest literature" is translation. Translating poetry seems very important to you. You've done a lot of work in this area. Do you feel this is a way to bear the burden of history or to quell the fear you've addressed in earlier interviews about losing your bilingualness? How does working with translation affect your poetry? Can you keep translations honest to the original?

MC: I started translating when I was an undergraduate at UMass, Amherst. I majored in Classical Chinese Language and Literature so that I could force myself to learn the classics. And that was a very important foundation for my lifetime work in poetry. This classical training, in conjunction with my grandmother's prodigious recitations, gave me a solid grounding for my fusionist aesthetics. The strength of my poems depends on my knowledge of both eastern and western literary history and to be able to give the muse roaming access. When I was in the Iowa Workshop in the eighties I worked as a translator/editor for the International Writing Program and met Ai Qing and Ding Ling. China was in the midst of ousting Chiang Ch'ing and the Gang of Four; and I was fortunate enough to have a chance to work with two pioneering Chinese modernists. Both had been banished to the harsh provinces for decades and were now released under Deng's "rehabilitation" campaign. I was very moved by their personal histories. In some countries art mattered; there were high stakes involved. What one scribbled down on the page could mean banishment, imprisonment, and even death. Right then and there, I decided that art must have a mission. It must have a reason for being and that if one day my muse should lose her urgency, I would stop writing. Of course, I live in the comfort of the U.S., under different circumstances. All the more, I want my work to matter in some historical/social context. Translating Ding Ling and most profoundly, translating Ai Qing—made me think about the role of the writer in society.

Eighth-grade picture, D. A. Grout School,
Portland, Oregon

In short, the act of translation made a deep impact on my muse during my earlier years. I don't publish everything I translate. I often give myself translation chores, e.g. a few poems of Tu Fu this week, a couple of Chuang-tzu's parables next week, so that I would not get rusty in my language skills. And I am appalled by all those so-called translators who don't even bother to learn the source languages from which they make their versions. I guess Pound gave way to that (well, this would be a topic for another time). I always tell my students to learn a second language, just so that they could have the experience of reading poetry in a different language.

TM: Because you work with translation, you understand how words get lost, displaced, or misinterpreted between languages and cultural or generational barriers. How so between the mind and the page? Even when you are not translating, how do you move from internal thoughts to those given to the reader? Any change in philosophy from say the poems of *Dwarf Bamboo* to the poems in your forthcoming collection, *Rhapsody in Plain Yellow*?

MC: Just the other day, in a Chinatown restaurant in Sydney, my

Taiwanese friend Irene, who is terribly myopic, misread "chicken" for "frog" and almost ordered fried frog. Ironically enough—it was I, a Chinese American, who corrected her. It just happened that I was paying attention. The translation process between poem and poem, between person to person, taught me to pay close attention. When I was in Taiwan for a Fulbright, I used to listen so hard that I would go home with a headache every night. My Mandarin was very rusty; and I was afraid that I would misunderstand something very important. I am a poet who believes in being very "honed." Sometimes, I would spend hours on a connective. I would spend years writing a short lyric, because of one technical difficulty or another: the balance of the poem is not quite right, one word is off, the sound of a phrase is wrong, etc. If the poem is not right, I won't let it go. Some of the long poems take four to five years to complete. My output is not abundant. It takes me seven years to publish a book. I have tried various methods and forms for writing my poems, but my patience has not changed. I don't care how others will interpret my poem, but I want to know my poem down to a phoneme. This attention, this knowledge is true love. I love poetry more and more as I grow older.

Sometimes in the process of reading poems in ancient Chinese, I would borrow ideas and motives and retranslate them into the here and now. I would reinvent an old cliché and make it serve a completely new context. In my poem, "Variations on an Ancient Theme: The Drunken Husband," I tried to refurbish two themes: one, of the drunken husband—as seen often in Tzu—poem after poem he would come in drunk, but of course, the woe-be-gone female would forgive "her lord." Two, the dog that kept barking "hung, hung" throughout Chinese poetry. I relocated the dog to be the harbinger of bad news in various vignettes in the American suburb. Here are five vignettes: each with a separate mixed-raced couple. The make up of the couple is: Asian woman and other. This proposition, itself, is polemical.

The dog is barking at the door
"Daddy crashed the car"
"Hush, kids, go to your room
Don't come out until it's over"
He stumbles up the dim lit stairs
Drops his Levis to his ankles

"Touch me and I'll kill you," she says
Pointing a revolver at his head

The dog is barking at the door
She doesn't recognize the master
she sniffs his guilty crotch
Positioned to bite it off
"Jesus, control your dog
A man can't come back to his castle"
"Kill him, Ling, Ling," she sobs
Curlers bobbing on her shoulders

The dog is barking at the door
He stumbles in swinging
"Where is my gook-of-a-wife
Where are my half-breed monsters"
There is silence up the cold stairs
No movement, no answer
The drawers are open like graves
The closets agape to the rafters

The dog is barking at the door
He stumbles in singing
"How is my teenage bride?
How is my mail-order darling?
Perhaps she's pretending to be asleep
Waiting for her man's hard cock"
He enters her from behind
Her sobbing does not deter him

The dog is barking at the door
What does the proud beast know?
Who is both Master and intruder?
Whose bloody handprint on the wall?
Whose revolver in the dishwater?
The neighbors won't heed her alarm
She keeps barking, barking
Bent on saving their kind

Marilyn Chin at Yaddo, summer of 1994

In my twenties I wrote a poem about eating dog. Now, I've come to full circle in having this dog be the loyal beast who is "bent on saving our kind." This is my Buddhist way of redeeming myself. This poem is a commentary on domestic violence and marital discord, of course, a contemporary theme—and perhaps, it's even considered to be narrowly focused, because the couples involved are mixed-race couples—but this very dog I had plucked out of ancient Chinese poetry is a universal dog, who would eventually bring us harmony. Through Chinese poetry, I learned to find the universal through the particular.

In myriad ways, too many and perhaps sometimes too subtle to mention, I believe that the act of translating poetry from another source language has taught me to be a better poet.

TM: I enjoyed reading that you feel "the act of translating poetry from another source language has taught (you) to be a better poet." It seems that you are one who can find connections to poetry in almost anything. What about teaching? You have taught other writers for many years. What do you take to your poetry from the classroom?

What do you bring to the classroom? Do you have a particular philosophy about the writer as teacher?

MC: It's strange to answer this after that terrible bloodbath in New York [September 11]. It makes one want to reevaluate one's life. All those cliché Japanese poems about our fleeting moment . . . We all want to teach less and write more. There are semesters that are complete migraines. My head would throb as if it were in a vice. Some semesters I would have a low-grade depression and I wouldn't know it until after the grading was finished and a dark cloud would suddenly lift from my shoulders. On a good day, I feel very blessed—proud that this peasant immigrant, child of illiterate grandmothers, could make her living by pontificating about poetry. Listen to this, she teaches Shakespeare sonnets to blonde surfers. Confucius said (well, he said a lot of things like men shouldn't be in the kitchen and women and "small men" are not tameable . . . but, I'm reading him lately.) . . . Confucius opened his "Analects" by saying, "Is it not pleasant to learn with constant perseverance and application? Is it not delightful to have friends visit from distant lands?" Yes, I believe that poetry has brought me much joy. Through poetry, I've met very interesting people and have traveled all over. Teaching is, of course, my "iron rice bowl." My knowledge is what I have to trade for my sustenance. I teach so that I can write and eat. Teaching is also part of my journey. Bashō used to meander from town to town with his walking stick, hang out with disciples, eat and drink and write poems. He did this to the very end. I still have reservations about writers teaching "workshop." I can't write when I'm teaching. Or, let's put it this way, I don't write well. This explains why it takes me seven years to publish a book of poems. Purely, I look at too much juvenilia and bad stuff—it can't be good for the muse. I know that some writers say that they get nourishment through this process. But, I don't.

However, as I grow older, I believe that I have much to impart to my students. A life of art, a life of teaching—is a life of love. This is very icky lugubrious, but this is how I feel now that I'm over forty. Confucius also said, "At forty, I had no doubts." I prefer what this young boy said to me in Taiwan—he appeared in my office with a lovely orchid, then sang, "At forty she's a blossoming flower."

After my Last Paycheck from the Factory, Two Thin Coupons, Four Tin Dollars, I Invited Old Liu for an Afternoon Meal

FOR THE CHINESE CULTURAL REVOLUTION
AND ALL THAT WAS WRONG WITH MY LIFE

I ordered vegetables and he ordered dog,
the cheapest kind, mushu, but without the cakes.
I watched him smack his greasy lips
and thought of home, my lover's gentle kisses—
his faint aroma, still with me now.

I confided with a grief too real,
"This is not what I expected"
and bit my lip to keep from crying,
"I've seen enough, I want to go home."
But suddenly I was seized by a vision

reminding me why I had come: two girls
in uniform, red bandanas and armbands
shouting slogans and Maoish songs,
"the East is red, the sun is rising;"
promises of freedom and a better world.

Trailing them was their mascot of Youth,
a creature out of Doctor Seuss or Lewis Carroll,
purplish pink, variegated and prancing.
I stood in awe of its godlike beauty
until the realist Liu disrupted my mirage.

"It's the dog I ordered and am eating still!"
he mumbled with a mouthful of wine.
And as it came closer I saw the truth:
its spots were not of breeding or exotic import,
but rampant colonies of scabies and fleas,

which, especially red in its forbidden country,
blazed a trail through the back of its woods;
and then, its forehead bled with worms,
so many and complex as if *they* did its thinking.
I rubbed my eyes, readjusted the world . . .

Then focused back on his gruesome dish
trimmed with parsley and rinds of orange.
One piece of bone, unidentified which,
stared at me like a goat's pleading eye
or the shiny new dollar I'd just lost.

Old Liu laughed and slapped my back,
"You American Chinese are hard to please."
Then, stuck his filthy chopsticks into my sauce.
"Mmmm, seasoning from Peijing, the best
since opium," then, pointed to a man

sitting behind me, a stout provincial governor
who didn't have to pay after eating the finest
Chinese pug, twenty-five yuan a leg.
He picked his teeth with a splintered shin,
burped and farted, flaunting his wealth.

Old Liu said with wine breath to kill,
"My cousin, don't be disillusioned,
his pride will be molested, his dignity violated,
and he as dead as the four-legged he ate
two short kilometers before home."

—From *Dwarf Bamboo*, 1987

A Portrait of the Self As Nation, 1990–1991

Fit in dominata servitus
In servitude dominatus
In mastery there is bondage
In bondage there is mastery

Latin proverb

The stranger and the enemy
We have seen him in the mirror.

George Seferis

Forgive me, Head Master,
but you see, I have forgotten
to put on my black lace underwear, and instead
I have hiked my slip up, up to my waist
so that I can enjoy the breeze.
It feels good to be *without*,
so good as to be salacious.
The feeling of flesh kissing tweed.
If ecstasy had a color, it would be
yellow and pink, yellow and pink
Mongolian skin rubbed raw.
The serrated lining especially fine
like wearing a hair-shirt, inches above the knee.
When was the last time I made love?
The last century? With a wan missionary.
Or was it San Wu the Bailiff?
The tax collector who came for my tithes?
The herdboy, the ox, on the bridge of magpies?
It was Roberto, certainly,
high on coke, circling the galaxy.
Or my recent vagabond love
driving a reckless chariot, lost

in my feral country. *Country,* Oh I am
so punny, so very, very punny.
Dear Mr. Decorum, don't you agree?

It's not so much the length of the song
but the range of the emotions—Fear
has kept me a good pink monk—and poetry
is my nunnery. Here I am alone in my altar,
self-hate, self-love, both self-erotic notions.
Eyes closed, listening to that one hand clapping—
not metaphysical trance, but fleshly mutilation—
and loving *it,* myself and that pink womb, my bed.
Reading "Ching Ping Mei" in the "expurgated"
where all the female protagonists were named
Lotus.
Those damned licentious women named us
Modest, Virtue, Cautious, Endearing,
Demure-dewdrop, Plum-aster, Petal-stamen.
They teach us to walk headbent in devotion,
to honor the five relations, ten sacraments.
Meanwhile, the feast is brewing elsewhere,
the ox is slaughtered and her entrails are hung
on the branches for the poor. They convince us, yes,
our chastity will save the nation—Oh mothers,
all your sweet epithets don't make us wise!
Orchid by any other name is equally seditious.

Now, where was I, oh yes, now I remember,
the last time I made love, it was to *you.*
I faintly remember your whiskers
against my tender nape.
You were a conquering barbarian,
helmeted, halberded,
beneath the gauntleted moon,
whispering Hunnish or English—
so-long Oolong went the racist song,
bye-bye little chinky butterfly.
There is no cure for self-pity,

the disease is death,
ennui, disaffection,
a roll of flesh-colored tract homes crowding my imagination.
I do hate my loneliness,
sitting cross-legged in my room,
satisfied with a few off-rhymes,
sending off precious haiku to some inconspicuous journal
named "Left Leaning Bamboo."
You, my precious reader, O sweet voyeur,
sweaty, balding, bespeckled,
in a rumpled rayon shirt
and a neo-Troubadour chignon,
politics mildly centrist,
the *right* fork for the *right* occasions,
matriculant of the best schools—
herewith, my last confession
(with decorous and perfect diction)
I loathe to admit. Yet, I shall admit it:
there was no Colonialist coercion;
sadly, we blended together well.
I was poor, starving, war torn,
an empty coffin to be filled,
You were a young, ambitious Lieutenant
with dreams of becoming a Prince
of a "new world order," Lord
over the League of Nations.

Lover, destroyer, savior!
I remember that moment of beguilement,
one hand muffling my mouth,
one hand untying my sash—
On your throat dangled a golden cross.
Your god is jealous, your god is cruel.
So, when did you finally return?
And . . . was there a second coming?
My memory is failing me, perhaps
you came too late
(we were already dead).

Perhaps you didn't come at all—
you had a deadline to meet,
another alliance to secure,
another resistance to break.
Or you came too often
to my painful dismay.
(Oh, how facile the liberator's hand.)
Often when I was asleep
You would hover over me
with your great silent wingspan
and watch me sadly.
This is the way you want me—
asleep, quiescent, almost dead,
sedated by lush immigrant dreams
of global bliss, connubial harmony.

Yet, I shall always remember
and deign to forgive
(long before I am satiated,
long before I am spent)
that last pressumed cry,
"your little death."
Under the halcyon light
you would smoke and contemplate
the sea and debris,
that barbaric keening
of what it means to be free.
As if we were ever free,
as if ever we could be.
Said the judge,
"Congratulations,
On this day, fifteen of November, 1967,
Marilyn Mei Ling Chin,
application # z-z-z-z-z,
you are an American citizen,
naturalized in the name of God.
the father, God the son and the Holy Ghost."
Time assuages, and even

Yellow River becomes clean . . .

Meanwhile we forget
the power of exclusion
what you are walling in or out—
and to whom you must give offence.
The hungry, the slovenly, the convicts
need not apply.
The syphilitic, the consumptive
may not moor.
The hookwormed and tracomaed
(and the likewise infested).
The gypsies, the sodomists, the mentally infirm.
The pagans, the heathens, the
non-denominational—
The coloreds, the mixed-races and the reds.
The communists, the usurous,
the mutants, the Hibakushas, the hags . . .

Oh, connoisseurs of gastronomy and *keemun* tea!
My foes, my loves,
how eloquent your discrimination,
how precise your poetry.
Last night, in our large, rotund bed,
we witnessed the fall. *Ours*
was an "aerial war." Bombs
glittering in the twilight sky
against the Star-Spangled Banner.
Dunes and dunes of sand,
fields and fields of rice.
A thousand charred oil wells,
the firebrands of night.
Ecstasy made us tired.

Sir, Master, Dominatrix,
Fall was a glorious season for the hegemonists.
We took long melancholy strolls on the beach,
digressed on art and politics

in a quaint warfside café in La Jolla.
The storm grazed our bare arms gently . . .
History has never failed us.
Why save Babylonia or Cathay,
when we can always have Paris?
Darling, if we are to remember at all,
Let us remember it well—
We were fierce, yet tender,
fierce and tender.

—From *The Phoenix Game, The Terrace Empty,* 1994

NOTES: Second stanza: "Ching Ping Mei"—Chinese erotic novel.

Sixth stanza: Exclusion—refers to various "exclusion acts" or anti-Chinese legislation that attempted to halt the flow of Chinese immigrants to the U.S.

Sixth stanza: Hookworm and tracoma—two diseases that kept many Chinese detained and quarantined at Angel Island.

Sixth stanza: Hibakushas—scarred survivors of the atom bomb and their deformed descendants.

Blues on Yellow

The canary died in the gold mine, her dreams got lost in the sieve.
The canary died in the gold mine, her dreams got lost in the sieve.
Her husband the crow killed under the railroad, the spokes hath
    shorn his wings.

Something's cookin' in Chin's kitchen, ten thousand yellow bellied
    sap suckers baked in a pie.
Something's cookin' in Chin's kitchen, ten thousand yellow bellied
    sap suckers baked in a pie.
Something's cookin' in Chin's kitchen, die die yellow bird, die die.

O crack an egg on the griddle, yellow will ooze into white.
O crack an egg on the griddle, yellow will ooze into white.
Run, run, sweet little Puritan, yellow will ooze into white.

If you cut my yellow wrists, I'll teach my yellow toes to write.
If you cut my yellow wrists, I'll teach my yellow toes to write.
If you cut my yellow fists, I'll teach my yellow feet to fight.

Do not be afraid to perish, my mother, Buddha's compassion is
    nigh.
Do not be afraid to perish, my mother, our boat will sail tonight.
Your babies will reach the promiseland, the stars will be their
    guide.

I am so mellow yellow, mellow yellow, Buddha sings in my veins.
I am so mellow yellow, mellow yellow, Buddha sings in my veins.
O take me to the land of the unreborn, there's no life on earth
    without pain.

(The verses could be sung in any order and could be repeated an
    infinite number of times)

—From *Rhapsody in Plain Yellow*, 2002

Chinese Quatrains
(The Woman in Tomb 44)

The aeroplane is shaped like a bird
Or a giant mechanical penis
My father escorts my mother
From girlhood to unhappiness

A dragonfly has iridescent wings
Shorn, it's a lowly pismire
Plucked of arms and legs
A throbbing red pepperpod

Baby, she's a girl
Pinkly propped as a doll
Baby, she's a pearl
An ulcer in the oyster of God

Cry little baby clam cry
The steam has opened your eyes
Your secret darkly hidden
The razor is sharpening the knife

Abandoned taro-leaf boat
It's lonely black sail broken
The corpses are fat and bejeweled
The hull is thoroughly rotten

The worm has entered the ear
And out the nose of my father
Cleaned the pelvis of my mother
and ringed around her finger-bone

One child beats a bedpan
One beats a fishhook out of wire
One beats his half sister on the head
Oh, teach us to fish and love

Don't say her boudoir is too narrow
She could sleep but in one cold bed
Don't say you own many horses
We escaped on her skinny mare's back

Man is good said Meng-Tzu
We must cultivate their natures
Man is evil said Hsun-Tzu
There's a worm in the human heart

He gleaned a beaded purse from Hong Kong
He procured an oval fan from Taiwan
She married him for a green card
He abandoned her for a blonde

My grandmother is calling her goslings
My mother is summoning her hens
The sun has vanished into the ocean
The moon has drowned in the fen

Discs of jade for her eyelids
A lozenge of pearl for her throat
Lapis and kudzu in her nostrils
They will rob her again and again

—From *Rhapsody in Plain Yellow*, 2002

IVAN DOIG

CONVERSATION WITH MIDDLE-CLASS COSMIC MECHANIC, IVAN DOIG

Derek Sheffield

*B*ORN IN White Sulphur Springs, Montana, Ivan Doig has been a ranch hand, newspaperman, and magazine editor and writer. His novels are *The Sea Runners* (1982), *Bucking the Sun* (1996), *Mountain Time* (1999), and his Montana Trilogy: *English Creek* (1984), *Dancing at the Rascal Fair* (1987), and *Ride with Me, Mariah Montana* (1990). Doig has also written three works of nonfiction: two memoirs, *This House of Sky* (1978) and *Heart Earth* (1993), and *Winter Brothers* (1980), a book which fuses excerpts from the diaries of James Swan, an early settler of the Puget Sound region, with entries from Doig's own journal evoking the same coastline.

Ivan Doig has received numerous writing awards, including a Christopher Award, the Pacific Northwest Booksellers Award for Literary Excellence, the Governor's Writers Day Award, and the David W. and Beatrice C. Evans Biography Award. *This House of Sky* was a finalist for the National Book Award in creative nonfiction, and in 1989 the Western Literature Association honored Doig with its Distinguished Achievement Award for his body of work. A graduate of Northwestern University, where he received degrees in journalism, he holds a Ph.D. in history from the University of Washington and honorary doctorates from Montana State University and Lewis and Clark College. Annie Proulx has called him "one of the best we've got" and Wallace Stegner wrote, "Doig knows this country and this life from the bottoms of his feet upward, and has known it, as he might say, ever since his legs were long enough to reach the ground. Here is the real Montana, and real West, through the eyes of a real writer."

Ivan Doig lives in north Seattle with his wife Carol. The interview took place on December 29, 2000, at their home where I found my gaze drawn occasionally to the sizable window of Doig's office, which looks, of course, west. Over a neatly gardened yard, past a steep bank, sailboats and freighters criss-crossed the Puget Sound. Beyond this slow and silent commotion, the Olympic Mountains stood sharply with such presence they managed to climb right into the dialogue. Around us, American history played along well-stocked bookshelves in the form of figurines: soldiers trudging, cannons aiming, and horses rearing. And one floor above, Carol Doig sipped tea and went about her business.

Though he has reached some impressive heights in his writing, Ivan Doig has remained grounded in the place he loves. He is congenial and has a rich and resonant voice that would have filled the airwaves, had Doig gone that way. His laughter riddles the interview as frequently as his Scotch wit. He loves language, spoken and written, and wades in it daily as his writing grows from considerable work habits. While thinking about how to describe Ivan Doig, I recalled some lines from Richard Hugo's poem, "Letter to Levertov from Butte":

. . . no matter what my salary is
or title, I remain a common laborer, stained by the perpetual
dust from loading flour or coal. I stay humble . . .

Derek Sheffield: I've read that you were sixteen when you decided ranch work wasn't in your future. When did you know that writing would be? That you would become the remembrancer, the talebringer?

Ivan Doig: Well, that turning point at age sixteen was in the midst of a summer when we were running sheep up above the Two Medicine River and a freezing rain just after the sheep had been sheared sent a lot of them over an old buffalo jump and made many others simply lie down and give up their ghost. I knew by the time I went back to high school that autumn that I was going to do something

Ivan with his grandmother, Bessie Ringer,
on a Montana ranch, 1942

else besides ranch work. I dropped out of Future Farmers of America
and took typing and Latin. That moved me a lot closer in my mind to
the high school teacher who became very influential in my becoming
a writer. Her name was Francis Tidyman, and she's described at some
length in *This House of Sky.* One of these impossible prairie tornadoes
who sometimes show up in small schools. She taught all the high
school English and then she would teach Latin some years, Spanish
other years, and she ran the high school paper, the annual, and so on.
When I came within her reach, she had me on the school paper pretty
promptly, and to a lesser extent, the school annual, and I took most of

her classes. My own inclination for turning toward trying to become a journalist emerged and so by the time I was seriously applying for scholarships my senior year, that's where it had all led.

I had no notion then that it was going to lead on toward books. It's not very well known that I was a broadcast journalism major in college. My intention, if anything, was to become Edward R. Murrow [laughter]. The radio had played an enormous role in our lives in Montana. It brought in whatever wafts of dream we had, like major league baseball, or drama, or comedy and it also brought in the news, which caught my attention. I think that kind of magnet has proven a historically sound one. The great newsmen, particularly the CBS news crew which Murrow set up, (the last of them, Robert Trout, died just a few weeks ago) did prove to be so superb that they were worthy models. It wasn't until I got my master's degree at Northwestern that I had to make the break between college and career—the one that so many guys my age had to, because the military was there waiting for me. I was in the Air Force Reserve during the Cuban Missile Crisis. When I came back out, my first job turned out to be a newspaper job, so that carried me on into writing.

DS: So it was the job that derailed you from broadcast journalism?

ID: It was. It's what was there. I came out of the Air Force at an awkward time of the year, March, when people weren't particularly hiring. Northwestern was well networked in placing its students and that happened to be the best-looking thing at the moment, a job as an editorial writer for a chain of newspapers in down-state Illinois so I promptly took it and stayed with print media from then on.

DS: How did your family take your decision to leave ranch work for writing?

ID: My dad always would say, "For God's sake, get yourself an education." Not unlike a lot of fathers who were working people. They wanted better things for their kids than they had had. Within him too, I now realize, was the Scotch respect for education, and his own limited education had been enough to show him that a little schooling could do quite a bit for you. He only went through the eighth grade, but he was good at arithmetic and went through life running crews of men where he had to keep track of wages and so forth.

DS: And he could count sheep.

ID: Could he ever count sheep. And he could measure haystacks, which is a fairly complicated formula [laughter]. Also he could write perfectly well. His commas are in the right place, words are spelled right. He had hellish handwriting [laughter], apparently the Spencerian method did not get down to the end of his fingertips, but in terms of handling the language he was really quite good. So that's a long way of saying that my father was always all for me getting an education, although his original notion of how far I could go—the pinnacle of jobs—was becoming a pharmacist, a druggist. One of his nephews had attained that and that's kind of what he could see. And I've realized since that was not too bad an idea from his viewpoint. All those little towns had drugstores in those days. There weren't malls or whatever. If indeed you wanted a portable career in the small-town West, druggist was a pretty good one.

My grandmother . . . (sigh) saw my going away as taking a piece of her heart with her. She was always all for whatever I wanted to do, and she would always end up telling me that. But she had so much more of an embrace of family and by the time I was leaving, she had lost one of her four children—my mother—through an early death. Another one was badly crippled with multiple sclerosis. A third one lived in Australia. So she had already seen a lot of people she cherished go from her, and my going out of state weighed on her.

DS: In *English Creek* you write, "Those firstborn always, always will live in a straddle between the ancestral path of life and the route of the new land." In the context of the book, you're speaking of Scotland versus America, but I want to apply it to ranch work versus word work. The physical, immediate, daily interaction with the world you had growing up was certainly hard work, but do you ever miss aspects of it? Or have you achieved a balance between time spent in the world and time spent re-creating the world?

ID: Those two very different looking kinds of work actually have a lot of similarities in the chores involved, the habit of doing the chores. I even keep pretty much the same working hours that I grew up with on a ranch. I'm up very early, always before dawn, down here starting to milk the thesaurus about the time I would have been milking cows on a Montana ranch. This is something I've tried to do some serious thinking about. There is a kind of physicality to the habit of writing too, of words coming out the ends of my fingers, and it's not always clear to me that they've lingered or ever been in my brain before they show up there on the keyboard. I've talked with some artist friends about this, the sculptor Tony Angell is one of them, and a jazz musician, and a watercolor artist. I've talked with them separately and we all feel what the sculptor has put a name on—"Getting it in the fingers." Often I'm surprised how the physicality of sitting and caressing the language produces, physically produces, the work I'm after. So there's that sort of mystical link to it.

The parts of ranch work I miss would be oriented to the land, I think, Derek. The way of life still is as tough as I figured out it was going to be. I keep in touch around the West as best I can and it's still pretty preposterous for a sixteen-year-old kid today to think he's going to be a farmer or rancher if there's no land in the family, and it's almost as difficult even if there is. So, as a viable fiscal way of life, there's still not that much to be missed there. Being under the Rocky Mountain Front on a good day on a tractor is a pretty damn fine thing, I know. One of the lessons of life in northern Montana is that you aren't gonna have that many good days sitting on tractors or trailing sheep. The ones that you do are going to be everlasting pageants in your head. But the incessant wind, the prospect of drought or enormous winters, just really kicks a lot of the romance out of the outdoor life. There are people, some of whom are my high school friends, who do seem to be cut out for that kind of life. Riley, the smart-mouthed newspaper writer I invented for *Ride with Me, Mariah Montana,* said something about guys not realizing they're working themselves to death because they're doing it out of doors. I've seen quite a lot of that. So I find it a lot more attractive and beneficial to my work to be able to go into the outdoors carrying a notebook and a pen and putting in dawn-to-dark days out there, looking at the country, listening to people, thinking it over.

DS: That reminds me of Van Gogh taking his canvas out into the fields.

ID: It's a pretty good idea to get out and feel the elements you're writing about. Some of them I've been able to bring into my work from memory. I saw enough blizzards in the time I was growing up out there that I don't feel compelled to rush out into a blizzard anymore. But the Montana droughts, I have gone there to experience because they weren't around as viciously when I was growing up. Apparently the warming of the earth is now wheeling them around.

DS: Well, I've read in Elizabeth Simpson's book about your thorough research habits, how you really take the time to know your material.

ID: Right. I've always tried to go take a look at the geography I'm writing about. Indeed, went to Scotland to see where the young men of *Dancing at the Rascal Fair* take off from the old life there.

DS: Did the story of the draft horse come from Scotland?

ID: It did, it did. The opening one. Now, this is the danger of being an interviewer, because notions about how carefully things are structured sometimes get disappointed by the time I'm done with them. I did come across, in a Scottish newspaper, an incident not far from the one that opens *Dancing at the Rascal Fair,* a horse being dragged into the Greenock harbor by a cart that flipped off the dock. But it must have taken me a year and a half, Derek, before I thought of having something similar toward the climax of the book. And even at that point when Rob goes into the reservoir on a horse, it wasn't because of that Scottish horse. It was a horse I had ridden across a similar reservoir. I made it safely, of course, but some years later on that same ranch a husky young ex-Marine did not. He drowned in an accident similar to what I have happen to Rob. Someone in an audience surprised me once by asking, "Now how did you carefully plan to have those two horse drownings?"

DS: That image of Rob and the horse drowning in that reservoir is as haunting to me, as a reader, as the elk in Craig Lesley's *Winterkill* and the horses in Linda Bierds's *The Stillness, The Dancing.*

ID: Well; good. I'm glad to be in that company because those are images that are permanently on the cave walls in the back of my head, too. I remember working long and hard on that scene of the horse going into the reservoir. You try to bring to a book everything you have and one thing I have is an experience of nearly drowning, as told in *This House of Sky.* Consequently, I don't know how many drownings there have been in my novels—one in *The Sea Runners,* two or three somewhere else. I've been able to draw on that as probably the closest risk I've ever been through and bring it into the fiction. At first I thought I should have gone out and taken swimming lessons after that. But I've decided since, "No, no, this is a very useful

Berneta and Charlie Doig at their sheep-herding
camp on Grassy Mountain, 1934

fear for me to have as a writer." It's like boating. I get seasick very
promptly, which was just a great help when I was writing *The Sea
Runners,* to give a character . . . uh . . .

DS: Misery.

ID: Yes . . . to give misery to Wennberg.

DS: Richard Hugo wrote, "Poets turn liabilities into assets."

ID: [laughter] Hugo was so great. He would sum up in one sentence
what we're trying in the whole damn interview to get at. I knew Hugo,
incidentally.

DS: Yes, I read that you had been acquainted with him in
Montana, and that whole group of Montana writers . . . Hugo,
Kittredge, Welch, and others.

ID: Yeah. It's kind of an odd loop in our case to Hugo. Carol, in her first job out of college, worked at the same college as Mildred Walker, a writer who ultimately became Hugo's mother-in-law.

DS: Oh, Ripley's mother.

ID: And this was many years ago, before Ripley and Hugo ever made eyes at each other in his class. When I first went into a Missoula bookstore with *This House of Sky,* it'd been reviewed in the *Missoulian* by somebody I'd never heard of—Ripley Schemm. Carol knew instantly what was going on. So, out of that came some unusually wonderful kidding opportunities on Hugo. We could always threaten to sic his mother-in-law on him. [laughter]

DS: Well, the connection does seem to run deep. Primarily two landscapes inhabit your work, the coastal one of the Puget Sound, and Montana. In this respect, you are like Richard Hugo, but in reverse as he went a bit east and you west. In fact, you two even have Scotland in common. He spent some time there in Skye on a Guggenheim to produce his book *The Right Madness on Skye.* Of Skye, he said the weather and vegetation reminded him of the Puget Sound while the starkness was all Montana. He claimed that he was a landscape poet. Are you a landscape writer? And what does that mean?

ID: You can get away with wearing the landscape sandwich board more easily if you are a poet than you can if you are a fiction writer, because reviewers and critics will quickly slap a fiction writer on the back of the sandwich board and leave the piece of paper that says *regional.* So I tend to balk a little bit at the notion that we're writers with a sense of place out here, when it's simply put that baldly, because I think there's so much more going on in the writing about the American West, from Norman Maclean, down through the younger generations to, say, Deidre McNamer, and somebody like Melanie Rae Thon. I'm mostly familiar with writers more or less my own age, including Jim Welch, Mary Clearman Blew, and Craig Lesley. You read their books and there's a lot of landscape in them but, God, there's pretty damn wonderful dialogue and I think a level of characterization in Western fiction which, if we hadn't put landscape in, the critics would say, "Well, it's a sense of *person* that these westerners grew up with." We're not just writing travelogues out here, as the sense-of-place tag can too easily suggest. I sometimes try to make the landscape a character. I did it consciously in *The Sea Runners.* I managed to keep a journal of the writing of that novel, and so I've got the old file cards and entries that show quite consciously after one of the trips to Alaska that, by God, the way to handle this Northwest coast is to put it in there as if it's the fifth character. Put it in in almost nonfiction terms. Just write a description of the coast and the tides and so on and maybe the humans are in the scene and maybe they're not. My other novels probably show it to a lesser extent. But the landscape, for me, is in the same creative territory as it is for Hugo. I'm aware that it triggers analogies in me. It sets me to thinking of ways to handle it and it keeps showing up when it didn't particularly have to in my books. How the mountains look to one of the characters. In the book I'm writing now, Susan Duff, who was a prized schoolgirl in Angus McCaskill's one-room schoolhouse, is going back to the abandoned homestead in Scotch Heaven in 1924, and the place has been abandoned since '18 or '19, and cows have gotten in the house as they tended to do in old homestead cabins. So she's there scrubbing up after the cows, but the mountains are out, too.

DS: The landscape is a character in your work. Is it a character in your life as well?

ID: Oh, yeah. It has let me down on the long rope of life to the Puget Sound here. Carol and I were married in Evanston, Illinois, a suburb north of Chicago. That's where we'd had our education and had pretty good magazine jobs, and we found ourselves driving into northern Wisconsin on weekends to see scrubby little pine trees. That began to tell us something. Within not much over a year, it had led us out here. The combination of mountains and water have always lured us. I'm not any kind of a mountain climber, or rock climber, but it still means something to us that we've been on top of Mt. Townsend across here [pointing across the Sound toward the Olympic Mountains] and Elk Peak and Deer Park. We've hiked much of the shoreline that we can see from here.

DS: When you came to Seattle did you have the feeling of familiarity that Angus does in *Dancing at the Rascal Fair* when he's picking out a homestead site?

ID: Let me try to describe as best as I can re-create it, pulling into Seattle on an August day in 1966. Carol and I left Chicago with the temperature and humidity both in the 90s, and we pulled across the floating bridge on a day when Mt. Rainier was out. Within a week or

Ivan, age 12, ca. 1951

two we'd found a house up behind University Village to rent and our neighbors, who were lifelong Seattleites—the guy had been born and raised across the alley there—they were hiding out in their basement because the temperature was almost 80. I very much have the memory of us looking at each other and saying, "This feels about right." [laughter] And Seattle had a lot of immediate attractions, including theater life. The university was a handsome campus to set foot on. The first time we walked in the quadrangle there we thought it looked like it had been there since Dink Stover came west from Yale. It was promptly a comfortable place. And I think your question does have a lot of carrying power because when it came time to look at leaving, once I had my Ph.D. and was in the job market, I couldn't bring myself to do it.

    DS: William Blake wrote, "We become what we behold." Does this explain how landscape shapes identity?

ID: I think it does, to a kind of intriguing extent.

DS: And how landscape, identity, and memory work their way into most of your work?

ID: Yeah, although when I'm sitting around here, what I *think* I'm working on is usually the language. But I'm generally pounding away on one of those three themes.

The way that the landscape of the West has fixed a lot of people into place and kept them there maybe even against their better interest, perhaps leading hopeless ways of life, as the larger world would look at it—yeah, there certainly has to be a lot of unarticulated love that keeps people there. And it's been one of the tugs that I've seen in a lot of friends. My own solution to it was that there are a lot of good places to live in the West, and I've chosen one which has its own appeal. It's not the Rocky Mountain Front out there, but pretty damn good mountains even so.

DS: Was it easier to love this landscape after first loving the Rocky Mountains?

ID: I think so. That's been on my mind lately too because I'm fairly recently back from a book tour in the upper Midwest. Saw many old friends there, one of my oldest friends from college, various people who have spent their whole lives on a flat disc of earth maybe a hundred miles across. And it apparently doesn't bother them that this geography is out here waiting for them because I've tried to coax them out, to shame them [laughter]. But indeed if I had been brought up in that, maybe I would prize the banks of the Mississippi River, or the Fox River Valley of Wisconsin, as deeply I do these places of the West. So, yes, I think where you land into life does put some kind of a parenthesis of vision around you. I know when I worked in Evanston on *The Rotarian* magazine as a young assistant editor, anything that came from the West was just handed to me, and my habit at lunch, one of the guys pointed out to me once, was that I would go off by myself down to Lake Michigan rather than going to the cafeteria. I certainly wasn't trying to mark myself off as "the lone westerner" but these guys I worked with knew I was.

DS: Do you have a greater allegiance to one landscape over another, Montana over the Sound? Or is it a tie?

ID: Well, it's pretty close to a tie. There are a few enlightened countries in the world—I think Ireland is one—that give you dual citizenship. And I've had something like that in my writing and the reception to it. I've been exceedingly fortunate being able to go back to Montana and have readers there ask me, "Why don't you live in Montana?" When I point out to them that I economically starved out as a young guy, my wife's job is in Seattle, and I'm in Montana as much as I can be, there doesn't seem any kind of rancor.

DS: In fact, they've been giving you honorary degrees.

ID: Right. I've felt very fortunate in that reception, and I haven't felt any rancor for living out here and writing the majority of my fiction about the Rocky Mountain Front area. The trellis of history and landscape that the McCaskills grow on certainly goes up along the Rockies there, Derek, but part of that is something I once heard Wallace Stegner talk about. Fortunately if was long after I started doing it myself, so it only confirmed me. He was speaking in Portland and someone in the audience asked him why he had stopped writing short stories, and he said, "Well, you use up your capital all the time." And he meant in terms of characterization. That certainly was one thing Faulkner did not do. Faulkner just kept the genealogy pasted on the wall and thought, "Okay, if X burns down Y's barn, how does that trigger what's going to happen in another generation here." And so I keep creating this long family line which serves as a kind of a trellis that my characters grow their lives on. That tends to be Rocky Mountain. It wouldn't have to be. When I was researching *Heart Earth* in Arizona, asking questions about that winter my family spent there, the Tucson newspaper's book editor grinned and said, "Well, if you hadn't left you might be writing about the Grand Canyon country, might you?" Yeah. Could be worse.

DS: Well, Keats wrote about Negative Capability, and I think part of what he meant by that term was distance from the subject, a bit of a cool remove. William Stafford wrote his best Kansas poems when he was living in Oregon.

ID: And the one I always cite. Joyce didn't write *Ulysses* about Paris. We don't have as good a book about Paris. In my case, I've always known that the writing is easier to get done here than it is back in Montana or somewhere else in the West. Part of that unfortunately means the shirking of perfectly good citizenship, which, if I lived in Montana I would feel quite compelled to pitch in on. Here, with the larger population in the state and with greater resources to the society, I've felt a lot more free to hole up in a suburb and work, and not do much of anything else.

DS: Are you talking about, say, devoting some of your time to protecting the environment?

ID: No, less that than participating in Montana's educational community or something else. Jim Welch served on the parole board in Montana something like ten years. Kittredge is kind of a circuit riding preacher, all the things he does. I think I would have to do, at the very least, writing conferences and poets-in-the-schools and so on.

DS: Seattle frees you up.

ID: It frees me up a lot. I'm able to try to pick my spots, and a lot of it does entail going back to Montana or to rural Utah through one of the state humanities councils or some kind of Nature Conservancy event. But I'm able to schedule those things outside of a writing stint. So in terms of sitting down and doing what I think I'm meant to do, a Puget Sound suburb is the most efficient place to do it.

DS: You mentioned earlier that your aim in the writing is to get the words right, not necessarily to evoke a theme, to get to what Maclean calls the "poetry under the prose." I mentioned to a poet friend a few weeks ago that I was going to interview you and she knew your name but unlike most of the folks around here hadn't read your books. So I read her a passage from *This House of Sky*, one of the memory sections, and she said, "Oh my God, that's beautiful. How did it ever get published?" I know she was responding to the poetry under the prose. Can you talk about that?

ID: Sure. I did keep a journal part-time when I was writing *This House of Sky*. It wasn't full-time because the work on *This House of Sky* was strewn across half a dozen years. But every so often I would put down what I was trying to do, and there is an entry somewhere back there—evidently after what I thought was a pretty decent day's work—that it would be wonderful to write it all as highly charge as poetry if I could just do it. And I think the clearest answer, about trying to get the poetry in, is that I simply worked on it and worked on it as if the book were an epic poem.

DS: Did you read it aloud as you worked on it?

ID: I would read aloud some. This goes back to broadcast journalism. I've always been aware of the power of spoken words and the power of rhythm, in particular. It maybe also goes back to a great stroke of luck in college, where the ungodly old scholarship dorm I landed in was also full of theater people and so you couldn't walk through the front door of that place without Richard Benjamin imitating Wrigley Field, or Ron Hogate singing as he later would on Broadway. And my best friend was a theater major, so I went to many of the rehearsals in what was a marvelous theater department, and I read a lot of Shakespeare, read a lot of dramatists, and was aware of the wonderful trickeries of the language. Allied with that was my own mercifully brief stint in trying to write poetry when I was in graduate school in history at the UW. All of these combine into the passion for the sentence and working within the sentence which meant going back over the words countless times—I don't know if I consciously did it on *This House of Sky* or not, Derek, but it's the same process. On some books I have taken a colored marker and either done it myself or hired somebody to mark every verb. Look at every goddamned verb. Look at how every paragraph begins and ends. Look at every adjective, whether to take it out or leave it in. Try to be a cosmic mechanic on the language.

DS: In my ear, the poetry under the prose is still alive. It is less overt than in *This House of Sky*, but nevertheless present in the more recent books.

ID: One of the things I'm embarked on now is, in fiction, to see how much I can drop it back a notch and still have lively language there, and maybe do something else within the story. Perhaps make a story move more quickly. Maybe extend the characterization or the interior. Maybe put the spotlight on something else within the story rather than on every showy verb. So I've been consciously tinkering.

DS: Much of the poetry in your prose, it seems to me, comes from the way people talk. In this respect, your work compares with William Stafford's. And I'm certain that you've nailed it, that you've leashed the colloquial with your language. Recently I was about to go skiing with some folks and one said, "Okay, everybody read-aye?" This was in La Grande, Oregon. And I realized that I had just read that "read-aye" the night before in *Mountain Time*. I don't know if I had heard it before, but it reminds me of another time, also in Oregon, in the Willamette Valley, when I saw two deer leap away from the road and I immediately remembered the phrase Mary Oliver uses in one of her poems to describe a startled deer, "silky agitation." She had re-created the deer in the language, just as you have re-created western speech in "read-aye." What's the value of these real voices in your writing?

ID: It seems to me there's an intrinsic rightness. To anybody who knows anything about the society or part of the country you're writing about, it punches that "validity" ticket. Perhaps it's the familiarity. Perhaps it entertains them in a certain way. But to have the characters sound right and sound memorable is one of the best fundamentals you can have for a story. You see these file cards back here? A lot of these are dialogue, and they're around here in various incarnations. There's one box which is largely Scotchisms, many of them picked up from trips to Scotland, various turns of phrases which the characters in *Dancing at the Rascal Fair* use. There's Montana lingo picked up in bars and cafes. The novel I'm working on now will have an African-American western guy who grew up there in the Two Medicine country. It's been interesting to find that lingo. I've given him a Sergeant in the black cavalry as a father, and so all these neighborhoods of colloquialisms are there to be visited and it's an aspect of language that constantly tickles at people's minds. You notice that computer geeks, who in many other aspects of life are just as dry and emotionless as they can manage to be, have produced almost instantly their own colloquial language as rich as cowboys'. And teenagers who don't seem to know the time of day are as busy at it as Shakespeare.

DS: And we still have "cool."

ID: And "cool" comes back and back and back. I think this is its third time around in my lifetime. I got a card today from the Nature Conservancy inviting us up to the Skagit River on their boat trip to see the eagles and the guy says, "It's going to be cold but it'll be cool." Lingo like that is one of the most fertile fields for a novelist to work in. What I say on love of lingo should be hedged in by something I should have mentioned earlier, that I'm a more natural editor than a first drafter, and I come at a lot of these things from the editing experience I picked up in journalism and probably from an inclination to tinker. I'm not particularly interested in immaculate conceptions. It maybe goes back to being used to doing chores. You have to get the firewood, you have to carry the water, you have to do thus and such. So I see my tinkering with the way my characters talk as a real part of the writing routine. But I've been thinking a lot lately too about how much to do it. Where do you draw the line? I feel fine in my own work, but I've been trying to put together a talk sometime for a speech request, about how other writers have done it, and how sometimes it's been overdone. Flannery O'Connor was pretty vocal on how much you do. Not very much, according to her. In fiction writing, it seems to me, you want people to sound like perhaps clever bits of vaudeville, in the Shakespearean sense with the wonderful clowns. You don't want them to sound like burlesque. So, it is a line to walk.

DS: You mentioned some work habits, like the early mornings. And I know Hugo had his sharpened, number two pencils.

ID: Steinbeck did the same thing, I've read. It had to be a certain kind of pencil. And I always respected that, but thought it was a bit much. Now I've discovered I *have* to have these goddamn Ticonderogas. I blame it on the pencil industry because it's getting harder and harder to pick up any pencil these days with a good dark lead. These small things. There's a famous Hugo story—I'm not sure this is craft or what it is—but he'd be working away with the coffee pot at his elbow, and he'd say, "Ripley, could you get me a cup of coffee?" [imitates Hugo's voice] He couldn't be disturbed that far.

In terms of habit for me, so many words a day is a good part of it. The output is pretty precisely measured—400 words a day— when I'm rough-drafting. Some of it is just the tiny touches I try to put into dialogue. As an example, in *Dancing at the Rascal Fair*— again, I'm aware of this because I consciously thought it up— Ninian Duff uses the Scottish "Ay" at the start of sentences, and Lucas Barclay uses it at the end of sentences. I've heard it both ways in Montana Scotch. I deliberately did that so that these characters— one's a Bible banger and one's a bartender—make a kind of dialogue parenthesis, to show that they have a commonality of language and expression, even though they may be opposed to each other. And that's a conscious touch. Another example comes from my current manuscript. My African-American ranch hand and singer is very raw, in terms of his talent, and he's never sung with the piano. At one point Susan Duff, in giving him lessons, says all right, it's time to go to the piano. And I think he's gonna say—instead of what I have had him say for the past six months—"I've never sang with a piano"—I think he's gonna have to say, "I've never sang with a piana." It's dawned on me that it needs an "A," the way I heard the bunkhouse guys on my dad's crews say it.

DS: How planned is your writing? Do you write from an outline?

ID: No, I've tried it a time or two. In fact I tried it with *Dancing at the Rascal Fair*. It had dawned on me that most of my books were turning out to have six or seven chapters or sections, and I thought, "Well, maybe I oughtta take a look at this." And so I took the yellow pad and tried to do an outline of where I thought *Rascal Fair* would go, and it didn't. It ended up with seven chapters.

What I actually start with is an arc of time, which I know: what the time span of the book is going to be. That becomes an armature to build a lot of the plot on because so much of my fiction relies upon people caught in the historical laws of gravity. World War One comes along and if you're a young male in Montana, why, you're swept away into it pretty surely. And if the 1919 flu epidemic comes along, it changes entire communities.

DS: So, the timescape and the landscape work together in your work.

ID: So the timescape is usually the plotting framework, and within that, various kinds of patchwork is done. How a character is going to talk will sometimes shape her personality. In *English Creek*, Jick fairly early says of his mother that when you start to hear her capital letters, you're in trouble. I simply knew I wanted some character who had that trait, and I didn't necessarily know it was going to be her.

DS: And Jick even gets his name from talk, from one of Stanley's quips.

ID: Yes. And in *The Sea Runners*, the blacksmith, probably the least likely candidate to have knowledge of the Bible, gets to be a Bible spouter because by the time it occurred to me that I needed one for nineteenth-century flavor the other characters were already shaped and I just thought, "Well, by God, let's make it interesting. Let's give it to the least likely guy." And so those kinds of decisions shape personalities and thereby the plots. Some turns in plots, skirmishes in them, will come about because you want to try something or see how far you can go out on the edge. I'm thinking of *Bucking the Sun*, the little sheriff there shoots a thief in the legs with a shotgun, because he's also a shrimp, as the sheriff is, and he's kind of snickering at the sheriff companionably. "We're both runts aren't we?" is what his laugh is saying. I have no idea where that came from.

DS: Sticks and stones.

Ivan and Carol Doig

ID: Sticks and stones. I had come across an old newspaper account of someone robbing jewelry stores across the Highline in Montana. It's a funny serial robbery to do because all the towns are about fifty miles apart. And you wonder: how smart is this? So I wanted this sequence of dumb robberies just to see what would happen. And indeed my sheriff is patiently waiting for the guy when he hits Glasgow.

DS: Facts, history, really seem to stir your imagination, which makes a lot of sense considering your background in journalism and your doctorate in history.

ID: It's pretty hard to make things up as strange as things happen. If I had written a thriller about the election that has just finished it would be preposterous to have Jeb Bush in that plot. The guy's brother is governor of the state? Come on. But that sort of thing seems to happen a lot simply because there's so many of us and the pinball clicks of us against each other produce all this strangeness.

DS: When I was reading *Dancing at the Rascal Fair,* I was sure, that people on long voyages would suck on limes. I was sure that that was some bit of history you'd come across in your research.

ID: I don't remember where I got that. I do remember something similar, coming across a bit of detail and saying, "Oh yeah, that's going in." Throwing the straw mattresses overboard when they're off Sandy Hook. I had not known that, although I had read quite a bit about immigration, but I came across that one in a letter in the Scottish archives. Details like that are often the little watch spring parts that I imagine from.

DS: Your books are a living record of the West, particularly Montana. If I knew someone who was interested in the history of Montana, I could just point him to a stack of your books.

ID: When I'm in Montana doing book signings, people do come up and say, "Oh I read your book and moved here." And this is a little more responsibility than I or my books want. But one of the wonderful, totally unforeseen bonuses of my books has been the friendship of Western historians that they've engendered. Bill Robbins down at Oregon State has used *English Creek* in history courses about the West. Carol and I were down at Stanford last summer to do a talk in a summer seminar they do for their alumni and I was introduced by Richard White. Richard is a friend of ours, but he's also one of the hottest Western historians, the most encyclopedic, and to my astonishment he introduced me as being more interested in history than historians are. At that moment I thought, "That's a funny way to put it." But I've spent part of this week sitting around here going back through a book called *Lost Country Life,* which is about Medieval agriculture, and how things were done, and what tools looked like, and how turns of phrase like "spitting image" came out of "splitting image"—cutting trees exactly in half so you would have matching beams in ships or house building. And I got to thinking that maybe Richard saw me in the right light.

DS: It vitalizes you and then you vitalize it in your writing.

ID: Yeah, it's kind of a shaped accident. I gave up dissipating it into magazine work. Now I am able to sit in one spot for two or three years at a time and shape it into a book. I don't drink it away, I don't talk it away, it is able to incubate its way into print. I see that as kind of a stroke of luck of personality, since I haven't utterly forged myself.

DS: Success can be a difficult experience among writers, an inhibitor. Since you have staked out a lasting homestead in the hearts and thoughts of so many readers, has it been difficult to keep going?

ID: I can say "no" pretty fluently. That has helped a lot.

DS: Well, I'm glad you didn't say "no" to this interview.

ID: [laughter] I haven't gone on some of the circuits of success, particularly the summer writing workshops that I think can take a lot of time, energy, and attention. I'm pleased that others are able to, and there are so many good writers that I'm not really needed there. I do go out and give occasional talks and so on, but my level of success has been a comfortable one. I'm a fairly rare bird: a middle-class novelist, in that my books don't sell at Stephen King, or John Grisham levels, but they sell healthily and consistently. So I've been able—largely on the basis of my writing and, always with the underpinning of Carol's teaching career, in terms of medical coverage and some kind of pension to look forward to—to come from a three-room railroad shack in Ringling to this place. That's been a reasonably comfortable arc of success to work within, Derek. One thing I was aware of at the time, when *This House of Sky* did not win the National Book Award, when *The Snow Leopard* carried the day, it dawned on me pretty promptly, "Well, this is going to make my life easier." And indeed it probably has. With that goes the realization that you probably only get one crack at the National Book Award or Pulitzer or other prizes. But life doesn't end if you don't get it on that one crack. As long as you've got other books to write, your health and a decent life and a good spouse and so forth. Hugo had, in a lot growlier way, that same attitude, because we were around him when he lost on the Pulitzer to Donald Justice and others year after year.

DS: Then there's Robert Lowell who said something like, "A few years ago I couldn't get anything published, and now I can't stop from getting everything published, and that scares me more."

ID: Well, I benefited from a kind of internal stroke of luck. When I was a magazine freelancer for ten years, I wrote incessantly. I wrote a couple dozen pieces a year. It turns out that working on the books weaned me off that entirely. I don't feel a compulsion now to do any of the shorter pieces that are asked of me.

DS: Financially speaking, you don't have to.

ID: Financially, I don't have to, and even though the topic may interest me, I don't feel I have to find out what I have to say on that topic. So I'm currently not even writing book reviews. I have reviewed more books than I will personally ever write, so I've contributed my bit to those great scales of reviewing justice. I worked very hard on book reviews, and had the habit—I got it in my magazine days—of including a paragraph which could be cut for reasons of space. More and more I found that paragraph was always cut so that the illustration could be goosed up. And I got to thinking, "Uh-uh. I'm not going to spend the weekend thinking up a good sentence or paragraph and then the graphic designer gets to yank it out of there."

DS: You referred to some early Doig poems.

ID: Well, they probably already show up in dabs in the novels. I'm not sure there's anything that hasn't been cannibalized and the bones licked clean by now. They pop up a little bit in *Mariah Montana*. Riley does a column about homesteads and he alludes to Thomas Jefferson and "the red school house of his head."

DS: "The red schoolhouse of his head." That's plundered from a poem?

ID: Yes. And I've written all of the songs in my fiction—to the detriment of my fiction, I must add—but I have written all the sons of bitches.

DS: I wondered about that. Particularly in *Dancing at the Rascal Fair* because the song is so integral to the book.

ID: None of that was early poetry, however. I wrote that song because I wanted to use the phrase as the book title. And I'm writing now, Lord help me, spirituals for the current book. I swiped a few lines I had left over in a notebook the other day for something there: "Does the hawk know its shadow?"

DS: So we have managed to get some Doig poetry in here.

ID: For free, no less, you clever devil. [laughter]

DS: Can you say more about the new book you're working on and maybe what's coming after that? What are Doig's readers going to see on the shelves five to ten years from now?

ID: Within two or three years, I hope they'll be seeing this novel about motives, and how much they can be read by other people, and even by ourselves, and what's mixed in with them. It has three principal characters. Susan Duff, grown from schoolgirlhood in *Dancing at the Rascal Fair,* has become a singing teacher in Helena. She's been a figure in the Suffrage Movement, and that was a vital piece of history in the West. The western states' suffrage amendments preceded the constitutional amendment by a number of years. So Susan's been

through those political wars. In the course of them she met and had
an affair with a Bull Moose progressive, a Teddy Roosevelt sort of
politician. But he's one of the Williamsons of the hated WW Ranch.
He's a World War One hero, but so far I'm running him against the
grain. He doesn't come out of it disillusioned in the same way as the
Lost Generation of the Twenties. I want him to have different scars
on him than the absolute kind of mandatory, stamped-out scars that
have been attributed to that so-called Lost Generation. He's not lost.
He's rich and he's a lot of other things. But he *has* lost the governor-
ship of Montana because he and Susan Duff were caught in this affair
and he got blackmailed out of the running. The book opens with him
showing up in her life four years later, in 1924. He surprises her, walks
into the house, and says he has a prize student for her. And it's his
black chauffeur: Monty Rathbun, a ranch hand who's grown up on
the WW, the son of the African-American laundress on the place. Out
of this comes the plot: What is everyone up to here with this singing
scheme? So it's a pretty interesting book to write. It's given me an
excuse to write some set places I didn't know were in me. The Monty
character, as it turned out when I sat down to write, has a background
as a rodeo clown. That's been his performing record so far, before this
yet-to-be career as a singer. So the first time you see Monty, he's in
that barrel they hop in when the Brahma bull takes after them. There
are any number of unforeseen scenes in book. There's probably going
to be one back in Scotland between Susan and the politician, flirting
tooth and nail outside the Castle in Edinburgh.

DS: It sounds pretty young still, full of intriguing possibilities.

ID: Yes, I'm about two-fifths of the way along. I'm able to put that
kind of a fraction on it because I sent the first chunk of the manuscript
to my editor just before the holidays. The one useful thing the computer can do for us is count every goddamned word now. Beyond that,
writing on a computer is a mixed bag. But you do always know how
many words you have anymore. [laughter] So that's the course of this
book. There are some flashbacks in it. It's a novel where time tunnels
backwards into what has happened to shape the motives of these
characters and how they respond to it.

DS: Doig Time. While reading your most recent book, *Mountain
Time,* I was thinking there is such a thing as Doig Time. Your prolific
use of the flashback and the historical perspective with which you and

your characters see the West. I'm thinking of Lexa hiking down that mountain in the steps of Bob Marshall. What a gift to see the landscape like that, to hear those old steps. And that gift is being passed on in your books.

ID: I feel lucky in being tuned in that way. I also see it as going with the storytelling impulse that a lot of my characters have, that I grew up around, and that I have, too. These historical flashbacks are technically analogous to the characters liking to tell stories. I've had reinforcement from readers, out on the bookstore trail, who tell me they like the flashbacks. They don't see them as intrusive or something to be fast-forwarded over with the eye. Anybody who's going to read my books soon knows they're going to have to spend some time with them. And so if you take readers back to tell them more about a character, they probably will like that. I don't know if I would ever try to write a book in the flat, contemporaneous straight chronology. I mean, there's a certain appeal if you just sit down and tell a story from finger snap to thunderclap. I admire that stuff, but I'm not sure it's in me. I've been reading John Fowles's book of essays called *Wormholes,* where his mind goes off in every direction. You can kind of see how we got *The French Lieutenant's Woman* out of that guy, that those great flashbacks are there if writers can just find the shutter to click.

DS: It seems that even though you are surrounded by teachers and teachers populate your books and have been prominent in your life, that it's been best for you to avoid the teaching life, against the stream of so many writers today, and make your living as a writer.

ID: This goes to the saying, "Life is choices."

DS: Your father used to say that.

ID: Yes, that's right. It comes straight out of the family. Very early on, probably in graduate school, I realized I do not have the energy or metabolism, whatever you want to call it, to teach and write both. I liked teaching a lot as a teaching assistant at the UW. I found it a vitalizing way of life. But it took me over, too. So it's a question of what are you going to be taken over by. And a lot of people can balance them, but I simply have a head that mulls only in one direction.

DS: And rather than shortchange one . . .

ID: And I felt I'd be shortchanging both, actually, by trying to do both. So if they advance from Dolly and clone all of us, why yeah, I'll be a teacher. But until then, I gotta be a writer.

WINTER OF '19

Ivan Doig

WINTER WAS WITH US now. The snow that whitened the foothills at the start of October repeated within forty-eight hours, this time piling itself shin-deep all across the Two Medicine county. We did the last of the autumn chores in December circumstances.

That first sizable snowstorm, and for that matter the three or four that followed it by the first of the week in November, proved to be just the thin edge of the wedge of the winter of 1919. On the fifteenth of November, thirty inches of snow fell on us. Lacelike flakes in a perfect silence dropped on Scotch Heaven that day as if the clouds suddenly were crumbling, every last shred of them tumbling down in a slow thick cascade. From the windows Adair and I watched everything outside change, become absurdly fattened in fresh white outline: our woodpile took on the smooth disguise of a snow-colored haystack. It was equally beautiful and dismaying, that floury tier on everything, for we knew it lay poised, simply waiting for wind the way a handful of dandelion seeds in a boy's hand awaits the first flying puff from him. That day I did something I had done only a few times in all my years on the Scotch Heaven homestead: I tied together lariats and strung them like a rope railing between the house and the barn, to grasp my way along so as not to get lost if a blizzard blinded the distance between while I was out on chores.

The very next day I needed that rope. Blowing snow shrouded the world, or at least our polar corner of it. The sheep had to be fed, somehow, and so in all the clothes I could pile on I went out to make my way along the line to the barn, harnessed the workhorses Sugar and Duke, and prayed for a lull.

When a lessening of the blizzard finally came, Rob came with it, a plaster man on a plaster horse. He had followed fencelines down from Breed Butte to the North Fork, then guided himself up the creek by its walls of willows and trees. Even now I have to hand it to the damn man. Here he was, blue as a pigeon from the chill of riding in that snow-throwing wind, yet as soon as he could make his mouth operate he was demanding that we plunge out there and provide hay to the sheep.

"Put some of Adair's coffee in you first," I stipulated, "then we'll get at it."

"I don't need—" he began croakily.

"Coffee," I reiterated. "I'm not going to pack you around today like a block of ice." When Adair had thawed him, back out we went into the white wind, steering the horses and hay sled along the creek the way Rob had done, then we grimly managed to half-fling half-sail a load of hay onto the sled rack, and next battled our way to my sheep shed, where the sheep were sheltering themselves. By the time we got there they were awful to hear—a bleated chorus of hunger and fear rendering the air. Not until we pitched the hay off to them did they put those fifteen hundred woolly throats to work on something besides telling us their agony.

That alarming day was the sample, the tailor's swatch, of our new season. The drought of that summer, the snow and the wind of that winter: the two great weathers of 1919. Through the rest of November and December, days were either frigid or blowy and too often both. By New Year's, Rob and I were meeting the mark of that giant winter each day on our routes to the sheep's feedground. At a place where my meadow made a bit of a dip, snow drifted and hardened and drifted some more and hardened again and on and on until there was a mound eight or ten feet deep and broad as a low hill there. "Big as the goddamn bridge across the Firth of Forth," Rob called it with permissible exaggeration in this case. This and other snow bridges built by the furrowing blizzards we could go right over with the horses and hay sled without breaking through, they were so thickly frozen. *Here winter plies his craft, soldering the years with ice.* Yes, and history can say the seam between 1919 and 1920 was triple thickness.

Thank heaven, or at least my winning cut of the cards, that we had bought twice as much hay as Rob wanted to, which still was not as much as I wanted to. Even so, every way I could calculate it now—and the worried look on Rob said his sums were coming out the same as mine— we were going to be scratching for hay in a few months if this harsh weather kept up.

It kept up.

Near the end of January I made a provisioning trip into town. Every house, shed, barn I passed, along the North Fork and the main creek, was white with snow. Gros Ventre's main street was a rutted trench between snowpiles, and no one was out who didn't have dire reason to be. All the more unexpected, then, when I stomped the white from my boots and went into the mercantile, and the person in the chair by the store was Toussaint Rennie.

"What, is it springtime on the Two Medicine?" I husked out to him, my voice stiff from the cold of my ride. "Because if it is, send some down to us."

"Angus, were you out for air?" he asked in return, and gave a chuckle.

"I thought I was demented to come just a dozen miles in this weather. So what does that make you?"

"Do you know, Angus, this is that '86 winter back again." I suddenly found myself at that supper of so long ago, when Rob and I journeyed north to look at the grass beyond the Two Medicine River. Before we were brothers-in-law, partners in sheep, enemies; before any of the snip snap between us. We had wagoned into Toussaint Rennie's place for the night and as Toussaint sauced the meal for us with his talk of the Two Medicine country, I was the one to ask him of the winter every-one told of in this Montana. *"The winter of '86, Toussaint. What was it like up here?"*

"That winter. That winter, we ate with an axe."

Rob made as if to clear an ear with his finger. "You did which?"

"We ate with the axe. No deer, no elk. No weather to hunt them in. I went out, find a cow if I can. Look for a hump under the snow. Do you know, a lot of snowdrifts look like a cow carcass?"

Rob was incredulous. "Toussaint, man, you mean you'd go out and find a dead cow to eat?"

"Any I found was dead," Toussaint vouched. "Chop her up, bring home as much as the horse can carry. West wind, all that winter, everything drifted east. You had to guess. Whether the horse could break snow far enough to find a cow." Toussaint seemed entertained by the memory. "That winter was long. Those cattlemen found out. I had work all summer, driving wagon for the cowhide skinners. That was what was left in this country by spring. More cowhides than cows."

"A once-in-a-lifetime winter," Rob summarized, "and I am glad enough I wasn't here to see it. Now we know to have hay and sheds, anyway. It's hard

luck that somebody else had to pay for that lesson, but life wasn't built even, was it."

"That '86 winter went around a corner of the mountains and waited to circle back on us, Angus," the broad figure planted by the warm stove was saying now. "Here it is."

"As good a theory as I've heard lately," I admitted ruefully. "Just how are your livestock faring, up there on the reservation?"

Toussaint's face altered. There was no chuckle behind what he said this time. "They are deadstock now."

February was identical to the frigid misery of January. At the very start of the last of its four white weeks, there came a day when Rob and I found fifteen fresh carcasses of ewes, dead of weakness and the constant cold. No, not right. Dead, most of all, of hunger.

Terrible as the winter had been, then, March was going to be worse. Scan the remaining hay twenty times and do its arithmetic every one of those times and the conclusion was ever the same. By the first of March, the hay would be gone. One week from today, the rest of the sheep would begin to starve.

A glance at Rob, as we drove the sled past the gray bumps of dead sheep, told me that his conclusion was the same as mine, with even more desperation added. He caught my gaze at him, and the day's words started.

"Don't work me over with your eyes, man. How in hell was I supposed to know that the biggest winter since snow got invented was on its way?"

"Tell it to the sheep, Rob. Then they'd at least that to chew on."

"All it'd take is one good chinook. A couple of days of that, and enough of this snow would go so that the sheep could paw down and graze a bit. That'd let us stretch the hay and we'd come out of this winter as rosy as virgins. So just put away that gravedigger look of yours, for Christ's sake. We're not done for yet. A chinook will show up, it has to."

You're now going to guile the weather, are you, Rob? Cite Barclay logic to it and scratch its icy ears, and it'll bounce to attention like a fetching dog to go bring you your chinook? That would be like you, Rob, to think that life and its weather are your private pets. Despite the warning he had given me, I told him all this with my eyes, too.

The end of that feeding day, if it could be called so, I was barning the workhorses when a tall collection of coal, cap, scarf, mittens, and the rest came into the yard atop a horse with the Long Cross brand. If I couldn't identify Varick in the bundle, I at least knew his saddlehorse. I gave a wave and he rode through the deep snow of that yard to join me inside the barn's shelter.

"How are you doing?" asked my son when he had unwrapped sufficiently to let it out.

"A bit threadbare, to say the truth. Winter seems to be a whole hell of a lot longer than it ever used to be, not to mention deeper."

"I noticed the sheep are looking a little lean." Lean didn't begin to say it, Varick. They were getting to resemble greyhounds. "You got enough hay to get through on, you think?"

"Rob and I were discussing that." I scanned the white ridges, the white bands of the North Fork, the white roof of the sheep shed. Another week of this supreme snow sitting everywhere on us and we had might as well hire coyotes to put the sheep out of their hungry misery. "Neither of us thinks we do have anywhere near enough, no."

Varick was plainly unsurprised. He said, part question and part not. "What about that Dakota spinach they've got at Valier?" Trainloads of what was being called hay, although it was merely a slewgrass and other wiry trash, were being brought in from North Dakota to Valier and other rail points and sold at astonishing prices.

"What about it?" I nodded to the east, across more than thirty miles. "It's in Valier, and we're here."

"I could get loose from Noon Creek for a couple days to help you haul," offered Varick. "Even bring my own hay sled. Can't beat that for a deal, now can you?"

I said nothing, while trying to think how to tell him his generosity was futile, Rob and I were so beyond help.

Eyeing me carefully, Varick persisted: "If you and Unk and me each take a sled to Valier, we can haul back a hell of a bunch of hay, Dad."

I stared east again, to the white length of Scotch Heaven, the white miles beyond that to the railroad cars of hay in Valier. Why try, even? A sled journey of that sort, in winter of this sort. *There is so much of this country, Angus.* That quiet mountaintop declaration of Adair's. *People keep having to stretch themselves out of shape trying to cope with so much. This Montana sets its own terms and tells you, do them or else.*

Or else. There in the snow of the valley where Rob and I had just pitched to them half the hay they ought to have had, the sheep were a single gray floe of wool in the universal whiteness. I remembered their bleating, the blizzard day we were late with the feeding: the awful hymn of their fear. Could I stand to hear that, day after day when the hay was gone?

Finally, I gave Varick all the answer I had. "All right, I'm one vote for trying it. But we'll need to talk to Rob."

"He'll be for it. Dead sheep are lost dollars to him. He'll be for it, Dad."

In the winter-hazed sky, the dim sun itself seemed to be trying to find a clearer look at our puzzling procession. A square-ended craft with a figurehead of two straining horses was there in the white nowhere, plowing on a snow sea. Then an identical apparition behind it, and a third ghost boat in the wake of that.

Three long sleds with hay racks on them, Varick at the reigns of the first, myself the next driver, Rob at the tail of this sled-runner voyage toward Valier, our convoy crept across the white land. But if slowly, we moved steadily. The big horses walked through the snow as if they were polar creatures. Copenhagen and Woodrow, my pair was named. Even American horses had the mix of two lands. Horse alloys, strong there in the dark harness in front of me.

We stopped at the Double W fenceline, half the way between Gros Venire and Valier, to eat from the bundle of lunch Adair had fixed us. Rob and I stomped some warmth into ourselves while Varick cut the barbed wire strands so we could get the sleds through. Of the four-wire fence, only the top two strands were showing above the snow. While Varick was at that, I gazed around the prairie. Cold and silence, stillness and snow. Once upon a time there were two young men, new to Montana, who thought they were seeing snow. *This is just a April skift,* was the freight wagon driver's assessment to us. That April and its light white coverlet sounded like high summer to me now. That flurry that had taken the mountains and the wheel tracks from our long-ago trek into the Two country was a pinch of salt compared to this. And Rob and I of then, how did we compare with what we are now? The journeys we had made together, across thirty years. Steamship and railroad and horse and foot and every kind of wheel. And by ash sled runners, enmity accompanying us. What, were we different Rob and different Angus, all the time before? Else how did the enmity manage to come between us? In all likelihood I am not the best judge myself. But I can tell you, from trudging through the days of this winter beside the unspeaking figure known as Rob Barclay, that this was not the Rob who would throw back his head and cockily call up to the hazed sun, *Can't you get the stove going up there?*

Onward from the fence, the marks of our sled runners falling away into the winter plain behind us. Silence and cold, snow and stillness. The murmurs within myself the only human sound. Adair asking, when Varick and I went into the house with his offer to make this hay trip: *Do both of you utterly have to go?* Reluctant *yeah* from her son, equally involuntary *yes* from her husband. From her: *Then I have to count on each of you to bring the other one back, don't I.* Toussaint, when I arranged for him to feed the sheep while we were gone, saying only: *This winter. You have to watch out for it, Angus.* And myself, here on this first ground I ever went across on horseback, scouting for a homestead site. Did I choose rightly, the high valley of Scotch Heaven over this prairie? That farmhouse there on the chalky horizon. If I had chosen that spot years ago, I would right now be in there drinking hot coffee and watching hay-hungry sheepmen ply past on their skeleton ships. No, not that simple. In the past summer of drought and grasshoppers and deflated prices, that farm, too, was bitter acres. The year 1919 had shown that farming could be a desperate way of life too. Maybe everything was, one time or another.

It was dusk when we came around the frozen length on Valier's lake and began to pass the stray houses of the outskirts. Valier did not have as much accumulation of winter as Scotch Heaven or Gros Ventre, but it still had about as much as a town can stand. The young trees, planted along the residential streets looked like long sticks stuck in to measure the snowfall. The downtown streets had drifts graceful as sand dunes. Stores peeked over the snow-banks. Pathways had been shoveled like a chain of canals, and at the eastern edge of town we could see the highest dike of all, where the railroad track had been plowed.

Along the cornices of the three-story hotel where we went for the night, thick icicles hung like winter's laundry. When we three numb things had managed to unharness the teams at the stable and at last could think of tending to ourselves, Varick gave his sum of our journey from Scotch Heaven: "That could've been a whole hell of a lot worse."

And Rob gave his. "Once we get those sleds heavy with hay, it will be."

At morning, the depot agent greeted us with: "I've been keeping your hay cool for you out in the icebox."

When no hint of amusement showed on any of the three of us, he sobered up radically and said: "I'll show you the boxcar. We can settle up after you're loaded."

We passed a dozen empty boxcars, huge husks without their cargo, and came to a final one with a stubby barricade of hay behind its slatted side. The agent broke ice from its door with a blacksmith hammer, then used a pinch bar to pry the grudging door open. "All yours," he stated, and hustled back inside the warmth of the depot.

The railroad car was stacked full of large bales like shaggy crates. Rob thrust a mitten under his armpit, pulled out his hand, and thrust it into a bale. The handful he pulled out was brown crackly swampgrass, which only in a winter of this sort would qualify as hay at all. "Awful stuff," Rob proclaimed.

"The woolies won't think it's as awful as starving," I told him. "Let's load and go." The weather was ever over our shoulder, and this was a lead-colored day that showed no intention of brightening. First thing of morning, I had taken a look out the hotel window to the west for the mountains and they were there, white-toothed as if they had sawed up through the snow prairie. As long as the mountains stayed unclouded we had what we needed from the weather today, neutrality.

Our work was harsh, laboring the bales from their stacks in the boxcar to the sleds alongside, as if we were hauling hundreds of loaded trunks down out of an attic. Oftener and oftener, Rob and I had to stop for breath. The smoke of our breathing clouded between us, two aging engines of work. To say the truth, without Varick's limber young strength I do not know how we ever would have loaded those three hay sleds.

When the last bale was aboard, even Varick looked close to spent, but he said only, "I guess that's them." A marker in our journey, that final bale: with it, the easy half of our hay task was over. Now to haul these loads, and ourselves, all the miles to Gros Ventre before nightfall, and on to Scotch Heaven the next day. Rob and I headed for the depot with our checkbooks to pay an outlandish price for this god-awful hay that was the only hay there was, and then we would have to get ourselves gone, out onto the prairie of winter.

We had our own tracks of yesterday to follow on the white plain west of Valier, smooth grooves of the sled runners and twin rough channels chopped up by the horses' hooves. The horses strained steadily as they pulled our hay loads. With every step they were rescuing us a little more, drawing us nearer to Scotch Heaven and out of this width of winter.

All was silence except for the rhythm of the horses' labor, muscle against harness, hooves against snow. Existence crept no faster than our sleds, as if time had slowed to look gravely at itself, to ponder what way to go next, at what pace. I know I had thoughts—you can't not—but the lull we were traveling in held me. Keeping the team's leather reigns wrapped in my mittened hands was the only occupation that counted in the world just then.

The change in the day began soon after we were beyond Valier's outlying farms and homesteads, where our tracks of yesterday went on into the prairie of the Double W range. At first the mountains only seemed oddly dimmed, as if dusk somehow had wandered into mid-day. I tried to believe it as a trick of light, all the while knowing the real likelihood.

In front of me I could see Varick letting only his hands and arms drive the team, the rest of him attentive to those dimming mountains. Behind me Rob undoubtedly was performing the same.

So the three of us simultaneously watched the mountains be taken by the murk. As if a gray stain was spreading down from the sky, the mountains gradually became more and more obscure, until they simply were absorbed out of sight. We had to hope that the weather covering the western horizon was only fog or fallow cloud and not a true storm. We had to hope that mightily.

The wind too, began faintly enough. Simply a lift along the top of the snow, soft little whiffs of white dust down there. I turtled deeper into the collar of my sheepskin coat in anticipation of the first gust to swoosh up onto the sled at me. But a windless minute passed, then another, although there were constant banners of snow weaving past the horses' hooves. I could see Varick and his sled as clear as anything; but he and it seemed suspended in a landscape that was casually moving from under them. A ground blizzard. Gentle enough, so far. A breeze brooming whatever loose snow it could find, oddly tidy in its way. Another tease from the weather, but as long as the wind stayed down there at knee-high we were out of harm.

I believed we were nearly to our halfway mark, the Double W fence, yet it seemed an age before Varick's sled at last halted. I knew we were going to feed our teams, and for that matter ourselves, at this midpoint. But when Rob and I slogged up to Varick, we found that he had more than replenishment on his mind.

"I don't know what you two think," he began, "but I figure we better just give up on the notion of going back the same route we came by."

Rob gave a grimace, which could have been either at Varick's words or at the sandwich frozen to the consistency of sawdust which he had just taken the first bite of. "And do what instead?" he asked skeptically.

"Follow this fence," Varick proposed with a nod of his head toward it, "to where it hits the creek." Half a fence, really, in this deep winter; only the top portions of the fenceposts were above the snow, a midget line of march north and south from our cluster of hay sleds and horses. "Once we get to the creek," Varick was postulating, "we can follow that on into Gros Ventre easy enough."

"Man, that'd take twice as long," Rob objected. "And that's twice as much effort for these horses, not to mention us."

Varick gave me a moment's look, then a long gaze at Rob. "Yeah, but at least this fence tells us where the hell we are," he answered. He inclined his head to the prairie the other side of the fence, where the wind's steady little sift had made our yesterday's tracks look softened.

"Even if it does, Varick, we know the country," Rob persisted. "Christ, man, the hills are right out there in plain sight." The bench-lands north of Noon Creek and Double W were like distant surf above the flow of the blown snow.

"We won't know an inch of it in a genuine blizzard," Varick insisted. "If this starts really storming and we get going in circles out there, we'll end up like the fillyloo bird."

Rob stared at him. "The which?"

"The fillyloo bird, Unk. That's the one that's got a wing shorter than the other, so that it keeps flying in littler and littler circles until it disappears up its own rear end."

Rob gave a short harsh laugh, but credit him, it was a laugh. I chortled as if I was filled with feathers. We were all going giddy, the cold stiffening our brains. Would they find us here in the springtime, with ice grins on our faces?

"All right, all right," Rob was conceding, as much to the notion of the fillyloo bird as Varick. If I had been the one to broach the fence route to him, Rob would have sniffed and snorted at it until we grew roots. But here he was, grudging but giving the words to Varick. "Lead on to your damn creek."

We began to follow the Double W fenceline south. The low stuttered pattern of the fenceposts could be seen ahead for maybe a quarter of a mile at a time, before fading into the ground blizzard. Occasionally there was a hump, or more often a series of them, next to the barbed wire— carcasses of the Double W cattle that drifted with the wind until the fence thwarted them. I wondered if Wampus Cat Williamson in his California money vault gave a damn.

A tiny cloud caught on my eyelash, I squinted to get rid of it and it melted coldly into my eye.

I blinked, and there were other snowflakes now, sliding across the air softly.

The stillness of their descent lasted only a few moments, before the first gust of wind hit and sent them spinning.

Quickly it was snowing so hard there seemed to be more white in the air than there was space between the flakes. In front of me Varick's sled was a squarish smudge.

The wind drove into us. No longer was it lazing along the ground. From the howl of it, this blizzard was blowing as high as the stars.

The horses labored. Varick and I and Rob got off and walked on the lee side of our hay sleds, to lessen the load for the teams and to be down out of the wind and churning whatever warmth we could into ourselves. I had on socks and socks and socks, and even so my feet felt the cold. This was severe travel, and before long the ghostly sled in front of me halted, and Varick was emerging from the volleys of wind and snow to see how we were faring. Rob promptly materialized from behind. A gather seemed needed by all three of us.

The wind quibbled around our boots even in the shelter of my hay sled. There we huddled, with our flap caps tied down tight over our ears and scarves across our faces up to our eyes. Bedouins of the blizzard. One by one we pulled down our scarves and scrutinized each other for frostbite.

"We're doing about as good as we can, seems to me," Varick assessed after our inspection of each other. In the howl of the wind, each word had to be a sentence. "I can only see a fencepost or two at a time in this," Varick told us, "but that'll do. Unk, how's it going with you, back there?"

"Winterish," was all that Rob replied.

"How about you, Dad—are you all right?"

That question of Varick's was many in one. I ached with the cold, the rust of weariness was in every muscle I used, I knew how tiny we three dots of men, horses and hay were in the expanse of this winter-swollen land. But I took only the part of the question that Varick maybe had not even known he was asking: Was I afraid? The answer, surprise to myself: I was not. Certainly not afraid for myself, for I could make myself outlast the cold and snow as long as Rob Barclay could. If one of us broke, then the other might begin to cave. But our stubbornnesses would carry each other far. We would not give one another the satisfaction of dying craven, would we, Rob?

"I'm good enough," I answered my son. "Let's go see more snow."

Trudge and try not to think about how much more trudging needed to be done. Here was existence scoured as far as it could go. Just the flecked sky, filled with fat snowflakes and spiteful wind; and us, six horse creatures and three human. Hoofprints of our horses, sliced path of our sled runners, our bootprints, wrote commotion in the snow. Yet a hundred yards behind Rob you would not be able to find a trace that we had ever been there. Maybe winter was trying to blow itself out in this one day. Maybe so, maybe no. It had been trying something since October. I felt pity for Woodrow, the horse of my team who was getting the wind full against his side. But he simply turned his head and persevered with his work.

I pounded my arm against my side and trudged. The wind whirled the air full of white flakes again. *Old mad winter/with snow hair flying.* This must be what mesmerism is, every particle of existence streaming to you and dreamily past. A white blanket for your mind. A storm such as this blew in all the way from legendary times, other winters great in their fury. The winter of '83. *The Starvation Winter, these Blackfoot call that, and by Jesus they did starve, poor bastards them, by the hundreds. Pure gruesome, what they went through.* Gruesome was the apt word for such winters, yes. The winter of '86, Toussaint's telling of it. *That winter. That winter, we ate with the axe.* And Rob saying, *A once-in-a-lifetime winter.* It depended on the size of the lifetime, didn't it.

The wind blowing, the snow flowing. Try to pound another aim's worth of warmth into myself and keep trudging. Every so often Varick, tall bundle of dimness ahead in the blowing snow, turned to look for me. I did the same for Rob. Rob. Rob who was all but vanished back there. Say he did vanish. Say he stumbled, sprawled in the miring snow, could not get back up in time before I missed him, next time I glanced back. Say Rob did vanish into the blizzard, what would I feel? Truth now, Angus: what? As I tried to find honest reply in myself, a side of my mind said at least that I would end it once and all, if Rob faltered back there in the snow and Varick and I could not find him, the poisoned time that had come between us—this entangled struggle between McCaskill and Barclay—would at least be ended. Or would it.

Whether it was a decision of just habit, I kept watching behind me periodically to Rob. The team he had were big matched grays, and against the storm dusk they faded startlingly, so that at a glance there simply seemed to be harness standing in the air back there, blinders and collars and straps as if the wind had dressed itself in them. And ever, beside the floating sets of harness, the bulky figure of Rob.

We were stopped again. Varick came slogging to me like a man wading surf, and reported in a half shout that the fenceline had gone out of sight under a snowdrift that filled a coulee. We would need to veer down and around the pit of snow, then angle back up once we were past it to find the fenceline where it emerged from the coulee.

"If we've got to, we've got to," I assented to Varick, and while he returned to his sled I beckoned for Rob to come up and hear the situation. He looked about as far from happy as a man could be, but he had to agree that the detour was all there was to do.

The horses must have wondered why they had to turn a corner here at the middle of nothingness, but they obediently veered left and floundered down the short slope.

Now the problem was up. The slope on the other side of the coulee was steep, and angling, the top of it lost in the swirling snow, so that as the horses strained they seemed to be climbing a stormcloud. This was the cruelest work yet, the team plunging a few steps at a time and then gathering themselves for the next lunge, all the while the loaded sled dragging backward on them. It hurt to even watch such raw effort. I sang out every encouragement I could, but the task was entirely up to the horses.

Up and up, in those awful surges, until at last the snow began to level out. The horses' sides still heaved from the exertion of getting us here, but I breathed easier now that we were atop the brow of the coulee and our way ahead to the fenceline would be less demanding.

Varick had halted us yet again. What this time?

One more time I waved Rob up to us as Varick trudged back from the lead sled.

"This don't feel right to me," Varick reported. He was squinting apprehensively. "I haven't found that fenceline yet and we ought've been back to it by now."

"We must not have come far enough to hit it yet, is all," Rob said impatiently, speaking what was in my mind, too.

Varick shook his head. "We've come pretty damn far. No, that fence ought to be here by now. But it isn't."

"Then where the Christ is it?" demanded Rob belligerently into the concealing storm. Our faces said that each of the three of us was morally certain we had come the right way after veering around the coulee. Hop with that first leg of logic and the second was inevitable: We ought to have come to the fence again. But no fence, logical or any other kind, was in evidence.

For a long moment we peered into the windblown snow, our breath smoking in front of our faces like separate small storms. Without that fence we were travelers with nowhere to go. Nowhere in life, that is. Bewilderment fought with reasoning, and I tried to clear my numb mind of everything but fence thoughts. Not even a blizzard could blow away a line of stoutly set posts and four lines of wire. Could it?

"There's just one other place I can think of for that fence to be," Varick suggested as if he hated to bring up the idea. "The sonofabitch might be under us."

With his overshoe he scuffed aside the day's powdery freshfall to show us the old hardened snow beneath. Rob and I stared down. Oh sweet Christ and every dimpled disciple. A snow bridge, was this? If it was, if we were huddled there on a giant drift where the snow had built and cemented itself onto the brow of the coulee all winter, fenceposts and barbed wire could be buried below us, right enough. Anything short of a steeple could be buried down there, if this truly was a snow bridge. And if we were overshooting the fenceline down there under the winter crust, we next were going to be on the blind plain, in danger of circling ourselves to death.

"Damn it," Rob seemed downright affronted by our predicament, "whoever saw snow like this?"

Varick had no time for that. Rapidly he said, "We can't just stand around here cussing the goddamn situation. What I'd better do is go out here a little way"—indicating to the left of us, what ought to be the southward slope of the long hump of drift we were on, if we were—"and take a look around for where the fence comes out of this."

His words scared my own into the air. "Not without a rope on you, you won't."

"Yeah, I'm afraid you're right about that," Varick agreed. The three of us peered to the route he proposed to take. Visibility came and went but it was never more than a few dozen strides' worth. I repeated that Varick was not moving one step into the blizzard without a rescue rope to follow back to us, even though we all knew the cumbersome minutes it would cost us to undo the ropes that were lashing the hay to the sled racks, knot them together, affix them around his waist." "It won't take time at all," I uttered unconvincingly.

Hateful as the task was, stiff-fingered and wind-harassed as we were, we got the ropes untied from each of our hay loads. Next, the reverse of that untying chore. "Rob, you're the one with the canny hands," I tried on him. He gave me a look, then with a grunt began knotting the several ropes together to make a single lifeline for Varick. One end of the line I tied firmly around Varick's waist while Rob was doing the splice knots, then we anchored the other end to Varick's hay rack.

"Let's try it," Varick said, and off he plunged into the blizzard. Rob and I, silent pillars side by side, lost sight of him before he had managed to take twenty effortful steps.

With my son out there in the oblivion of winter, each moment ached in me. But I could think of no other precaution we might have done. If Varick didn't come back within a reasonable time, Rob and I could follow the rope into the blizzard and fetch him. I would do it by myself if I had to. It might take every morsel of energy left in me, but I would get Varick back out of that swirling snow if I had to.

The rope went taut.

It stayed that way a long moment, as if Varick was dangling straight down from it instead of out across a plain of snow. Then the line alternately slackened and straightened, as Varick pulled himself back to us hand over hand.

His face, strained and wincing, told us before his words did. "I didn't make it to the fence. Ran out of rope."

Rob swore feelingly; I tried to think. We needed new rope, more line of life, to explore again into that snow world, and we did not have more rope. We just had ourselves, the three of us.

"Varick," I began. "Can you stand another try of it?"

"Floundering around out there isn't really anything I want to make a career of," he admitted, breathing as if he'd been in a race. "But yeah, I can do it again if I have to."

"Then this time I'll go out with you, for however far he can still see me." I jerked my head to indicate Rob. "You give us a yell when we're just about out of sight, Rob. Then you go out beyond me, Varick, while I hold the rope for you. What do you think? It would gain us that much distance"—I nodded to the edge of visibility out there—"for looking, at least."

"That sounds as good as any," Varick assented. Rob only bobbed his head once; we McCaskills could take it for yes if we wanted.

Varick and I set out, the wind sending scythes of snow at us. The cold sawed at us through every seam in our clothing. Quickly we were up to our knees in a fresh drift. Varick broke the way and I thrashed after him. A drift atop a drift, this last dune of snow would be. And other layers beneath that as we slogged. October snow, November on top of that. And December atop that, and January, and February . . . How many tiers of this winter could there be? This wasn't a winter, it was geological ages of snow. It was a storm planet building itself layer by layer. It was—

Abruptly I stopped, and reaching a hand ahead to Varick's shoulder, brought him to a halt, too. When he turned, the apprehension in my manner made words unnecessary.

We looked back. Nothingness. The white void of snow, the blizzard erasing all difference between earth and sky. No glimpse of Rob. No sound in the air but the wind.

We stood like listening statues, our tracks already gone into the swirling snow we had come out of. Again, yet, no voice from the safety of there.

The bastard.

The utter betraying triple-slippery unforgiving bastard Rob had let us come too far. I ought to have killed him with my own hands, the day we fought there on Breed Butte, the day it all began. He was letting the blizzard eat us. Letting Varick and me vanish like two sparks into the whirl of this snow. Letting us—

Then sounds that were not quite the wind's.

. . . arrr . . .

. . . ough . . .

The blizzard swirled in a new way, and the wraith figure of Rob was there, waving both arms over his head.

"*Far enough,*" his voice faintly carried to us. "*Far enough.*"

Varick's heavy breathing was close to mine. "He always was one to press the luck, wasn't he," my son uttered. "Particularly when it's somebody else's."

We breathed together, marking the sight and sound of Rob into our senses, then turned ahead to squint for any sign of the fenceline. None.

"You ready to go fishing?" asked Varick, and away he plunged again, the rope around his waist and in my mittened hands.

Through my weariness I concentrated on the hemp in my hands. *To see a world in a grain of sand . . .* Would grains of snow do? By the dozens and hundreds they fell and fell, their whiteness coating my sleeves and mittens . . . *Hold infinity in the palm of your hand . . .* Would mittened palms be deft enough for that? I had to force my cold claw of a hand to keep making a fist around the moving line of rope. The rope paying out through my grip already had taken Varick from sight, into the snow cyclone. Thoughts swarmed to fill his absence. What if he stumbled out there, jerking the rope out of my stiff hands? Hold, Angus. Find a way to hold. I fumbled the end of the rope around my waist, clutching it tightly belted around me with my right hand while the left hand encircled the strand going out to Varick. If he fell I would fall, too, but nothing would make me let go of this rope. I would be Varick's anchor. Such as I was, I would be that much. A splice knot caught in my grip an instant before I let it belly out and away. The knots. Rob's knots. Lord of mercy, why hadn't I done them myself? What if he hadn't tied them firmly, what if just one began to slip loose? No. No, I could trust Rob's hands even if I couldn't trust him.

Only a few feet of rope left. If Varick did not find the fenceline now, we never would. My heart thundered in me, as if the enormity of clothing around it was making it echo. A quiver of chill went through me each time the wind clasped around my body. If we couldn't go on we would need to try to hide ourselves in caves of the hay, try to wait out the blizzard. But if this cold and wind went on through the night, our chances were slim. More likely they were none. If any one of us could live through, let it be Var—

Tugs on the rope, like something heavy quivering at the end of the hempen line. Or something floundering after it had fallen.

"*Varick!*" I shouted as loud as I could. The wind took my words. I might as well have been yelling into a bale of that Dakota hay.

The tugs continued. I swallowed, held firm, clutching the jerking rope around me. I resisted a hundred impulses to plunge forward and help Varick in his struggle. I resisted another hundred to whirl around in search of Rob, to see whether he still was there as our guidemark. The distance back to him and the hay sleds was the same as it ever had been, I had to recite to my bolting instincts, only the snow was in motion, not the white distance stretching itself, as it gave every appearance of. Motion of another sort as the invisible end of this rope, the tugs continuing in a ragged rhythm that I hoped had to be—

Varick suddenly coming hand over hand, materializing out of the whirl. A struggling upright slab of whiteness amid the coiling swirl of whiteness.

He saved his breath until he was back to me, my arms helping to hold him up.

"It's there!" he panted. "The fenceline. It comes out of the drift about there"—carefully pointing an angle to our left, although everything in me would have guessed it had to be to our right. "The sleds are actually on the other side of the sonofabitch. We about went too far, Dad."

Fixing ourselves on the figure whose waves and shouts came and went through the blowing flakes, we fought snow with our feet until we were back beside Rob. Varick saved him the burden of asking. "We got ourselves a fence again, Unk."

Laboriously we retied the ropes across the hay loads, as well as men in our condition could. Then Varick turned his team to the left—they were glad enough to, suffering in the wind as they had been—and I reined Woodrow and Copenhagen around to follow them, and Rob and his grays swung in behind us. Once our procession was down off the mound of snow, the tops of the fenceposts appeared and then the topmost single strand of barbwire, the three strands beneath it in the accumulated white depth. The white iron winter, with a brutal web in it. That single top strand, though. That was our tether to the creek, to survival. I had never known until then that I could be joyously glad to see barbed bramble.

Now how far to the creek? We had to keep going, following the line of fence, no matter what distance it was. There was no knowing the hour of the day, either. The storm had made it all dusk. The complicated effort of trying to fumble out my pocket watch for a look, I couldn't even consider. Slog was all we really needed to know, really. But how far?

Another laborious half-mile, mile. Who knew? This day's distances had nothing to do with numbers.

Then thin shadows stood in the snowy air.

Trees, willows of the creek. Dim frieze that hung on the white wall of weather. But as much guidance as if it was all the direction posts on earth, every one of them pointing us to Gros Ventre and safety.

A person is never too weary to feel victory. Blearily exultant, I stood and watched while Varick halted his sled and began to slog back to meet Rob and me. Now that we had the creek, consultation wasn't really needed anymore. But maybe he simply had to share success with us, maybe— then as I squinted at the treeline of the creek, something moved in the bottom corner of my vision, there where the fence cornered into the creek.

I blinked and the something still moved, slowly, barely. A lower clot of forms beneath the willow shadows: Double W cattle, white with the snow coated onto them, caught there in the fence corner.

"The two of you go ahead and take your sleds across the creek, why not?" my son said as nonchalantly as if our day of struggle was already years in the past. "I'll snip the fence for these cows and give them a shove out into the brush, then catch up with you."

"Man, why bother?" Rob spoke bitterly. He still wore that bleak look, as if being prodded along by the point of an invisible bayonet. "They're goddamn Williamson's."

"That isn't their fault," Varick gave him back. "Head on across, you two. I won't be long."

I made my tired arms and tired legs climb atop the hay on the sled, then rattled the reins to start Copenhagen and Woodrow on their last few plodded miles to town, miles with the guarantee of the creek beside us. When we had crossed the narrow creek and made our turn toward Gros Ventre, Rob and his gray team copying behind us, I could hear faintly above the wind the grateful moans of the cattle Varick was freeing from the blizzard.

In the morning, our procession from Gros Ventre west toward home was a slow glide through white peace. New snow had freshened everything, and without the wind the country sat plump and calm.

As we passed the knob ridge at the mouth of the North Fork valley, branchloads in the tops of its pine trees were dislodging and falling onto the lower branches, sending up snow like white dust. The all-but-silent plummets of snow in the pines and the sounds of our teams and sleds were the only things to be heard in Scotch Heaven. The lone soul anywhere here in the center of the valley was George Frew, feeding his sheep beside the creek. George's wave to us was slow and thoughtful, as if he was wondering whether he, too, would soon be making such a journey as we had.

And now we were around the final turn of the valley to my homestead, mine and Adair's, and there on their feedground beside the North Fork were the sheep in their gray gather, and the broad bundled figure of Toussaint distributing dabs of hay. For a long minute he watched our tiny fleet of bale-laden sleds. Varick in the lead, next me, Rob at the tail. Then Toussaint gripped his pitchfork in the middle of the handle, hoisted it above his head and solemnly held it there as if making sure we could see what it was, as if showing us it was not an axe.

From *Dreamers and Desperadoes*, ed. Craig Lesley and Katheryn Stavrakis (New York: Bantam, Doubleday, Dell, 1993)

WILLIAM STAFFORD

TALKING RECKLESSLY: AN INTERVIEW WITH THE STAFFORD FAMILY

Derek Sheffield

*T*HE *INTERVIEW* took place at the Stafford home in Lake Oswego, Oregon, on April 30, 2002. Dorothy, Kim, and Barbara were present. Kit joined in later via e-mail.

Derek Sheffield: Dorothy, how did you and Bill meet?

Dorothy: That's a story. My father was a minister in the Church of the Brethren, one of the three peace churches that supported the other camps. I was home for the weekend from Riverside, where I taught. It was my father's turn to go to the camp in Santa Barbara to preach, and he asked me if I wanted to go along. I always liked talking to my father, so I said sure. There we were in Santa Barbara at the camp, and it got dark. There was a full moon—isn't that a good setting? Bill asked me to go for a walk. We walked a long way that night, across a dry creek bed, the way California streams are in the summer. I quoted something from Willa Cather that I liked: "pale stars in the sky, but I remember them all as flooded with the rich indolence of a full moon." And Bill asked, "Do you like Willa Cather, too?" Then he told me about his family in Kansas, about how they moved from one little town to another. It was hard for the children, leaving friends and

*William Stafford. Photo reprinted by permission
of the Estate of William Stafford*

schools and familiar places, but a library was always waiting in the
next town, with friends on the shelves to welcome them.

Bill described his family making weekly trips to the library, and I
added the memory of my mother quoting a Dickens character at any
appropriate moment and growing up with our parents reading aloud
from works of Browning, Wordsworth, Longfellow, the Psalms.

Five dates from that conversation, on another moonlit night, Bill
said to me, "How are you always going to feel?"

"Just like this, but you don't even know if I can cook."

And Bill said, "That doesn't matter. You don't know if I can bring
anything home to cook." Well, we gambled. It was a lucky gamble,
and it lasted for forty-nine years.

DS: What year was that?

Dorothy: 1944

DS: Was he the same person then that he became?

Dorothy: I think so. I think that was one thing about Bill. He was consistent, all through those years, knowing who he was and never swerving from that knowledge.

DS: He was forty-six in 1960 when his first book of poems, *West of Your City*, was published. Was he anxious between 1947, which was when *Down in the Heart* was published, and 1960?

Dorothy: Maybe inside, but not outside. No. He sent a lot of poems out to every little magazine going and when he got a request he sent something in. He was always active and publishing, and I don't remember him ever saying anything about being impatient.

DS: So he felt, maybe, that he was reaching an audience?

Dorothy: I think he just liked to write and wanted to share this writing with others. He was delighted, of course, when a book came together. His University of Kansas Master's thesis, *Down in My Heart*, came from experiences in camp, and his University of Iowa Ph.D. thesis was poems from the Iowa City Writers' Workshop.

Kim: He had three pieces of advice for being a successful poet. The first was—delay as long as possible the publication of your first book of poems. The second was—send out a lot of poems to magazines. And the third was—write better than anyone else.

DS: Kim, I understand that you have written a memoir of your life with your father. Can you say a little about it?

Kim: It's a mysterious process to sit down and try to put together all the different things you remember, for all the different reasons you remember those things and not others. But I tried to follow not Daddy's story and not my story so much as the story of how we knew each other and the context of our family that was so rich a source for honoring stories and words and a life of witness. When we reprinted *Down in My Heart*, we added a subtitle, *Peace Witness in War Time*, and I think that subtitle speaks for the book I've written.

DS: What's your book called?

Kim: *Early Morning*. There's one story that my editor wanted me to take out of the book. To protect me from reviewers, she said. The scene is when Daddy and I are talking, and he shakes his head and says, "Baroque prose. First Annie Dillard, now everybody." I said, "Well, Daddy, that's kind of what I write." And he said, "You're one of the worst."

I can see why my editor wanted to take this out but I find that a precious and a very characteristic response to a fellow writer. Not so much to a son, but just to another writer. The subtext is that praise can do more damage than . . . something other than praise. Also, it exemplifies his love of talking recklessly. He would often start a conversation, "Let's talk recklessly." And I think he was marking my distance from him. He was pointing out my independence in kind of an odd way. Of course, he wrote a few Baroque things himself.

DS: Did you win the battle with your editor?

Kim: Oh yeah. It stayed. No dithering around.

DS: No dithering around, yeah. Barbara, you've done some collaborative projects with your father, pairing your illustrations with his words. Can you say a little about what that was like?

Barbara: Dad was always trying to get me to come forward with something visual. He never said no to anyone who would ask him for poems, and I think every now and then he felt he could say, "Hey, I have a daughter. Let's get her work alongside mine."

I remember there was one project, right before Dad died; someone approached us about doing a show together. So, Dad would send along poems to me and I would show him what I was coming up with. That was really, a wonderful process, poems and paintings coming from each other. I will often still use one of Dad's poems to get me started on a painting.

DS: I heard a story about a time when you were a little girl and started waking up early to be with your dad when he was writing because you thought he was lonely. Is this how you remember it?

Barbara: I remember, and I think that all of us would probably share this feeling—we had no sense that we were getting in Dad's way with his writing. But he would get up so early so that he could have his writing time, and I did get this idea that maybe he was lonely. So, for a brief period of time, I would get up to keep him company, and he never said a word to me about it being his writing time. He would just get up earlier.

DS: What did you do while he was writing? I assume he'd be lying out there on the couch . . .

Barbara: I'd sit or stand on the register and my nightgown would billow with the heat and I'd just talk to him. But he would get up earlier. I don't know how long this went on, but I would get up earlier

William fishing. Photo reprinted by permission of the Estate of William Stafford

and he would get up even earlier and finally I couldn't do it. I couldn't get up any earlier.

DS: What kind of father was he? My perspective as a reader, knowing him only by his work, is that he was like the father in his poems, the one who could hear little animal steps, the one who invited his son to hear the first bird. In other words, he wasn't controlling, but participatory. Is my vision close to home?

Kim: He was *the best* as a daddy. I think because he would accompany you. It wasn't that he was interested in you—this is what I felt—but he was interested in everything. So, you would be accompanied in whichever way your life turned. As you grow up, you get interested in different things. He says in his daily writings, "Some people take a conscientious interest in the hobbies of their children. I would make the best bow in the world." He was following his own appetites and interests and curiosities. You didn't feel patronized, or ignored. You felt accompanied.

Barbara: In response to something we'd say, he'd say, "Oh now, Shakespeare said something about that." There were these presences around our table that made you kind of sit up a little bit and talk more. He would say, "Tell me more," when you would offer an idea, without judgment, just wanting to follow it out. Mom and Dad both did that.

Another enduring memory for me is coming home after I'd left, coming home to visit. Whatever Mom and Dad would be doing, they'd stop and come and sit at the table and hope the visit would last as long as possible. They would always walk us into the front yard as we left and stand until we were gone. The message was, "You're welcome here and we want to know all about your life."

Kim: It was how he taught also. This was the whole idea of interviewing the students, rather than teaching them. To draw everything forth and then notice a little unusual part of what's been drawn forth and follow that. This is one of the things I really miss about Daddy—his ability to interview an individual or a group, and activate everyone in the group. I think that's one way he dealt with fame. He refused to be famous, even though he was.

DS: I've noticed his tendency in dialogues with other writers such as Richard Hugo and Robert Bly to turn the question back at them and say something like "That sounds like a Hugo line."

Barbara: He was great at turning things around and inside out.

Dorothy: I always thought of it as the way my mother did when she did the washing. She'd take the socks and turn them wrong side out. You know, things I had taken for granted for years, he would just get upset and make me take a new look.

Barbara: And the humor too. Sometimes he'd say, "Oh you're gonna be so mad." He would throw out a word and say, "Now you know what that means, don't you?" Well, nobody knew what that word meant.

Dorothy: When we were first married—I think it was the first morning—he said, "Well Dorothy how is your Weltanschauung?" And I said, "What does that mean?" "What, don't you know what Weltanschauung is?" It was always like that. Do you know what Weltanschauung is?

DS: Sounds German.

Dorothy: Worldview. "How is your worldview?"

Barbara: But, I will say this: there were some things that were so clear about right and wrong. He wouldn't meddle with the little things, but he would come down so hard, very clearly, with the big things. It got us to monitor the conscience of our lives because we knew we had to do it. There's nobody telling us. That's my experience.

DS: Okay, let's talk recklessly. If you had to pick one animal to identify with William Stafford, what would it be, and why?

Kim: Well, I think it depended on the day. Sometimes, he was definitely the wolf, in charge, alpha. And other times, he would be the quail or the dove or the antelope. There is that poem about the antelope that ends, "There will be that form in the grass."

Dorothy: Or the monkey, reaching out with all its fingers, to get the nuance of the conversation, or the action.

Kim: I would say he's not a herd animal, but the individual. The fox might be in there.

Barbara: Definitely an animal with a good nose.

Dorothy: Maybe a dog. At Christmas, he'd always smell the present before he opened it.

Kim: He said one time that when he starts writing a poem, he doesn't always know what it's going to be about but he knows what it's going to smell like. "Love the earth like a mole, fur near."

Barbara: When we'd be out looking for arrowheads—I know I'm not supposed to say that we did that—but when we did, Dad would say, "Let's just think like a deer, or let's think like a rabbit." Often, it brought forth a beautiful point.

Dorothy: You know, when you get married, you have no idea what kind of person you're marrying, really, or what kind of father he would make. Bill never went around cooing at babies, ever. But then when we had babies, he was wonderful, and so at home and so loving. It was a very nice surprise.

DS: And as I was listening to Kim and Barbara speak of him as a father, I was thinking of the many times that his children have entered his poems, and several times, verbatim. He was interested in the way they used language. In fact, Dorothy, you mentioned a manuscript comprised of things the children said.

Dorothy: Yes, *Lost Words*. He wrote every morning anyway, and

From left: *Bret, Kit, Kim, Barbara, Dorothy, and William Stafford. Photo by William Stafford; reprinted by permission of the Estate of William Stafford*

he'd jot down what the children said. He gave the collection to me for Christmas. Then I kept track too.

DS: Now, that brings me to a question that I don't have written down, but one I've wondered about. You mentioned he would write every day and he would write down things the kids said. Then add all the correspondence he did for his writing and all the work he did for his classes—did he ever leave the desk?

Dorothy: Oh yes. After writing in the mornings, he would teach and then afterwards would be tired and take a nap, and then the minute the mail came, he'd go right to his office and answer it every day. That's how he kept going, which was wonderful. Then in the afternoon, often we'd go to the yard, to the vegetables and the flowers.

Now, there was one wonderful thing to me, about Bill—he didn't ever view himself as a special person or a special poet. Poetry was down-to-earth and he was down-to-earth. I asked him once if he hadn't been a writer and a teacher, what he would have been. He said, "I'd have a bicycle shop." He loved to do that kind of thing, fix things, and make them better. When we moved here, this was just a square of grass, and he planted all the trees. Every time I'd get an idea about the yard, he would make it happen. It was great.

DS: He has that wonderful anthem to handy folks. I think it's called "Fixers," where the dog barks when the engine starts. That was my feeling, that he managed to spend a lot of time out in the physical world, but at the same time, here is this guy who—well, let me share a story with you. I have a friend who sent him a book; it was a little self-published kind of venture. This was in the early 1980s and my friend sent Stafford and several other luminaries his book. Stafford was the only one who wrote back. He sent a little note that said, "Thank you for the book. I like it, and I'm still grocking on it."

Barbara: What's that from?

Kim: *Stranger in a Strange Land.*

Dorothy: Oh; it's a wonderful word.

DS: After my friend told me this story, I began referring to Stafford as the King of Grock and Roll.

Dorothy: When I met Bill, I was so impressed because he talked so well, so magically, to me. And after that everyone else sounded prosaic. I think I'd been looking for that all my life. He just made everything . . . different.

Kim: Do you think we seemed prosaic to him?

Dorothy: Probably so. No, I don't. He thought we were all okay, I think. I wish he were sitting here. I get restive sometimes when people make a saint of Bill, because he wasn't. I loved him dearly and they take him away from my life when they get too precious about him. Can you understand that?

DS: Well, one thing I remember hearing Barbara say back at the N.C.T.E. conference in 1997 was that he loved chopping down the trees as much as planting them.

Dorothy: I had a problem with that. He retired two years before I did and I'd come home and he'd be up in a tree. He would call it pruning, but it was scary . . . He'd love to be up in trees, doing stuff like that. He was up in trees 'til the day he died.

DS: Did he do some of that as a C.O.?

Dorothy: He fought forest fires and worked on trails.

Kim: Physical labor. There was no shortage of that.

Dorothy: He used to say, from Falstaff, I guess, "They hate us youth." He was so full of things we keep saying, wonderful Bill sayings that he repeated many times.

Kim: And they were always funny. If you were clamoring for a drink of water, you would find out years later he was quoting Sir Phillip Sydney with, "Thy need is greater than mine." How do you take that? I guess he was saying go ahead and be first, even though you don't deserve to be first.

Dorothy: We had company once and we were all sitting out on the deck and—I don't know how this came up—but Bill said, "Sometimes I don't really like my friends." And everybody was thinking, "Are you talking about me?" That's what you call reckless talk.

Kim: Where did you go from there?

Dorothy: I don't remember that. I just remember the startling moment. Everybody felt fine. They knew how he was, but people that didn't know Bill were sometimes offended. What he would say was true, but he didn't always couch it in tact.

DS: Do you think he was verbalizing his own self-awareness, a passing realization that "sometimes I don't like my friends?"

Kim: Sometimes, you realize, you're in a conversation where everyone knows the next thing you're supposed to say. But he wouldn't say it. He'd say something else. I remember one time he was giving a reading at the University of Oregon. One of my professors didn't go to the reading, saw him later, and said, "Bill, I'm sorry I didn't see your reading." Daddy is supposed to say, "Well that's okay." But instead he said, "Well, you can get away with that for awhile, but eventually you'll miss your chance."

DS: Did he have a smile on his face?

Kim: Not really. If you're his friend, or his child, it's just, well, Daddy told the truth that time. But if you don't know him, I imagine that would be devastating.

DS: What do you think provided the greatest challenge for William Stafford? Did you ever think there was anything that Caesar couldn't handle?

Kim: Well, I don't know where I got this, but I feel like he personally believed he was supposed to be able to stop World War II. He was able to see so clearly how countries go wrong. People are cruel to each other. He had such a clear sense about that. I think he held himself to a very high standard for writing, teaching, or witnessing in some way that would rectify the world.

Dorothy: And he said about World War II that it was a hard one to object to. He said, "Well, once you're in it, what can you do?" But the steps that led up to it, the increments, little by little, that made a Hitler. . . . In other words, we ought to start way back with whatever happened, find out the causes and situations.

I remember him talking about an ocean-liner coming to the dock, and it's headlong to get there. It's going at such a speed that you can't do anything about it, but you should have given it warnings, way back there. Made the chart of the course different.

Kim: On Pearl Harbor day—and I think this probably did happen— if his friends said to him, "Well, what would you do?" That's that moment on the ocean-liner when you take the wheel ten feet from the dock and going 30 knots. But the pacifist is the one who's trained to see beyond, and before.

DS: The one who stops and pulls the deer off the road because he's thinking about future travelers.

Kim: In terms of his inability, I think he carried a burden that he couldn't take care of his brother. His younger brother Bob who had a hard life, some depression.

DS: The bomber pilot.

Kim: He was a bomber pilot in the war. In some ways, he was the brother less capable of prevailing in the world. When his brother died of alcoholism that was really hard on Daddy. And when my brother died, it was I think another iteration of that inexplicable event in the world that he blamed himself for not averting. And he responded by withdrawing from us.

Dorothy: It was very hard for me. Our sorrow wasn't shared.

Kim: He has that poem, right at the end: "It's heavy to drag, this big sack of what / you should have done." I think, like a lot of people,

Summer 1972, University of Washington. From left: *Beth and Nelson Bentley, William Stafford, Madeleine DeFrees, Michelle Birch, and Richard Hugo. Photo reprinted by permission of the Estate of William Stafford*

he carried a sense of, you could say, miracles he hadn't performed, but things he held himself to account for, all the same. Big things.

Barbara: Well, I think, how can you have it both ways? If he was a father who wouldn't guide us, "This is what you do," then when life takes turns, you can't blame yourself for not being there. I'm not expressing this very well . . .

Dorothy: When Bret died, Bill was in Iowa, and you [Kim] called him, and he came home the next morning. I started to talk about it, and he said, "in the night, I worked it out." So, I didn't talk about it after that. I couldn't quite understand it. I could see, at that point, why parents, when they have a tragedy like that, separate because it's so lonely for one person, or two people who can't share. But he was a loving person.

Barbara: Well, Dad was partly a loner.

Dorothy: He said that the war set him apart.

Kim: What do you think that meant, Mother, "I worked it out?" What did he mean by that?

Dorothy: I just assumed he'd thought about Bret's life and figured that he couldn't have made it not happen, his death, that he'd found some kind of peace. I don't know.

Kim: But why does that mean he couldn't talk about it?

Dorothy: I don't know . . . the hardest time of our lives.

Kim: I would think he hadn't worked it out. I think it continued as a self-accusation.

DS: He was writing about it up until his death.

Dorothy: Beautiful poems. Well, it was so unheard of. We'd always thought our little flock would stay together.

DS: There is a lot of assurance in his poems: "There will be that form in the grass." This is one of the things that appeals to me in his work because I need such reminders. Was he reminding himself? Did he need that?

Dorothy: I think he talked about his own family so much because that was the place where he didn't have these tremendous problems, and you were surrounded by the people you loved, and were encouraged. He was a Kansas boy, and then he was far from his original home, and I think he just went back to that in his poems, over and over.

Kim: You know, I never thought about this, but Bret couldn't talk to us, and, took his life. In a way, Daddy was like his son.

Dorothy: I never thought about that, Kim, but I think that's right. And he would never talk about death. That was a lonely thing too because we were getting older, and he never mentioned what would happen. In our business file he had a category called "if we ever die" for the wills and things. In the big things of life, Bill was so wonderful, when we were happy. But anything that was on the dark side. . . . I don't know what it was.

Kim: He held himself very much to account in his daily writings. Always accusing himself, and he overstated it. He overstated a quality that was real.

Dorothy: When Bill died, three people called me up from different parts of the country and said, "Did Bill believe in God?" And I said, "I don't know." But I said he was certainly a spiritual person and I think believed in what other people call God. It was the spirit that made a difference in living and it would go on—I had that feeling. It's very strange to live with somebody fifty years and not know if he believes in God. Kim had an answer. He came out one morning from his nap and said, "You know what? God is dead." He was about three.

Kim: Well, there was the report of the neighbor kid who went home and told her mom, "The Stafford kids don't have to watch T.V. They get to go camping and stuff like that."

Dorothy: And then the woman across the street, the neighbor whose daughter, Debbie, was Barbara's age. Her mother was always sewing pretty dresses for her when she was little and Barb was always getting hand-me-downs. Debbie said to her mother, "Why can't we have an attic like the Staffords?"

Barbara: Oh, and then we had wonderful rituals. We had a sacrifice meal once a week where we would have cornbread and give what part of our allowance we felt ready to contribute.

Kim: We would pool it in the center of the table.

Dorothy: Whenever things were going right, we'd say, "This is Brothers and Sisters Day." Then we'd go out to dinner and everybody got a little present. What else did we have?

Kim: We made pizza every Sunday. And there was the anchovy part of the family, and the non-anchovy part of the family.

Dorothy: Bill made the dough.

Barbara: Oh, and bread.

Dorothy: Yeah, we'd make bread. We took turns. He liked his best, although he didn't say so, and I liked mine best, although I didn't say so.

DS: Did he ever write poetry at any other time than the morning?

Dorothy: Now and then.

Kim: I remember the scene in Washington, D.C., when Portland mayor Bud Clark had commissioned him to write a poem about the great blue heron, our city's bird.

DS: "Spirit of Place."

Kim: Yes. And I remember Daddy lying on the bed in the motel jotting this poem so he could hand it off to me to fly it back to Portland.

Dorothy: I remember once someone called and asked Bill, "Do you have any poems about tomatoes?" And he said, "Well, I think I could

*William Stafford teaching at the
University of Washington*

find one." And so he wrote a poem about tomatoes. They had a magazine that was called *Tomatoes.*

Kim: Actually he got an old poem and put some tomatoes in it.

DS: Well, the secret's out. The real Stafford process. Based on what
I've read, it seems that he did not workshop his poems in a group or
through correspondence, or often even share them with the family. Is
that right?

Dorothy: Sometimes he shared them with us, but not usually.
Mostly we would see the poems when they were published.

Kim: In the correspondence we have an example where he submitted a poem to *Poetry Northwest* and Carolyn Kizer was editing and she
wrote a long list of suggestions for changes he might make—none of
which he made.

Kim: Did he workshop his poems? He came home one time from
the East and said, "I learned a strange custom. There are some poets

who have a committee and they submit their poems to a committee and eventually the committee puts together a book for them. Then they send the book out, and the committee writes reviews about what a wonderful book this is." He said, "I don't understand why an artist, who has the freedom to do what they want to do, exactly the way they want to do it, would ever squander that freedom for a committee. I just don't understand it."

DS: It's my impression, too, that he traveled frequently. Given the number of poems he wrote in his life, I must surmise that he wrote many of these on the road.

Dorothy: He often wrote a poem for the place where he stayed.

Kim: I did a workshop this year at Quartz Mountain out in Oklahoma. Before I went, I stopped by the Stafford Archive and archive director Paul Merchant asked, "Well, do you want to take all the poems your father wrote when he was at Quartz Mountain in 1978?" There they were, and some of them were really good.

DS: Somewhere he said, "To me, poems are expendable, but the process is not expendable, it is lifelong." He also said, "I would trade everything I've written to write the next poem." In this way, he takes poetry out of the reach of capitalism, of productivity, which is a beautiful place to be.

Kim: If you interrupted him in his writing time, it was no problem. There was this inexhaustible source.

Dorothy: Never once did he close his study door to the kids. But he did wistfully talk about being at Yaddo where they didn't even have vacuum cleaners going during the writing hours.

Kim: Well, that's where he wrote "Traveling through the Dark," "Ceremony," and some of the others.

DS: Robert Bly said that he thinks that Stafford's secret, abiding topic is aggression. I would also like to add relaxation. The way he focused on process over product in his writing, the way he kept his door open to the kids, and even the way he physically wrote, lying down on the couch—these approaches allowed him to relax into his life the way he would into a poem. So, in that trance-like state, the true self and the true language would emerge. And through his poems and his prose, he invited his listeners to do the same. What do you think about that?

Dorothy: I think that's right. In fact, he was kind of a missionary with this message. It was consistent through all his readings and talking about life.

Kim: I have a chapter in my book called, "It Was All Easy," which is a line from his last poem. I ask myself, "Well, it wasn't *all* easy, was it?" The relation between aggression and that kind of Zen stepping back . . . if you're like Daddy and you recognize the true dangerous aggressive habits of the world, and all your life you practice living in a non-confrontational way with those dangers, then you take a deep breath, write a poem, love your family, and you teach your students in the presence of those dangers. You conduct yourself in a very calm way. You have to.

DS: You mentioned Zen. What do you think of the notion of William Stafford as a modern day mystic? When I read Rumi or Thoreau, I hear flashes of Stafford, in the many ways. They all say, "What can anyone give you greater than now?"

Kim: Well, I'm thinking about one of the poems, "Malheur before Dawn," and in the poem he's listening to the frogs: "I didn't know a ditch could hold so much joy." That's a very domestic kind of Zen. It's nothing precious or Oriental. It's more Kansas, the bounty of the world.

Barbara: It defies a kind of label. Yes, without ever defining it, Dad was a mystic, but there's nothing about him that would make you want to define it.

Dorothy: I can't remember the name of the group, but definitely a mystic group invited him to come, and he said no. I think he kept it inside.

Kim: Well, in a way, it goes back to God. Did he believe in God? It's sort of like when the reporter asked Carl Jung, "Dr. Jung, do you believe in God?" And Jung said, "*Believe? I know.*"

Dorothy: I remember a dinner party where he made everybody so mad, including me. We were talking about religion and Bill said, "Well, I'm saved. How about the rest of you?"

DS: If he were here, what would he be saying at the dinner table in this time of the war on terrorism, in this time of generalized aggression? I understand that President Bush has something like an eighty percent approval rating for his militaristic response to September 11. Would Stafford's stance be as unpopular today as it was when he dared to be a C.O. during WWII?

William and Dorothy Stafford

Dorothy: I've often wondered what he'd say.

Kim: I think in some ways his best or most direct utterance in response to those conditions appeared following the Gulf War. He had a series of questions: What does it mean to celebrate victory when we've conducted a war that has demonstrated the effectiveness of terrible means to our adversaries? What do you think they've learned from this? How will they act on what they've learned from this? What will be our next escalation in order to continue to prevail based on our use of force?

He would ask questions, very trenchantly Socratic questions. But he would also be mystified. I think he'd be the first to say that a pacifist is not someone who has the answers but someone who will not augment the terror with one's own life. But as far as solving the terror, that's the work of many.

Dorothy: He'd know that many present answers are wrong.

Barbara: And he'd say about Bush, "We didn't elect him by that much."

Kim: He would go further though. He would sympathize with Bush's plight: "Eighty percent approval rating? That's pretty coercive. He can't easily stop doing what he's doing. How could we help him think of another way that wouldn't lose his support?" It's odd to use the word "strategic," but he would think "strategically" on behalf of someone in the predicament of waging war. Do you think?

I just remember in the Vietnam War one of the things he said was, "Our leaders need to know that it's okay with us if they become less hawkish."

Dorothy: There was a wonderful photograph. It was during the Vietnam War and Bill was by a podium downtown reading, and in the foreground is a policeman, heavy, big, with his arms folded. You know, just looking on, and here's Bill way off, kind of little in the picture, and it's wonderful. Not might, but right.

DS: This interview will appear on the shelves close to the time of the 10th anniversary of his death on August 28, 1993. How does it feel nearly ten years out?

Kim: I still feel like he's in the next room.

Dorothy: I do too, except when I go to bed and he isn't there. He would often say, "Do you hurt anywhere, Dorothy?" I'd say, "No." And he'd say, "Well then let's celebrate."

Barbara: Well, there's so much he said with his silence. I look back over these years . . . someone has lived so well and given in a way that— at least as a daughter or someone who knew him fairly well and had many discussions—I find myself filling in what he might be saying, what he did say going over all those conversations. Often it was what he didn't say.

DS: Somewhere he wrote, "The things you do not have to say make you rich."

Kim: And he said—I don't remember the poem—but the Eskimos indicate time to depart by saying, "I feel rich enough."

Dorothy: Rich is a good word to go with Bill and our life with him.

After reading the interview via e-mail, Kit Stafford had some thoughts to share:

There is so much we have in common—looking back on our family culture. Things we count on in our individual lives now. The consistencies that Mother, Barb, and Kim talked about were in a pool back home. One we can draw on anytime. When we fanned out in our grown up lives we each experienced new relationships with Daddy.

In 1984 I crossed the Cascade mountains to visit, then stayed. The folks would come over to their place at Indian Ford. I had time to walk and talk, to cover new terrain with each of them. Maybe because I was so far from the fold in Portland—out of the loop—like I am now, not being with the family for the interview—there was a tendency and an almost urgency to share close thoughts. It was out of these times that I began to coax Daddy to tell me what he really thought about things and how he felt. I asked for advice (we'd been trained not to need it), his opinions (I wanted details). We talked about Bret. I heard how it was for him. And from my mother, how it was for her. It was liberating and safe— far from the patterns they each were known by.

On the morning of the day he died the folks gave me a call—both on the line—catching up on the news and "something important." I told a friend just after the call, "I just don't know what it is." At the close Daddy said, "I love you my friend, give the dogs a pat on the head and take care of the place, adios." "Adios."

I'm thinking just now of how Daddy made my childhood meander-ings into a kind of poem. I think I was five or six years old when he'd take me with him to Tillamook on the Oregon coast to teach a night class. To keep him awake on the long drive I'd talk about how good life was going to be when I grew up:

The Way We'd Live

We'd have an old car, the kind that gets
flat tires, but inside would be wolfskin
    on the seats and warm fur on the steering
    wheel, and wolf fur on all the buttons. And
    we'd live in a ranch house made out of
    logs with a loft where you sleep, and you'd
    walk a little ways and there'd be the barn
    with the horses. We'd drive to town, and
    we'd have flat tires, and be sort of old.

I live on an old farm now with my husband Clay (a teacher of horses) and our three dogs. Daddy would have loved this place where that poem is coming true—ten acres, an old barn, places in the grass where the deer bed down, an arrowhead once in a while.

NOTE: Special thanks to Melinda Crouchley for her transcription assistance.

HOLDING THE ROETHKE CHAIR:
WILLIAM STAFFORD'S PROSE JOURNAL

*T*HE PROSE FRAGMENTS that follow are scattered among William Stafford's daily writings between mid-June and mid-August, 1972, when he was in Seattle (with occasional weekend forays back to Oregon) during his tenure of the Roethke Chair in Poetry. They present a thoroughly characteristic mixture of notes on his current teaching, thinking, and reading, and they close with a dream.

20 June 1972

Yesterday in poetry writing we agreed to keep track of what struck us as poetry. This brown ink somehow relates. And the statement in *Encounter:* "a thought if expressed grows dishonest." And a workman unnoticed high on the corner of a hotel tapping the last parts together.

If you glimpse, you should mention.

20 June 1972

The world is a long poem I am falling through—I just tell about it.

25 June 1972

Children are near death—they remember it, they have just come from it. They look around at a world new. The old have forgotten. The world is theirs, life is a habit, they have had it long.

3 July 1972

Reading Wallace Stevens. Yes, we perch for our thinking on limited territory. And there are dizzying glimpses from here. Most people forget the vertigo that should be natural here. But the sense of height must be limited, lest people not fear *helpfully* any more. The sense of being human derives from many vantages, of which Stevens represents an extreme.

9 July 1972

Analyzing poetry in terms of its references continues to pose disquiets for me, e.g. "and then the lighting of the lamps," in Eliot's Prelude: not lamps, not lighting, but "and then" strikes me as significant.

And if you start writing with just *anything*, then the significant result is in an element other than the reference?

"Prose is when the language is not noticeable." But what if poetry could be like that? In the sagas there is an understated progression.

Maybe the language could get unnoticed, and the *content* could get unnoticed, and only the ride would be left. God needs nothing but style.

Remember: the *actual* influence of particular syllables is a cumulative effect more important than doctrines.

9 July 1972

You feel bad if a bad proportion exists, even if it is out of sight. Similarly, for someone like Wittgenstein certain unresolved puzzles nag at one; like having a closet you know is filled with a jumble that will clutter your life if you open it.

10 July 1972

We live after the deadlines set for us by the most fanatical of our present soothsayers.

10 July 1972

Since "The Wasteland" my generation have enjoyed so lavish a lifetime that wasteland viewers today cannot forgive us for it.

11 July 1972

So many people think poetry is in the wording, the poetic words, that it would be helpful to live a while in a culture in which literal and literary are the same.

17 July 1972

Why do most people head into the drive and back out?

18 July 1972

Richard Hugo told about being almost hypnotized by watching wind across a grassfield, and of forgetting the war in Italy, but of not feeling like a monster when he was dropping the bombs. (But why did he watch the field?)

20 July 1972

Anyone very old talking about the danger and violence of the world is a walking contradiction: there would be no survivors in the scene many people depict.

23 July 1972

Some leaves don't try very hard. But the sun shines anyway.

26 July 1972

You think help is out there. All the operations of the world lead you to expect the crucial elements to come from somewhere your self needs. But in some endeavors the direction of help is the other way; and surfacing in your own feelings and thoughts come the new, needed elements. The golden bough grows from your hand.

28 July 1972

Pascal said eloquence is vanity. In our Northwest Writers Conference yesterday were we in a stance that smacked of vanity? I believe so. For me there was an air I now suspect, in the way I *felt* the interchanges. When someone admired what you said, you felt proprietary. Not to be credited, nor to be guilty, but to be present—is that the sustaining way to be?

2 August 1972

In class, it's like a chess game. Too headlong a move will end the game too soon, without the rewards of making encounters that help. We hardly ever finish the game. If I make this move, what move best extends our whole game?

8 August 1972

In conversation we can say, "This will sound strange, but . . . " and we put our personal credit on the line. A poet has no personal credit. Poetry is language predicated on neutral receivers. When a poem asks for a loan, it fails.

8 August 1972

Brevity is disability. You can't bring all into your life, but a perfect sensibility would encompass the whole harmony of the world. Some people celebrate their limits. Mostly, I am sorry.

8 August 1972

A writer senses that he can't deliver something expeditiously enough, or paced right, or in a sequence that is convincing, or under circumstances that compel assent. That material, he must abandon, not for reasons of principle, but just out of inability. He says something like, "It doesn't ring true, somehow." And a bystander can't see what the trouble is. The issue is not a question of worth, but one of whether the language will carry conviction.

9 August 1972

Some make writing the avoiding of mistakes—don't offend anyone. It's like my job as electrician in a refinery: no switches at certain times, no iron hammers. But I want to run, hammering oil drums.

9 August 1972

A poet like Elizabeth Bishop is paid to up the attention: by enhancing the scene we deepen our lives.

One way to stay oriented in language is to *extreme* it: you know where you are. But you leave the middle out.

Eliz Bishop poems often achieve at the end a metaphor like an ex post facto emblem: retroactively, the elements of the poem line up with the ending.

14 August 1972

Kim said Richie Lyons talks of the "control" in a story—it is what locates a theme or prevalent lead, like the river in *Huckleberry Finn*.

19 August 1972

Dream: one person away from others just watches. A police-job? I talk to him, and he is easily cynical about his job and about his *apparent* acceptance of isolation.

PROLOGUE FROM EARLY MORNING:
REMEMBERING MY FATHER

Kim Stafford

*I*T'S MORNING, before first light, 1965. I'm with my brother Bret at the tailgate of the family station wagon on the gravel shoulder of a road. We grope by dark in the back of the car where our bikes lie tangled in a heap, the pedals and handlebars locked together. We drag them out, work them free, then stand them side by side. "Ready?" Our father's voice from the dark. "I guess so." My brother. "You lucky kids." Our father puts one hand on my shoulder and another on my brother's. I'm shivering, partly with joy. Daddy has given up his writing time before dawn and brought us to the top of Chehalem Mountain, so we can start our bike ride to the Pacific with a long coast downhill. The real work, the climb over the mountains and the thickening traffic, will come later, but he has given us this easy beginning. Then he is in the car, turning back across the road, heading east, and we watch his tail-lights dwindle, toward home. My brother is older, so he goes first, clambering onto his bike and gliding west down the dark road. He disappears into the gloom. Then it's me in a rush-cold wind in my face, knuckles clamped, damp smell of the forest, gravel popping from the wheels. In time, the sun rises behind us, touching everything green with gold— fields and trees, a blur of mailboxes, the dashed centerline of the road. Then sweat. Fire in my lungs. My brother a speck at the top of the road's long climb. No water. That tight passage called the Van Duzer Corridor where giant trees crowd the twisting highway. Cars on a curve ripping past within inches, and my wheels skidding in gravel toward the ditch. How long can you feel a hand, steady on your shoulder, after that hand pulls away?

NOTE: "Reprinted with permission of Graywolf Press, Saint Paul, Minnesota

Lake Union

I

This negative of the world, a reflecting
glass, hooded, closed over carefully—
you can trail your fingers in it, stir
the pride and the ruins there upside
down, all given to the waves
till it smoothes again.

Some pictures open beyond our
picture of them—another frame they are in,
and its frame, and the soft sailing day
fitted to grommets on the horizon.
When you touch that world it trembles,
dissolves, comes back steady, reformed
again and again, pressed smooth on the water.

II

None of us has found, serene enough,
a face that knows and accepts. Why should we
honor these tantrums that prevail, these people
who posture around us, and ourselves, too,
giving and grabbing?

After some Fourth of July or Christmas, a wind
comes back and a fog gathers in every
scrap of skyscraper, and the crowds and bridges.
And we—noted or not, numbered and then
passed over, a census where nobody counts—

we stand unjudged and unjudging,
open and serene and ready,
quietly jubilant like a pier in the tide
or a wisp of moss caught on a thorn.

We merge with that lost whistle groping
and the long erasing swish of the rain.

29 JUNE

There Is a Weight in the World

I

There will be a tap at the door, but
you won't hear. In all the slide
of the minutes and hours—no change.
Miles will help—I like to think
of that—and the days. You will rest
your cheek on your hand. Was there
a time when someone tapped lightly
and went on by? There was. There is.
It is right now, this time.

II

We can reach the mountains,
but the air that comes will
touch with a lasting touch.
The crown of the sun won't move.
In an album somewhere the rocks
get ready, suspended. I hurry among
them conducting their frozen song.
Be my witness, wanderers. Call the bird calls home.
Day, move under my hand.

III

A person happens to glance your way,
someone, anyone, a girl, a man,
a woman. That person has become
weighted. You cannot let the glance
just end. It does, though. You go
on—hundreds of these chance looks
extend into a crowded future never
letting go. There is a weight in the world.

Reaching new things, you have to leave the old.

4 JULY

Meditation

Trying like someone called in the night
and muffled by sleep, wanting to wake
and be clear, you hurry the words
but then they don't know, don't know.

And you fall back and in the morning
you say, "Someone called." But you can't
remember the message or what you said.
By noon it is all a part of everything.

That ring around you, the barrier thought
can't get over, it shows up as those
crisscrossed part-knowings, each one
partly holding down the next, but almost clear.

When you can't get out, you sing. Wave
by wave as the ocean counts the sand,
you open and open the world, and in your cell
the stars stand forth. They are, you are—

And being is a shining thing.

6 JULY

A Farewell Letter to Whoever Finds It

Every morning when light gives back
all there is, I turn from inside and
look along the earth where some have taken
high place and some blame them and renounce
the world, and all are clenched where
they are, sustained.

I wouldn't want to tell them another game.

Leaving my books and all of that
intellectual catnip, I walk around.
Much of this town is play: the man
whose big truck has dog hutches along
the side, the woman who trains horses,
tourists with cowboy boots. . . .

I wouldn't want to tell them another game.

We take what we like of all
this changeable time. Everything we own
can last, become still, be a clear
part of the great world. Look at it
this way—it was always ours.
Some of us keep remembering.

This far stone floats through the sky.

23 JULY

Books

A leaf drops down. A face betrayed
speaks through its words. A voice
leads out. No one follows.
We go back and play the salmon through
the falls again, or have some year
come over the bars at us, then
be less than it was, or more.

We want to tell so fast that
the story leads the world: books
on the war blockade before submarines
can dive. I tell my face
to watch out. I live in the shade
of myself. What can I do for all
who will need me tomorrow?

I go back through the book, fending
the past, and fall where the world
is going.

I AUGUST

For Wallace Stevens

He celebrates what celebrates, a party
for the party-goer, to loose the reins
and follow—every horse play horse
across a world that says
not to be, or be.

So—take a hand, sing it. Forward—
not too fast! The kind of spin
the world has holds us still,
then sends us out
where dreams begin.

Just loose the reins and
stamp and follow.

2 AUGUST

TWO DRAFTS OF A POEM:
"TWO OF A KIND"

S OMETIMES A SINGLE PAGE of manuscript can open a window into unfamiliar areas of a poet's thought. The two facsimile pages reproduced here are the manuscript and typescript drafts of a poem written (with a dedication to Nelson Bentley) in 1988, and published in *The Seattle Review* the following year. The manuscript page from 29 May 1988 contains three poem drafts. The first, broken off before completion, is an early memory, one of a number of accounts of near-death experiences. Other memories of this kind appear to have surfaced in poems of the late 1980s. For example, the poem written two days later, on the 31st, "This Is for Everyone," begins "Avalanche. / Been buried, been part of the earth." This in turn is a memory of the collapsed trench described in "Life Work" (written 1986, and published in *Passwords* and *The Way It Is*). And again recently, another reminder of mortality had visited the poet and some of his friends on the 6th May. The occasion was described in the unpublished poem "One Day:"

Not yet really afraid when the floor shook
we all looked at each other. Then the chandelier
swayed. Was this the time? . . .

I held it all still while I turned back to my friends
and caught across each face a new wince, a truth:
All of this would be gone if I should die some day.

The abandoned fragment of May 29th gives way to a complete draft of a poem celebrating life in a tiny detail, a grass leaf stuck to the heel. It was first titled "Among the Grasses," then "Grass," and finally, after the change from a singular to a plural subject, "Two of a Kind." It may be significant, in light of the previous fragment, that the only idea not carried forward from the manuscript to the typed draft is an oblique reference to death: "And cool night waits all of my days." The poem leaves unexplained what has rendered the two friends "immune" in the first stanza, or what assures their innocence in the last, but there is no doubt about the confident acceptance of the whole range of experience: the hours, the friends, the great cauldron burning bright, the great shock of the world, and finally the gift of the two selves.

The third poem on the page, from the following day, and (like the first) never typed and sent out, shares some of the themes of those from May 29th. It begins with a phrasing borrowed from a frequently-anthologized poem of May 1967, twenty-one years earlier, "Earth Dweller" [*Allegiances* and *The Way It Is*]:

It was all the clods at once become
precious; it was the barn, and the shed,
and the windmill, my hands, the crack
Arlie made in the ax handle: oh, let me stay
here humbly, forgotten, to rejoice in it all;
let the sun casually rise and set.

A similar excitement fills this fragment:

It will be all the leaves become
tongues, every hill shouting. It will be
night sprung into the sky with its darkness.

"Earth Dweller" ended with a much-quoted statement of comfort with the world's gifts:

The world speaks everything to us.
It is our only friend.

Twenty-one years later, the poet accepts the same gifts, yet with resignation:

What the years [packed], that convolution of snake
without end, will return sudden, turned into now,
no past and the spread that made it bearable,
no future and the perspective that allows pain to be art.

And the page has one last surprise, an aphorism that calls into question the relationship between memory and imagination:

Does it make any difference that what I saw really happened?

Of the three poems on this page, the first may well be an invention, the reverie of a persona; the second is surely a true reminiscence of a walk in the company of Nelson Bentley; and the third removes "the perspective that allows pain to be art." No wonder Stafford felt free to raise the double question: how much do we depend on the truth of what we experience, and how much less true is an invention? As readers, we can guess at his answer to the question, already signaled in the title of the Collected Poems of 1977: *Stories That Could Be True.*

29 May 1988

Bicycle downhill, no hands, I lived
so many times the rats ran away
growling. But one year I died — a truck,
a hole in the pavement. They brought me back,
a pessimistic doctor, a hospital.
That luck had built, odds

Among the grasses
I found on that hill one strange leaf
stuck to my heel, and I walked immune
after that day.

all hours come swarming, parts of
what is; all purple, all prickle return
into the great cauldron a ouzel brings —
And cool night writes all of my tears.
from that strange glass all of this
come: every dark, the world can girl,
but also this tonight being a all
walking through this town with stuff on my heel,
even noisily grass

It will be like this

of the world

the life of
being

an innocent walker with grass on
my heel.

30 may
It will be (like) all the leaves become
tongues, every hill shouting. It will be
night opening into the sky with its darkness.
That the years without, that convolution of packer
without end, will return sudden, turned into now,
there no past and the spread that makes it bearable,
or future and the perspective that allows pain to be art.
Does it make any difference that what I say happened?
really

packed
completed

Two of a Kind

Found on the same hill, one strange leaf
stuck to our heels. And we walked immune
after that day.

Hours came swarming, parts of what is;
all people, all friends, burned bright
in the great cauldron of sunset.

From that strange leaf all of this came:
the great shock of the world, but also
this gift, our two selves—

Walking,
innocent,
grass on our heels.

SHARON OLDS

AN AESTHETICS OF BEAUTY AND THE SOMATIC POEMS OF SHARON OLDS: WHEN FLESH BECOMES WORD

Linden Ontjes

—*"The body does not lie." Martha Graham*

"The sources of poetry are in the spirit seeking completeness." Muriel Rukeyser

*S*HARON OLDS knows the world through her body; her somatic poems challenge the reader to reexperience the world with her through the use of kinesthetic imagery. After praising Olds's art, some critics turn quickly to her poetry's utilitarian effects: bearing political witness to injustice; scriptotherapy; or feminist proof that the personal is political.[1] Other critics remain mired in an exhausting debate over first principles. Can the egotistical "I" of confessional narrative speak the truth? What are the implications of adopting body as subject matter?[2] This essay argues for a different approach: understanding the dynamics of the somatic poem through an aesthetics of beauty.

What do I mean by the somatic poem and why apply an aesthetics of beauty? Olds's somatic poems closely describe the human body in all its imperfect glory and, from a first person perspective, invite the reader to experience what the body knows. A somatic poem acts as a sort of poetic equivalent to the direct evidence rule: the body speaks for itself and its direct testimony is the original, the truth. From her first collec-

Sharon, age 4, Berkeley, California, ca. 1946

tion *Satan Says* through her recently published work *The Unswept Room*, Olds's poems startle with visual acuity. Her poems accumulate layered sensory detail, often in a series of tight close-ups, then move forward through linked chains of kinesthetic imagery. As in contemporary figurative painting and feminist art criticism,[3] Olds assumes that bodies are beautiful. Not because one among many may adhere to the Classical definition of proportional beauty, but because every individual body, in all its particularity and knowledge, is beautiful. In Aristotelian terms, the "made thing" or poem, has as its "final cause" or purpose, the effect achieved by its inherent operation. The inherent operation of Olds's somatic poems presents us with what Elaine Scarry[4] calls the three sites of beauty: the generative object or body, the beholder—both Olds and reader—and the creation, the poem.

1 / The Body as the First Site of Beauty

As originally defined, "aesthetics" held closely to its etymological origins: the Greek word for sense experience leading to knowledge.[5] For Olds, full knowledge of beauty can be apprehended through its external manifestations and its attachment to a particular object. In poems such as "The Knowing," "A Vision," "Little Things," and many others, Olds asserts that close observation and sensory impressions are how we know beauty.[6] This position leads Olds to cast aside poetic decorum and

New mittens, San Francisco

depict as beautiful, even sacred, a used diaphragm,[7] pubic hair matted with dried semen and vaginal fluids,[8] and aspects of an aging woman's body that "if a young woman saw on herself she would / scream, as if at a horror movie."[9] Beauty is not a matter of artistic good taste but full knowledge. Olds makes the reader an accessory by re-creating the act of beholding. Thus, the reader "contracts (her) own submission—having established by free consent, a reciprocal, contractual alliance with the image."[10]

Still, can knowledge equal beauty when Olds's close descriptive eye turns to the horrific: the speaker of these poems is tied to a chair as a child, is burned and pissed on, and survives a father's alcoholism and a mother's abuse? I would argue that these poems fall within a contemporary tradition of transgressive beauty which encompasses the dual qualities of attraction and repulsion. Beauty is "the agency that causes visual pleasure in the beholder—by showing us something of which we may not approve in such a way that we cannot resist it. The evocation of pleasure through discomfort is . . . a deliberate form of transgression."[11] This transgressive form of beauty relies upon the willingness of poet and reader to overturn the Classical definition of beauty[12] linked to good-

ness and the definition of its opposite, the ugly linked to evil.[13] By writing about "the ugly" so lavishly that we unwillingly find the poem itself
beautiful, Olds invites us into a conscious or subconscious awareness
of the nature of good and evil, participation and complicity. Nothing less
is at stake than the apprehension of the sacred, nothing less than the
definition of beauty.

2 / The Beholder as the Second Site of Beauty

As discussed above, Olds draws the reader into a joint act of beholding beauty. There, as Olds and reader experience an overwhelming sur-
feit of sensory intake, i.e. beauty, a crucial cognitive process occurs.[14] Scarry
argues that this cognitive process leads the joint-beholders toward the
sacred and the just. First, upon viewing the generative object, here the
body, the beholder experiences the conviction that the object is beauty:
unique, incomparable, unprecedented. Then, the beholder experiences
error: while attempting to comprehend by describing, the mind makes
comparisons. How can an object compared be unique? Yet error is tran-
scended when the mind reaches back and back for the comparison that
will capture best the beautiful object and finds that it has reached the
sacred. The feature of "unprecedentedness" stays stable across two
objects.[15] "Something beautiful fills the mind yet invites the search for
something beyond itself, something larger or something of the same
scale with which it needs to be brought into relation."[16] Finally, the
beholder experiences a radical decentering of self which serves a social
good by creating a desire for justice.[17]

A poem's features should reinforce the operation of an aesthetic of
beauty and make it more available to perception.[18] For Olds, these features begin with the overall action of the poem. Olds's somatic poems
are Aristotelian actions animated by a unifying final purpose—a poem
"that both imitates an action and is itself an action."[19] What has been
called the lyrical epiphany in poetry, with the obligatory closing salute,
is nothing more than an enactment of Scarry's cognitive process of
encountering beauty.

Olds's poetry contains multiple images which describe the poem's
subject (using simile and metaphor), develop associative chains which
move the poem forward, and call forth a physical response from the
reader: kinesthetic imagery. Olds defines metaphors (as opposed to sim-

Sharon at Boulder Creek, California

iles) as literal equations and so, claims not to use them in her work.[20] This essay uses the term "metaphor" in the more generalized sense of a trope which figuratively equates two objects through imagery. Whether we label Olds's poetic devices of imagery as similes, metaphors or kinesthetic imagery, these devices lead the reader through an experience like Scarry's cognitive process. To understand this mimetic, let us look at just one example among many. In "Frosted Elfin," the speaker of the poem views her pubes as a child's slipper conch, the brown purple fur of a woman's pansy, her mother's crown of thorns with a spear's slash, a possible sideways Bridalveil Falls. "But my love says / it is a wing, a pair of wings wherein / we fly to paradise, and through it,/ and to what lies beyond it." Alicia Ostriker has written brilliantly about the function of metaphor, sometimes referring to Olds's work directly.[21] Ostriker's description of how a metaphor operates parallels the beholder's cognitive process described by Scarry. Beauty is "a greeting": the beholder's delight comes from a sense that "a welcoming thing has entered into and consented to, your being in its midst."[22] In metaphor, the two objects compared remain separate yet the distance between them is canceled by the recognition of a likeness "whereby each illuminates some inner truth belonging to the other."[23] This dynamic unavoidably invites comparison to falling in love or more literally, to sexual intercourse and the postcoital moment which figures so prominently in Olds's work.[24] Indeed, Ostriker states that Olds, the poet, achieves "self-integration through visionary integration."[25]

This dynamic of contact between bodies as a reconciliation of dualities that leads to enlightenment is often overt in Olds's work. In "The Source," there's "nothing between us / but our bodies, naked, and when those dissolve, / nothing between us." Then, in a sequence of images, Olds resolves dualities between father, daughter, brothers, sisters, and self by returning to the Source: semen. Olds variously refers to her somatic approach toward the world and the word as a prayer[26], a psalm[27], and a vision.[28] In "Prayer," Olds begins "Let me be faithful to the central meanings": and moves back and forth between the physical intimacy of giving birth and having sex, using linked kinesthetic images. Both acts represent a submersion of self into the body's "holy" demands. Olds ends, "[L]et me not forget: / each action, each word / taking its beginning from these." "Am and Am Not," places the soul firmly in the body; a soul made all but corporeal by a linked chain of associations from vagina, to penis, to throat, to belly. "[S]he is asleep in there, vertical / undulant one, she is dancing upright in her dream." For Olds, knowledge of the sacred seems unlikely without knowledge of the body: a sort of reversal of Eve's Fall from Grace once she bites into forbidden fruit. In "Sex Without Love," Olds asks:

> How do they come to the
> come to the   come to the   God   come to the
> still waters, and not love
> the one who came there with them, light
> rising slowly as steam off their joined
> skin?

Neither a church nor a minister is necessary for the sacred wedding vow: "In truth, we had married / that first night, in bed, we had been / married by our bodies."[29] Going Song of Solomon one better, Olds finds, less metaphorically than ideologically, that the body stands in for the church.

Issues of complicity, shame and guilt arise constantly in Olds's poems of the telling incident and poems of relationship of self to

Sharon Olds with Lucille Clifton, September 2002

Sharon Olds with Ruth Stone, Sheffield, Vermont. Photo by Barbara K. Bristol

world.[30] In the somatic poems, however, when guilt asserts itself, the body defeats it: another move toward the sacred as forgiveness.[31] Olds sees "the whole body as blameless and lovely."[32] The husband of the speaker in the poem rescues her from the "Calvinist shudder[s]" of her parents, by learning with her that the senses, the body are pungent and part of "the sweet / grease of life." She is his "girl in oil" who has awakened "from the dream of judgment."[33] In the most prolonged example of this approach, Olds devotes an entire book, *The Father,* to resolving a tormented daughter-father relationship by close attention to and attendance upon his dying body. One quotation will suffice; in "The Look," Olds gives her father a back rub as if "his body were his soul."

Some of the poems in *The Unswept Room* anticipate a future crisis, presumably divorce, by begging to stay in the body. Toward the end of the book, several somatic poems end with heartbreaking lines, using the plasticity of time in poems as a dramatic device. In "Past Future Imperfect," Olds speaking from the present looks back on a time when they were "lying together, then, / jetsam, high tide line" knowing now that they had "weeks left. I'll look / back and see the silence, the ignorance / moving in the air around them, while the one who / knew gathered strength, and the one who did not / know kept vigil." Again, in "If, Someday," she anticipates her self looking backward at a time of bliss. She begs in "Psalm" devoted to their lovemaking, "Do not / tell me this could end. Do not tell me." She opens the book with a wish "to eat a last meal in her old neighborhood," an epigraph by Adrienne Rich. The closing and title poem, "The Unswept," presents the poems in this collection as crumbs dropped on the floor after a feast. The reader must await Olds's next book to find out what happens after the central action of the body; intimacy as an expression of love in a first marriage, no longer applies. As Olds insists, her poems are not strictly autobiographical[34] but the trope is so closely informed by experience that we are left stranded with her when "A Time of Passion" ends:

> Locked together, or one
> finger of one touching one
> nipple of the other, we were flying head
> first into the earth and out, as if practicing.
> It never crossed my mind that he no longer
> loved me, that we had left the realm of love.

3 / The Creation as the Third Site of Beauty

Although Olds's poetry, as creation, must come from a maker's hand, Olds's transparent style removes her thumbprints. Olds uses common diction, vocabulary, and syntax, to preserve "natural speech." She limits her use of poetic devices, relying primarily upon kinesthetic imagery, as discussed above. Olds's titles serve merely as labels for the poems' subjects, common nouns such as mother, father, daughter, son. No gloss which sets Olds apart as a personae or expert separate from the experience related. By such transparency, Olds retains her close link to the reader as joint-beholder. In "The Changing Face of Common Intercourse," Marjorie Perloff argues that "natural speech" is another deliberate linguistic strategy, designed to manipulate the reader into a set of reactions by proving the speaker's authenticity as if only recording his actual sensations.[35] Manipulated or not, readers clearly approve. Even when they consciously recognize that Olds's work can never be direct speech taken as literal truth, they want to enter into the act of beholding with her in a deeply felt "aesthetic intimacy."[36] Olds's strategy of transparency serves her aesthetics: the first site of beauty, the body, dominates the act of beholding and the creation of poem. Accordingly, the poem's language must try to get as close to the body as possible without inserting itself between the generative object and its description.

Likewise, Olds writes in "organic form" meant to mimic the sensation of beholding beauty, rather than in one of the more stylized forms, ranging from the traditional to the deconstructionist. Her headlong poems create a rushed pace playing off against a slow and steady background beat of awe. Olds says, "The grid over which I discovered I have been improvising is a four-beat line, mostly in quatrains, much as in the Episcopalian hymn "A Mighty Fortress Is Our God.'" She often sets the pattern in the first four lines, then plays with it. "Another reason for the rush was my fear of self-censorship. I was sometimes afraid of what I was saying, so I had to hurry. Also, I wanted to look self-confident."[37] In poem after poem, collection after collection, Olds succeeds in bringing the body to the page. Her poems seize and hold the reader. Together, poet and reader experience an aesthetics of beauty in which Flesh is made Word.[38] Together in *The Unswept Room*, we encounter Body as Soul.

NOTES

1. For two outstanding collections of recent scholarship, see Kate Sontag and David Graham, eds. *After Confession: Poetry as Autobiography* (Saint Paul: Graywolf Press, 2001) and Molly McQuade, ed. *By Herself: Women Reclaim Poetry,* (Saint Paul: Graywolf Press, 2000). For a good overview of recent scholarly pub-

lications, see Maryjo Mahoney, "Women and Autobiography," *NWSA Journal* v. 13:1 (Spring 2001): 56; and Kathryn Kirkpatrick, "Poetry Matters," *NWSA Journal* v. 14:1 (Spring 2002): 185–196.

2. For a selection of negative criticism, see William Logan, "No Mercy," *New Criterion* v. 18:4 (December 1999): 60; Marjorie Perloff, "The Changing Face of Common Intercourse: Talk Poetry, Talk Show, and the Scene of Writing," in *Radical Artifice: Writing Poetry in the Age of Media* (Chicago and London: The University of Chicago Press, 1991); Adam Kirsch, "The Exhibitionist," *The New Republic* (Dec. 27, 1999): 38, and Louise Glück, "The Forbidden," in *After Confession*, 247.

3. Olga M. Viso, "Beauty and Its Dilemmas" in *Regarding Beauty: A View of the Late Twentieth Century* (Washington, D.C.: Hirshhorn Museum and Hatje Cantz Publishers, 1999), 102. See also Viso's discussion of artists Marlene Dumas and Kiki Smith, ibid., 101–104.

4. Elaine Scarry, *On Beauty and Being Just* (Princeton and Oxford: Princeton University Press, 1999).

5. Ibid., 89.

6. Olds's reliance upon imagery to carry poetic meaning, compares to what T.S. Eliot called the objective correlative, Ezra Pound the Image, Robert Bly the Deep Image, and to William Carlos Williams's Imagism.

7. Sharon Olds, "Diaphragm Aria" in *The Unswept Room* (New York: Alfred A. Knopf, 2002), 44.

8. "The Releasing" in ibid., 42.

9. "The Older" in ibid., 68.

10. Arthur C. Danto, "Beauty for Ashes," in *Regarding Beauty*, 185.

11. David Hickey, *The Invisible Dragon: Four Essays on Beauty* (Los Angeles: Art Issues Press, 1993).

12. David Hickey quoted by Olga Viso, "Beauty and Its Dilemmas," in *Regarding Beauty*, 97.

13. Viso, ibid, 87–89. Classics held that "beauty was a quality present in objects, possessing identifiable characteristics and forms, and they quantified beauty in terms of conceptual formalisms such as order, symmetry and proportion." They looked to nature as a model and sought to rationalize beauty in a formula of ratios and proportions. Selective beauty was an ideal composite of these deductions.

14. Scarry, *On Beauty*, 117.

15. Ibid., 24.

16. Ibid., 29.

17. Ibid., 117.

18. In a conversation with Neal Benezra, David Hickey said that in coming years, beauty will not be "an attribute of objects but a pattern of response." Neal Benezra, "The Misadventures of Beauty," in *Regarding Beauty*, 36.

19. Scarry, *On Beauty*, 102.

20. Sharon Olds interview on *Fresh Air with Terry Gross*, KUAC-FM 89.9, National Public Radio, September 25, 2002.

21. Alicia Ostriker, *Stealing the Language: The Emergence of Women's Poetry in America* (Boston: Beacon Press, 1986), 194. See also, Alicia Ostriker, "A Meditation on Metaphor," in Molly McQuade, ed. *By Herself: Women Reclaim Poetry* (Saint Paul: Graywolf Press, 2000), 157–162. See *Stealing the Language* for

Ostriker's development of the argument that women's use of the body as subject matter in literature can help transform literature and politics through the reunification of false dualisms. See pp. 111, 95, 101, 196–197. This argument is derived in part from Adrienne Rich's ground breaking work, *Of Woman Born: Motherhood as Experience and Institution* (W. W. Norton & Company, New York, 1976), pp. 97, 101–102.

22. Scarry, *On Beauty*, 23.

23. Ostriker, "A Meditation on Metaphor" in *By Herself*, 159.

24. For example, Olds, "True Love," in *The Wellspring* (New York: Alfred A. Knopf, 1996), 88.

25. Ostriker, *Stealing the Language*, 194.

26. Olds, "Prayer" in *Satan Says* (Pittsburgh: University of Pittsburgh Press, 1980), 72.

27. Olds, "Psalm" in *The Father* (New York: Alfred A. Knopf, 1992), 29.

28. Olds, "A Vision" in *Blood, Tin, Straw* (New York: Alfred A. Knopf, 1999), 51.

29. Olds, *The Unswept Room*, 30.

30. Olds, *The Unswept Room*, 3, 88, 43, 19, 79, 97. In a series of "telling incident poems," Olds suffers guilt from a range of sources. In "Unknown," transitive guilt applies to Olds after her relative drives drunk and kills a family in a collision. In "The Headline," Olds feels empathetic guilt for a son who killed a father. In "The Clasp," she feels individual guilt for a harsh moment with her daughter. In several "self in the world" poems, Olds feels racial guilt.

31. See Olds define personhood as body in "This" and "The Month of June: 13 1/2" in *The Golden Cell*, 63, 86. In "The Quest," Olds treasures "Every gold cell of her body" and protection of a daughter's body stands in for all forms of maternal protection (p. 70). Elsewhere, life is a physical entity, compared to food (pp. 27, 74, 77, 81). Lastly, all knowledge is derived from knowledge of how another's body acts (p. 90).

32. Olds, "Sunday Night," *The Unswept Room*, 15.

33. Olds, "Fish Oil," ibid., 70.

34. Dinitia Smith, "The Examined Life, Without Punctuation," *New York Times*, 9 September 1999, sec. E 1.

35. Marjorie Perloff, "The Changing Face of Common Intercourse: Talk Poetry, Talk Show, and the Scene of Writing," in *Radical Artifice: Writing Poetry in the Age of Media* (Chicago and London: The University of Chicago Press, 1991), 30.

36. Billy Collins, "My Grandfather's Tackle Box: The Limits of Memory-Driven Poetry," *Poetry* v.178:5 (August 2001): 278; See also, Ostriker, *Stealing the Language*, 205. "But women's poetry is in fact filled with the idea that the reader is and should be engaged in an active personal transaction with the writer. The imperative of intimacy may finally account for the confessional or self-exploratory mode in women's poetry precisely because of the intimacy this mode imposes on the audience. One cannot read, for example, Sexton or Wakoski without feeling that the objectivity of readership is under attack. In both cases the pull on the audience is directly related to an erotic ideology."

37. Laurel Blossom, "Sharon Olds: An Interview," *Poets & Writers Magazine*, v. 21:5 (September / October 1993): 36.

38. Ostriker, *Stealing the Language*, 198–199.

LOOKING BACK AT SOME REVISIONS

Sharon Olds

*T*HE HONOR of Colleen's invitation sort of blurred my attention to the word *retrospective*. Then, when I woke up to the concept, it wasn't clear to me how to do a retrospective without autobiography— and of course I don't *have* an autobiography! Then I thought of some poems of mine which I had revised after their appearance in a book, and I thought maybe I could look back at that.

I don't remember anyone telling me what was wrong with the poem in *Satan Says* (1980) called "That Year"; what I remember is rereading it years later and feeling repelled and dismayed by its foolishness. It was written when I was maybe thirty, and I was maybe forty-five when I went back and tried to lay down a level and a compass atop it. This is the revised version that appeared in the next printing.

That Year

The year of the mask of blood, my father
hammering on the glass door to get in

was the year they found her body in the hills,
in a shallow grave, naked, white as
mushroom, partially decomposed,
raped, murdered, the girl from my class.

That was the year my mother took us
and hid us so we would not be there
when she told him to leave; so there wasn't another
tying by the wrist to the chair,

or denial of food, not another
forcing of food, the head held back,
down the throat at the restaurant,
the shame of vomited buttermilk
down the sweater with its shame of new breasts.
That was the year
I started to bleed,
crossing over that border in the night,
and in Social Studies, we came at last
to Auschwitz, in my ignorance
I felt as if I recognized it
like my father's face, the face of a guard
turning away—or worse yet
turning toward me.

The symmetrical piles of white bodies,
the round, white breast-shapes of the heaps,
the smell of the smoke, the dogs the wires the
rope the hunger. This had happened to people,
just a few years ago,
in Germany, the guards Protestants
like my father and me, but in my dreams,
every night, I was one of those
about to be killed. It had happened to six million
Jews, to Jesus's family
I was not in—and not everyone
had died, and there was a word for them
I wanted, in my ignorance,
to share some part of, the word *survivor*.

    Some time later, I came back to a hotel room, in Boston, from a reading where I'd been introduced as "one of our leading incest poets." Magic Johnson was on the T. V., speaking for the first time about his HIV—I sat a while with that great face and demeanor. That evening the fresh dawning on me of the carelessness of my writing seemed to fill the hotel room—except for that face of truth and courage on the screen.

    Hard to believe, now, that I had not, before that, thought of a reader who might read the poem "What if God" and believe what the poem said,

that the actual, legs, as well as the soul legs, of the child in the poem
were "pried apart." That evening I felt I was meeting my melodrama
and entitlement face to face, and went back to the poem to see what I
could do with it (I guess, throughout, the whole business of actual and
imagined has not been too clear to me). This was the revised version.

What If God

And what if God had been watching, when my mother
came into my room, at night, to lie down on me
and pray and cry? What did he do when her
long adult body rolled on me
like lava from the top of the mountain
and the magma popped from her ducts, and my bed
shook from the tremors, the cracking of my nature
across? What was He? Was He a bison
to lower His partly extinct head
and suck His Puritan phallus while we cried
and prayed to Him, or was He a squirrel
reaching through her hole in my shell, His arm
up to the elbow in the yolk of my soul
stirring, stirring the gold? Or was He
a kid in Biology, dissecting me
while she held my brain carapace apart
so He could fork out the eggs, or was He a man
entering, while she pried my spirit
open in the starry dark—
she said that all we did was done in His sight
so He must have seen her weep, into my
hair, and slip my soul from between my
ribs like a tiny hotel soap, He
washed His hands of me as I washed my
hands of Him. Is there a God in the house?
Is there a God in the house? Then reach down
and take that woman off that child's body,
take that woman by the nape of the neck like a young cat,
and lift her up, and deliver her over to me.

Some while after that, my high school offered me a reading on what was to be my fiftieth birthday—it seemed a great way to leave town and avoid facing that zero! I'd had some correspondence with the Creative Writing teacher, and with the new Women of Color Club of this old New England boarding school, and the trip would give me a chance to have a meal with them.

It was very moving to me to be there, and at dessert I asked if anyone wanted to ask me anything about studying Creative Writing, or about the New York University graduate program, or about Poetry, and the president of the club said, graciously, "Yes—we'd like to talk to you about the racism in your poems."

Now, I almost have to laugh at the picture of this rather pompous grey-haired secret-birthday-girl white girl schoolteacher type hearing that! I said, "What a good idea, tell me where it is and we'll see what we can do about it." And they walked me through "On the Subway," helping me see it as they saw it, and in the old, cold dorm room that night I worked on the revision in the margins of my reading copy.

On the Subway

The young man and I face each other.
His feet are huge, in black sneakers
laced with white in a complex pattern like a
set of intentional scars. We are stuck on
opposite sides of the car, a couple of
molecules stuck in a rod of light
rapidly moving through darkness. He has
or my white eye imagines he has
the casual cold look of a mugger,
alert under hooded eyelids. He is wearing
red, like the inside of the body
exposed. I am wearing old fur, the
whole skin of an animal taken and
used. I look at his raw face,
he looks at my dark coat, and I don't
know if I am in his power—
he could take my coat so easily, my

briefcase, my life—
or if he is in my power, the way I am
living off his life, eating the steak he may
not be eating, as if I am taking
the food from his mouth. And he is black
and I am white, and without meaning or
trying to I must profit from his darkness,
the way he absorbs the murderous beams of the
nation's heart, as black cotton
absorbs the heat of the sun and holds it. There is
no way to know how easy this
white skin makes my life, this
life he could break so easily, the way I
think his back is being broken, the
rod of his soul that at birth was dark and
fluid, rich as the heart of a seedling
ready to thrust up into any available light.

Then my attention wandered to two other poems in *The Gold Cell,*
which now looked to me exaggerated and a little masochistic in their
voluptuary self-pity. If poems written around age forty could now have
their act cleaned up by an older and hopefully less Puritan hand, I would
try to bring that about.

Now I Lay Me

It is a fine prayer, *Now I lay me*
down to sleep, the power of the child
taking herself up in her arms
and laying herself down on her bed
as if she were her own mother,
Now I lay me down to sleep,
I pray the Lord my soul to keep,
her hands folded knuckle by knuckle,
feeling her heart beating in the knuckles.
Knees on the fine dark hair-like hardwood
beams of the floor, she commended herself

to the care of some reliable keeper
so all night there might be a part of her no one
could touch. Unless while God had that part
she did not have it, but lay there a raw
soulless animal for someone to do dirt on . . .
If I should die before I wake seemed
possible some nights, the father with the blood
on his face, the mother down to eighty-two pounds, it was a
mark of doom and a benison
to be able to say *I pray the Lord*
my soul to take—the chance that, dead,
she would be safe for eternity,
which was much longer than one of those nights—
she herself could see, each morning, the
blessing of the dawn, like some true god coming,
she could get out of bed, and wade in the false
goodness of another day.
It was all fine except for the word *take,*
word with the *k* like a claw near the end of it.
What if the Lord were another one of those takers,
what if the Lord were no bigger than her father,
what if those noises through the wall were not
her mother and father struggling to do it
or not do it, what if those noises
were the sound of the Lord wrestling with her father
on the round, bedroom rug, and what if the
Lord, who did not eat real food,
got weaker, and her father, with all he ate
and drank, got stronger, what if the Lord
lost? *God bless Mommy and Daddy*
and Sister and Brother and Grama and Grampa
in Heaven, and then the light went out,
the last of the uneasy kisses,
and then she was alone in the dark,
and the darkness started to grow there, in her room,
as it liked to do, and then the night began.

San Francisco

When we'd go to San Francisco, my father
seemed to seek out the steepest streets,
he would sit behind the wheel and smile
to himself, his face red as a lobster
at Fisherman's Wharf after they drop it
green and waving into boiling water.
His eyes would snap as if popping from a pod,
his black hair would smoke in that salty
air, he would tilt the nose of the car
up and press on the gas. We'd begin
the ascent, nearly vertical,
tires about to lose their grip on those
slanted cobbles, he'd inch us up, like an
engineering experiment
we'd barely rise, till we hung in space from
nothing, like driving up an elevator shaft,
the black pull of the earth's weight
sucking us back, he'd slow down more and
more, we'd barely rise past buildings
pressed to the side of the precipice
like trees up the face of a cliff. I do not
remember my mother, but she was there,
this may have been for her. As we neared the
top he went slower, and slower, and then
shifted into first, I think he was smiling,
and in that silence between gears
I would break, weeping and peeing, the fluids of my
body bursting out like people from the
windows of a burning high-rise.
We'd hit the peak, tilt level,
but what was life when the man who had made my
body liked to dangle it over space as if
teasing me with death. He sat there sparkling, a
refuse dump, the wheel loose
in his hands, the reins of my life held slack.

We'd climb out, my knees shaking
and trickled on, to look at the world spread
out at our feet as if we owned it,
as if we had power over our lives,
as if my father had control of himself
or I of my fate—
              far below us,
blue and dazzling, the merciless cold
beauty of the Bay, my whole saved life ahead of me.

Then this fall, 2002, a poet to whom I'd sent my new book, *The Unswept Room*, wrote me that, as a Jew, he was offended by the poem "The Window." It seemed to him to be a WASP mother-daughter poem using the Holocaust as background scenery. When I first hear a criticism of my work, I tend immediately to see that the critic is absolutely right. I had passed that poem by ten or so poets before I'd first sent it to a magazine, knowing that I couldn't see the poem from outside my own experience. Now I went to the same ten, and an additional ten poets, and scientists, and psychoanalysts, and scholars for help. After a series of, for me, extraordinary conversations, I was able to let go of my initial breast-beating rewrite, which actually smelled even more of poet's narcissus than the old version. (Lucille Clifton called the lines of that kind of rewrite "wink-wink nudge-nudge" lines, in which the poet says to the reader "this is how I want you to see me, I'm a pretty good person really.")

None of the colleagues I went to for help saw the poem in need of a different ending, or spirit. Each one said moving, complex, and plain common sense things about history, poetry, art and life, Jew and Gentile and Muslim and pagan. One said she thought the end was O.K. but the part about sanctuary was a little sanctimonious. Another said he'd never understood the part about "the ark consumed"—the Ark of the Covenant? Noah's? Had it been consumed? The poem in the hands of many workers struggled toward a better form. (And it's hard for me to believe now that it wasn't until the last moment—the edited proofs for the British edition were due—that I decided there shouldn't be any laughter— *mein Gott*, as the grandmother in C. K. Williams's triolet would say.)

The Window

Our daughter calls me, in tears—like water
being forced, under great pressure, from densest
stone. *I am mad at you,* she whispers.
You said in a poem that you're a survivor,
that's O. K., but you said that you are
a Jew, when you're not, that's so cheap. You're right,
I say, *you're so right. Did you see the Holocaust*
movie, she asks, in a stifled voice,
there's a window on the third floor of the barracks
and I know it's a little bathroom, I used it
in Poland the day I was there, and she sobs,
a sound like someone swallowing gravel.
And the rooms hadn't been dusted, *it was*
as if everything was left as it was,
and some of the same molecules
might be there in the room. And there were exhibit cases,
one with hair—hair. In my mind
I see the landscape, behind glass,
the human hills and mountains, the intimate
crowning of a private life
now a case of clouds, detritus,
meshes. *And there were eyeglasses,*
a huge pile of liking to read,
and of liking books, and being able to see, and
then . . . then there was a display case
of suitcases, and an Orthodox guide was
taking a tour through. She is able, while she cries,
to speak, in a small, stopped-down voice
as if a pebble could talk. *He was telling*
a class of Bar Mitzvah boys
to look at the names on the suitcases—
some of them had believed . . . they were going . . .
on vacation, she says—or something like it,
I cannot hear each word
but sometimes just the creak of rock

on water. I do not want to ask her
to repeat. She seems to be saying she had to
leave the room, to find a place
to cry in, maybe the little bathroom,
I feel as if I am there, near her,
and am seeing, through her, the horror of the human,
as if she is transparent, holding
no gaze to herself. *There were people not
crying, just looking,* she says, then she says
so much about us is unbearable.
We talk a long time, we are coming back
up from inside some human ground,
I try to tell her it was not weakness
in her, that it was love she felt,
the helpless sacredness of each life, and the
dread of our species. *Yeah yeah,* she says,
in the low voice of someone lately
the young in the nest, maybe soon the nesting one,
within view the evidence
of the ark consumed, and no thought of herself
to distract her, nothing distracts her, not even
the breathing of her own body as she sees.

    Last is a poem from a year ago—fourteen months ago, September, 2001.

    With one co-worker I had had several conversations about a few lines in the middle of the poem. I thought it made clear sense to describe the speaker's former husband's present life as

unknown to me, unseen by me,
unheard, untouched—but known, seen,
heard, touched.

but my friend said it seemed as if these lines could be read as "unknown to the speaker—but really known to her, too; unseen by her—and yet in some way seen by her, too."

    I argued stubbornly against "overclarifying" and "spelling things out too explicitly," but at the last moment (though just too late to change it

in *The Atlantic*) I saw that it wasn't clear, and I understood that something in me hadn't wanted it to be clear, and I changed it. And now, when
I read the poem aloud, when going on rounds, during my Poetry rota-
tion, I slow down a little—to get it said, and said, and said (sung).

A Week Later

A week later, I said to a friend: I don't
think I could ever write about it.
Maybe in a year I could write something.
There is something in me maybe someday
to be written; now it is folded, and folded,
and folded, like a note in school. And in my dream
someone was playing jacks, and in the air there was a
huge, thrown, tilted jack
on fire. And when I woke up, I found myself
counting the days since I had last seen
my husband—only two years, and some weeks,
and hours. We had signed the papers and come down to the
ground floor of the Chrysler Building,
the intact beauty of its lobby around us
like a king's tomb, on the ceiling the little
painted plane, in the mural, flying. And it
entered my strictured heart, this morning,
slightly, shyly as if warily,
untamed, a greater sense of the sweetness
and plenty of his ongoing life,
unknown to me, unseen by me,
unheard by me, untouched by me,
but known by others, seen by others,
heard, touched. And it came to me,
for moments at a time, moment after moment,
to be glad for him that he is with the one
he feels was meant for him. And I thought of my
mother, minutes from her death, eighty-five
years from her birth, the almost warbler
bones of her shoulder under my hand, the

eggshell skull, as she lay in some peace
in the clean sheets, and I could tell her the best
of my poor, partial love, I could sing her
out, with it, I saw the luck
and the luxury of that hour.

RICK BASS

FITTING IN THE WEST:
A CONVERSATION WITH RICK BASS

Douglas Heckman

*I*MET RICK AT HIS HOME in the early afternoon.
His two daughters—Mary Katherine and Lowry—were in town attending the one-room school, while his wife—Elizabeth—was off for a cross country ski. The December sun was low-angled, but had warmed the day enough to cause melt. Over the howl of his hounds, Rick told me I was lucky to have caught a sunny day, the Yaak receiving only a handful of such days over the winter. We sat in the living room to talk; he offered me the couch, a seat with a fine view.

Douglas Heckman: In an NPR interview in November 2002, you mentioned that "you'd rather be called a western writer than an eastern writer." Are you indeed a western writer?

Rick Bass: Absolutely a western writer. I can write anywhere and about anything, and I will and have, but I am absolutely a western writer. I remember my reaction when I used to hear Wallace Stegner or William Kittredge say that, and I'd think, oh man, don't sell yourself short. But I realize now that they weren't selling themselves short. It's not better or worse than eastern or southern; it's just what it is. It's a source of place and of strength.

Rick fishing, Texas, ca. 1963

DH: How do you define western writer?

RB: I wouldn't try and get too fancy with it. You could really tweak it out and come up with certifiable attributes. Nature writer/scholar Scott Slovic, had this anthology called *Being in the World*. It refers to the notion that for writers, writing is an act of how they are in the world, their way of being in the world. The way any other animal, any other species, fits in the world. I guess that might be a common theme of a western writer. This notion of fit that is so dramatically and readily observable in the west. An individual fitting in a place, or not fitting in a place. That notion of fitted-ness which is inherent drama and story. Place is story to a westerner. The way to a southerner, time is story: your family's history going down vertically through time. There is a place aspect of southern literature, but it's more a time- or history-based connection. But for a westerner—white westerners are so new here, in this landscape—that everything we see is about fit. We're just looking around with this open-mouthed wonder and awe at the power of the landscape and the puniness of humans upon it. It's the hubris of our hopes and lives against such massive space and geological time.

DH: Is there any such thing as an American writer?

RB: I suspect that there is. And that's not necessarily a good thing to say about somebody. Which is why I'm hesitating to list who might be one. For instance, I'd say we have an American president right now.

DH: Do you believe a writer like Annie Proulx, a writer whose books have focused on numerous regions of North America, could be classified as an American writer?

RB: I don't think of her as an American writer. I see how she could be represented as one, but she's so much better than that. There's no doubt in my mind that she could go to Russia and make a great novel. I was thinking more in terms of theme. The great American novel is *All the King's Men*. I think it's the destructiveness of rampant ambition. Politics or love: which do you choose? One guy chooses one and is broken. The other guy chooses the other and is broken. We just can't get it right.

DH: Richard Ford once commented that his novel, *The Ultimate Good Luck,* allowed him to move beyond a Faulkner influence and to become a writer in his own right. Is there a book, or a story, of yours which had a similar effect for you?

RB: No, there wasn't a conscious effort, but there was a story in *The Watch* that's set in Montana called "Choteau." It was written the first or second year I was up here; I think all the other stories were Texas and Mississippi stories. I think of those other stories in the collection as having a lot of green and yellow it in; in my mind, "Choteau" is just full of blues and whites. That story is a distinctive break from the jungle greens and yellows of the other stories.

DH: I loved the story, "Cats and Students, Bubbles and Abysses" from *The Watch*. Your bastardization of grammar, analogies, and all things writerly is wonderful. Where did you find the idea for this story?

RB: I remember desperately wanting to write and be a writer and be accepted as a writer and be successful as a writer; by successful I mean, making something of worth and power and import and value, all of those abstractions, art. And being surrounded by it in Mississippi, being stimulated by that, and yet frustrated by not knowing how to do that, not knowing how to step into that flow of art, of making pretty things, important things. So those two tensions are at work in that story, and a lot other similar, lesser, but parallel tensions. The whole magnified polarity of the south.

DH: It's also a very funny story.

Rick with his mother, Mary Lucy Robson Bass, Texas, 1958

RB: Humor is a weird thing. I've heard it said humor comes from despair. I think that's true. I write about one funny thing every three years. And it strikes me whenever I do it. But, there's long, dry spells between. Too long, too dry. It's a good sign when you can write something funny.

DH: It's not a skill?

RB: No. It's like a malarial fever. The funny stories get fewer and farther between. It gets more and more jaded, less and less innocent. I definitely tend to take stuff too seriously. But that's where humor comes from. You brood and brood for years and years and finally it pops out in one sentence and it's funny. But as far as calculating or manipulating or utilizing humor as a tool or technique, I could no more do that than I could control the weather.

DH: Do you read reviews of your own books?

RB: I see them sometimes. I used to worry about it, that it could tinker with the creative process, the self-awareness, and all that stuff, but I've seen so many thousands of reviews of my work. It's like how many thousands of times have you read the weather in the paper? Sometimes it's right, sometimes it's wrong, but whatever it is, it's all in the past and getting further and its not going to be much different from what's coming. I was laughing earlier, because really, what does it matter? My sales are really tiny. It's humbling to realize how few people read my work in book form.

DH: Even your fiction, particularly your new collection, *The Hermit's Story*?

RB: Oh yes. It's [*The Hermit's Story*] a significant investment of everything I've got and it's just invisible. It can be depressing. But it can also be liberating. It's good to remember that you don't write for other folks, you write for yourself. It's a cliché, but it's good. It reminds me of when I started off, when I was writing *The Watch*: I was twenty-some odd years old and nobody was reading me then either. I had fun sitting out at the table in the field working on stories and working with imagination rather than self-consciousness.

DH: Can your advocacy work, like the *Book of Yaak*, be effective without a large readership?

RB: Yes. The idea that there's this guy living back in the woods that wrote a book about where he lives and why the roadless lands should be protected, the fact that people know that's going on, is almost as effective as the fact that someone goes and reads the words. That's not how it is for fiction. You've got to read the story. You've got to experience the fiction to be able to relate to it. But to relate to a book like the *Book of Yaak* you don't even have to read it. It's enough just to know it's there, like a roadless area itself. Much like the wilderness idea that Wallace Stegner espoused.

DH: How do you split your time between writing fiction and non-fiction advocacy? Is there any sort of pattern to it?

RB: The catalyst or genesis for those transitions back and forth are, for me, really just an opportunity. When the activism demands or pulls me in unavoidably, then I'm there in it and with it and for it, and anytime I can escape it I duck out and work on fiction.

DH: Do you ever feel your fiction writing is being shortchanged due to your focus on environmental causes?

RB: I've been hugely fortunate in the last few years to be working with some folks locally, the Yaak Valley Forest Council, and we've got this great executive director. We can work together to buy me that time and I can stay close to the story emotionally. I used to just glimpse an opening and say, here comes two weeks of free time and I'm going to try and compress a story in there. To some degree that could be helpful, but more often than not, it wasn't. It was an artificial constraint

Rick Bass with his daughter, Lowry, 2000

on an organic being, the story itself wanting to be what it wanted to be. Now those boundaries have been made more flexible and supple as a result of the Forest Council's work.

DH: Do you find a similar pleasure in writing essays versus short stories?

RB: I think each year I feel less and less that pleasure of completion when I make an essay about the Yaak. It's just so hard to find new perspectives to argue that case. Whereas with fiction you're constantly, or should constantly be, creating something new, or observing something new, or discovering something new. Advocacy non-fiction is taxing. Your goal remains the same and either you're moving closer to it or being pushed back from it. It's pretty fixed. In fiction, the goal is not fixed. You don't even have a goal. You're just following what you see or sense.

DH: Michael Cunningham commented in an *Other Voices* interview that "your arm either moves like this (small movement) or it moves like this (large movement). You are, with very few exceptions, somebody who paints a certain size. If you're a big painter, your small paintings are going to look funny. And vice versa. It's the same with short stories and novels." Do you agree with this statement?

RB: I'll answer with another metaphor. I know that when I'm in the woods, I notice things that other folks don't notice. And I notice that other folks notice things that I don't notice. I'm a hunter and gatherer, not an agricultural kind of guy, not even an fisherman. I'm more terrestrial than aquatic. We're just keyed to different things. Either through instinct or experience or a combination of both.

DH: But you've written both stories and novels.

RB: I'm glad it's a free world. I'm glad that even though I'm stronger or more naturally suited for short story writing, that I have the ability to try and write a novel, to embrace that challenge. I love how difficult it is, how hard it is. Of course, I deplore it also. I come in from work every day feeling whipped. But, I also wake up in the middle of the night and come downstairs and work from two to six in the morning just because I can't wait to move it farther downfield.

DH: Were you happy with your first novel, *Where the Sea Used to Be?*

RB: I am happy with it. I was very happy when I finished it. It's the most challenging thing that I've done as a writer. And that was gratifying to be challenged and to make something that I'm proud of and admire and respect. I think the book is smarter than I am and that pleases me.

DH: How long did the process take you?

RB: There's a novella by the same title that I wrote in 1985. I finished the last line edit in 1999. So, I guess it took me bits of four-teen years and tens of thousands of pages.

DH: Did you believe in it the whole time?

RB: No, not the whole time. The worst thing of all was believing in it when I shouldn't have believed in it. Knowing the drafts that existed before the final book were so bad, and yet when I was making them, I believed deeply. And that's the worst to look back and see how duped I was. Because if you can be duped into thinking something that's bad is good and alive and vital and meaningful when really it's just doggy, and then you can also be tricked into thinking that what you're doing is not meaningful when perhaps in fact it is, then the odds are two out of three against your opinion mattering anything. Those aren't good odds.

DH: What's the most difficult part of writing novels?

RB: The hard thing for me with novels is what I guess is hard for everybody: focus, sustaining, knowing where you've been, and know-ing the accruing pace and obligations attended to your creative past.

I like to just inhabit each day's fiction fully and imaginatively for its own sake. I really don't have the discipline to give any energy or awareness back to the past. I just want to be in the moment with the imagining and the creating and the writing. And that's really fun, but that's not what makes a novel; that's just what makes a lot of pages. To shape, and sculpt and force that mass of text and images into a syncopated, moving, living thing, with the interconnected parts coming from the past is difficult for me.

DH: Will you write another one?

RB: I'm working on a novel now. I'm having the same difficulties: thousands and thousands of pages with some really fine scenes, some really fine images, some really fine stories embedded within those pages. And some meaning and theme and plot developing from the richness of the text; and yet, it's longer than it is high. They always just seem to go so long. That's partly my bias. I would rather read a long novel than a short novel. And I'd rather make a long novel than a short novel.

DH: Do you find writing this second novel a more familiar process?

RB: To some extent it's a help to have done it once. But that said, what pleases me most about fiction writing is when I'm utterly lost and don't know what's going to happen, even in the next day's work. It's that moment of surprise, discovery, etc., that is fulfilling to a writer in which something is created and you are the vessel of observation for that creation. So, in that vein, the less you know the more powerful your sense of discovery's going to be, which is to say the more powerful your text or writing can become.

DH: What ideas are you working with in this new novel?

RB: I'm really intrigued by notions of repetition and variation in cycles. Where you tell the same story with a second set of characters or a third set of characters, or in the second or third landscape, or in the second or third century, all with slight variations. Actually, Annie Proulx's *Accordion Crimes* is an example of that notion. It doesn't necessarily make for the most dramatic or vibrant or fresh novel, because actually what you're selling with that idea is anti-freshness. To some extent, it can be viewed that you're saying, "Look, give me a story and I'll tell you that story a hundred different ways and I'll make it slightly different each time." That's how life is. It's marvelous. I don't think that's demeaning or diminishing of life's power or force; I think it illuminates it. This repetition of sameness in stories of nature and landscape and people and cultures and generations.

DH: Was this theme of cyclic storytelling in your first novel?

RB: No, that's not something I did with the first novel. But it is something I'm working with now. It's definitely in the second novel in spades. I've seen it come up both in my fiction and nonfiction.

DH: Are you conscious of the novel's themes before you write it? Or do they come as you write?

RB: I start out being conscious of it. I have dozens of pages of notes on theme. And little charged images or moments or metaphors which have a fidelity to those themes. But once I get into the story those things fall away. I either forget them or they become irrelevant to what's going on. Usually that initial theme falls away and another theme develops from beneath it and then I've got to edit the draft and pull out the previous theme and reshape and pay attention to the newly discovered theme. Which is a sloppy and inefficient way to work, for sure.

DH: Does your activism work inhibit or complicate this process?

RB: It's already a difficult enough process, winnowing through what you thought you believed, or what you did believe, into what you now realize you believe. That's a pretty traumatic artistic and emotional experience, to be ripping and gutting the stitches of your old theme and building up this strange new theme. And then to have this other stuff, activism, intruding from a ninety degree perspective. It's kind of like a jackhammer going on in your mind.

DH: Sounds like it can be a challenging, if not frustrating process.

RB: Listening to you paraphrase that old theme–new theme stuff, it reminds me of what hunting season is like. If you're out forty days hunting, just pounding the hills looking for tracks, looking for sign and for animals, there's only going to be probably one moment when you intercept your quarry, your goal. But there's all those hours and days invested before that time. In the end, you're lucky, you're fortunate and happy, if you can take that animal. But if you don't, you've still got that whole season of looking that's a value. The wrong paths, the days which you didn't see anything are really just an investment toward the days when you did, somehow a necessary part of it. But what the activism is like is that you're out there hunting, working into

Rick Bass in Yaak, 1990

the wind, new snow, good tracking conditions, feeling good, up early before light; then there's these paratroopers in pink parachutes, banging drums, floating down from the sky by the hundreds. All of a sudden, there's no longer a quality experience, whether your working with the old theme or the new theme, whether there's game in the basin or not.

DH: When a story doesn't work, what do you usually find at fault?

RB: When I fail it's a failure of courage, a failure of effort, a failure of will, a failure of imagination. It's me trying to shortcut. It's me not leading fully, headlong, fully in love with the subject and characters. It's not technique. It's me, not the English language that fails.

DH: You've been publishing for nearly twenty years now. Can you track any specifics in terms of your evolution as a writer?

RB: I'm sure so, but I'd be the last person to ask about that. That may not speak well to me. This piece that I'm working on right now that's called *The Elephant,* I'm that far away from it. I'm in it. I've never done anything before this. *The Watch* is just like somebody else's book. And certainly somebody's else's themes. The only thing I'm thinking about artistically is tomorrow's work, certainly not yesterday's. And certainly not twenty years ago. I don't think I'm dodging a responsibility. What's behind me is behind me. What's in front of me is alive and shouldn't be controlled.

DH: You picked the short story, "Penetrations" to be included along with this interview. When did you write it? Why this particular story?

RB: It was in Mississippi, so it would have been 1986 or 1987. I liked how far away it was, how ancient, and yet it has themes that I'm still, especially in this second novel, fooling with: crossing borders and boundaries.

DH: How did these themes come across in "Penetrations?"

RB: When I think of that story the one thing I think of is the kids being in class, and there was a line they drew, an imaginary line, and they would try to cross that threshold and it was a thrill for them to see how close they could get to it before it snapped that hypnosis and they would come back to the other world. The comfort level of being close to boundaries. From an ecological perspective, that's where usually the greatest diversity of life is; it's in the those transitional areas between ecotypes and territories. And that's certainly what those kids were pushing between: adolescence and adulthood.

DH: You seem to enjoy working with very solid metaphors.

RB: An image that becomes a metaphor is incredibly old-fashioned, but it really pleases me. It's something more than a symbol; it's a living symbol, an organic symbol. I love the richness in it. That's what art, to me, is: how one thing is like another that previously you would not have imagined.

DH: Penetrating, diving and boring seem to accent many of your stories. Is this a metaphor which still interests you?

RB: It still is, almost to the point of worrying about it. But I continue to be fascinated by the choices of exploration, vertical or horizontal, and the tradeoffs that come in choosing to take one path over another. Breadth versus depth. What is it about a person's character that makes him or her more comfortable with descending or ascending as opposed to traveling laterally or horizontally?

DH: There seemed to be both aspects in "The Cave" from *The Hermit's Story.*

RB: Definitely. There's that very crude framework of vertical depth and then they're on the tracks and there's the horizontal depth, and then there's that strange notion of them being absorbed by the earth and remade and coming out on the other side refashioned and their senses are sharpened through the elements.

DH: Was that a conscious effort?

RB: Oh my God, no. It's a journey, a path, a marker, a discovery, an intuitive, creative, organic path, and quite frankly, I'm not smart enough to do it any other way. Even if I can't think, I can feel. Again, we're back to the athletic concept, of being sturdy enough to shoulder the weight and the unruliness of those emotions and then painting pictures that represent those emotional truths. It's quite frankly hard to not make a good story when you access those deepest truths and feelings.

DH: Do you have a favorite story in the new collection?

RB: I think "The Distance" is a really interesting story. That's one of those stories that I step back and look at and think, "Wow, that's a smart son of a gun that wrote that story." But, not knowing where it came from or how it was made or how I took loose parts and made it into a story. I feel pretty lucky to have made that one, to have gotten away with that one. "The Hermit's Story" is gratifying to me in that it pleases so many people.

DH: How much do you use editorial advice?

RB: A huge, huge amount. I use my editors heavily, not just line edits, but structurally, thematically. I rely on editors more than any other writer that I've known or met, unless they're keeping secrets from me. I wish I had a page to show what editors do for me. Actually, I'm glad I don't.

DH: Do you think there are important steps in the writer's journey? Important milestones or experiences?

RB: I went to some writers' workshops, so I was exposed to that philosophy of teaching, but I learned more directly through reading and through editors. I'd send a manuscript off and the editor would send back a form of rejection. Then I'd send another story and it'd be a different kind of form letter. And another story and then there'd be two words and the editor's initials and I'd have to look at the masthead to figure out what those two initials were and I'd send another story and they'd say, "interesting, but lacks focus"; "nice, but lacks craft" and so on. And I learned through week by week, month by month, year by year, word by word, comment by comment. Which was a good pace for me as opposed to the intenseness of the workshop.

DH: In *Winter* you discussed, partly tongue-in-cheek, some advice you had gleaned from other writers. For instance, Larry Levis used a black Parker, while Jim Harrison used a black pen at night and a gold pen during the day. What would your advice be to young writers?

RB: It'd be fun to say something funny, but no. When I was writing *Winter*, I sure wanted it to be out there and to make a difference. I wanted to be able to say, "Okay, I have this black pen; I'm halfway there." Whatever crutch I could grab, I went for it. But I suppose I might say to fall headlong in love with your subject, your story, your setting, your character, place, theme . . . something. Just give yourself totally to it and completely. Not be looking at what color of pen is in your hand.

DH: Here, roughly twenty years into your career, how would you like people to recognize you and your writing? Fiction writer? Environmentalist? Novelist? Essayist? Naturalist?

RB: Its comes and goes. What fulfills me day by day is just being a parent, a father. It pleases me sometimes to think that someday the girls might enjoy reading this story, this essay, or seeing that this roadless area is protected. So, they're kind of the lens for that kind of musing. And frankly the creative act of thinking of how to make them laugh or smile when they get home from school is what is dominant on my mind more than the element even. What I find most important in writing is making pretty images that will last in people's minds and bring peace and beauty into people's minds. I'm very proud of the hours I've put in on behalf of wild places and the gains that have been made. I got this award last week from the Montana Wilderness Association. It meant more to me than any prize I ever got in writing. Ultimately, protecting a wilderness area is far more important than leaving a beautiful image in someone's mind. A roadless area is not a beautiful image; it is the image. It's not the memory of a thing, it's not a symbol of a thing; it's the thing. You didn't make it, but you kept it from crashing.

PENETRATIONS

Rick Bass

MY *OLDER* brother Sam was a ladies' man. When I was seventeen, he was twenty-two, and during my junior year of high school, to my great initial horror, he began dating my biology teacher, Miss Heathcote, and then worse yet, fell in love with her, and worst of all, she fell in love with him. I asked Sam to try to keep it a secret from her, that I was his brother, because I was worried that it might make trouble for me in class.

My brother was not right—and though he is better today, has been treated, and has also straightened up some, I still fear that a rough road lies ahead of him—but then, the time that I am speaking of now, he was only beginning to go wrong, to unravel—to feel ungoverned by any laws or constraints.

Sam lived at home, with my parents and me. He had been a fireman for a while, but had been let go from the force for "general irresponsibility;" the fire department believed that he had almost a *fetish* for danger, for daring.

Sam had wanted to be a policeman, after that, but he had a couple of shoplifting convictions, and that was out of the question. I think he would very much have enjoyed being a policeman.

I do not mean to make him sound like such an ogre. He was a good brother, and even today, we're still close. He has been married and divorced once. He's never gotten into any kind of legal trouble, since the shoplifting thing. He was eighteen when that happened. Both times, it was a coat that he tried to walk out with— mink, the first time, and lynx, the next—for his girlfriends, on a dare. The same security guard that had caught him the first time was on duty the second time—Sam wearing the coat as if it were a windbreaker, as if it were his—walking, then sprinting for the doorway, in his jeans and tennis shoes—and Sam still talks about going back to school, or about opening a restaurant, or maybe joining the Peace Corps. Will they take a man in his early forties? I don't know.

I remember my parents being distressed, that Sam was drifting off on a wrong course—they were not so wild about him living at home, though, as I heard my father say once, "Better here, at least, where we can keep an eye on him"—but back then, I did not recognize so well that it was a wrong course, and I simply enjoyed being around the danger of Sam—or rather, the way Sam was drawn to danger, and to heat.

What Sam did, during the time that I am speaking of—when he was twenty-two—besides court women (and women loved him)—was to chase ambulances, and chase fire trucks, after the fire department let him go, and even before. Sam had a police scanner radio in his room, and another one mounted beneath the dash in his truck, and fire extinguishers in the back of the truck. I don't mean three or four extinguishers, but a whole truck load. He had purchased them, he said, from the fire department at "a substantial discount," and he used them at will.

Part of this makes me sad, to remember it now. But I thought it was exciting, then. Sam wore a fire chief's helmet, which he would don whenever any of the calls went out. He had a city map in the glove box, which he used to study all the time. He would listen to the scanner and try to get to the scenes of disaster before anyone else—before the authorities— and sometimes, he did.

Sometimes, I went with him. Sam and I had certain rules, when we went out on fire calls, and we had, on the times that we could not get there in time to be the heroes, made it into a game that we called "Penetrations." The object of the game was to see how close to the center of the disaster you could get, or "penetrate"—to go from the outside, and the ring of spectators, into the center, so that you were part of whatever was happening—so that you were as close to it as you could be, so that you could reach out and touch it, if you wanted.

If a home were burning, we would try to get inside it—we would pretend it was our house, and that we'd left something valuable inside. We'd put on an act, pitch a fit, and struggle, when the firemen grabbed us, to break free; so close that we could feel the wind from the fire, so close that the heat blistered our bare faces. Sometimes we got close enough to actually touch the front door. We never made it inside a burning building, but we tried; for whatever crazy reason, Sam tried, and I followed him; I tried, too. We never got in, though; there was always someone to restrain us and keep us from going any farther. I don't know how far we really would have gone. We never really found out.

Miss Heathcote was thirty-two or thirty-three, and beautiful. She was the only attractive teacher in the school, and as such, was always an outcast, away from the other teachers. The women were distant or catty to her—even then, we could see that, and knew it for what it was—and the men were worse, they were fawning, slobbering pigs, coming around her all the time like pigs checking out a trough, even though the trough is empty. There was the delicious and wild rumor that Miss Heathcote had been a Playmate in her younger days, in that magazine— ruined!—and there was not a student among us who did not believe it, or who had not researched the rumor, but no such issue was ever produced—though we knew it was out there, in the past, we could picture it as clear as day, until, in our minds, we believed that maybe we *had* seen it, but had just misplaced it . . .

Sam and I managed to keep it a secret for about three weeks, that we were brothers, before Miss Heathcote found out. She came over to the house one afternoon, and I simply forgot to hide—it suddenly seemed natural to me, to be sitting there out in the open—and though she was a little annoyed with Sam about having kept it a secret, she didn't take it out on me. In fact, she was gentle and kind with me. Some mornings the three of us would have coffee and donuts together, before driving to school—and so that made me feel badly about what I told my classmates.

"On weekends, when my parents are out, she comes over and swings from the chandeliers naked," I told them. "She pulled one out of the ceiling once."

Such tales were easily believable, in the heat of our adolescence, and I made up worse ones than that, too. I simply couldn't help it. We would sit there in class and watch her calm beauty—and the startling depth of her eyes, the deep, relaxed peace she cast over us—murmuring the complexities of biology, telling them to us like a fairy tale, rather than a hard science—these things seemed only to enhance the stories I made up about her. Her placidness, her great gentleness, seemed certain to implicate a raging, lusty inferno lying just below the surface, a surface thin as ice. She'd been at the school forever—ten years, the only school she'd ever taught (Sam had gone to a private boy's school, sort of a disciplinarian retreat, when he was my age).

The students believed the stories I made up about Miss Heathcote and Sam as they had never believed anything before.

My parents were not that terribly much older than Miss Heathcote—they were in their mid-forties—and were a little uncomfortable, at first, not knowing whether to treat her as a friend, on her own power, or as a friend of Sam's—but I'd heard them talking about her, and about Sam, too, when Sam and Miss Heathcote were out—"She's a calm glass of water," my mother kept saying, "she's exactly what he needs"—to which my father always replied, illogically, it seemed to me, "She's a beauty, all right"—and by Thanksgiving, it felt as if Miss Heathcote were family. We were all comfortable with her—Sam, too, I think—in a way that we had never been comfortable with his other girlfriends.

Sometimes, after a fire, or an accident, Sam and I would drive by Miss Heathcote's house. We'd circle the block, again and again. She lived in the same house she had bought when she first moved to town, ten years ago. So beautiful, and never married! We'd cruise past that small house as if she were a teenager. Whenever any of my brother's old girlfriends called, he had instructed me, if I answered the phone, to tell them he wasn't home—to tell them he'd moved away, to tell them he'd died, to tell them anything. Sometimes he and Miss Heathcote went on picnics. I did not go on any of them, but on Friday nights I would watch him packing their lunches into the wicker basket, getting everything ready, and I could imagine what the picnics were like. Sam owned a canoe, with only one paddle, and he took her out in the early days of spring. It was not easy to picture Miss Heathcote laying back in the canoe watching Sam, or anyone, paddle, but I assume that was how it went. I think I was in love with Miss Heathcote too, a little, and I was afraid Sam was going to botch it.

Still, I could not help but continue to create the stories. Horrible, awful stories, which stir me to shame, even now.

"She dances in the street, naked, at night," I said. "The neighbors turn on their lights, and look out their windows and watch. She's a good dancer," I added.

I knew that some of these stories were getting back to Miss Heathcote—I knew that they *had* to be—and she would look at me, sometimes, over at our house—a look passing between her and me, a look not in any way for Sam—a look that told me she knew, and that she did not like it at all—but she was so in love with Sam—forever holding his hand, forever running her hand through his hair, as if trying to calm him— the way a man or woman might try to gentle a nervous horse in a burn- ing barn, with the smell of smoke just beginning to drift in—that she never said anything to me, not wanting to stir the waters, not wanting to rock the boat. I think she thought that if she were nice enough to me, and gentle enough, that she could calm me, too, and that I would grow weary of creating the rumors; and I think, too, that she simply had too much pride to admit that she knew, or that it bothered her; and gradu- ally, as the year went on, I did slow down on the stories, though I could still be counted on by my classmates, when pressured, to come up with a good one.

Something I *had* seen, which I did not tell the class, haunted me then, and still does. One time, when Sam had to go to the fire station, she begged him not to; she wrapped her arms around his leg, and wouldn't let him go. They weren't fighting—not yet—she just didn't want him to go. Sam didn't know what to do. This was before he had been fired. He loved his job and he had to get to the fire station. I had never seen such a thing: a woman trying *physically* to restrain a man from doing something. It seemed to me that Miss Heathcote's cool blue eyes—that her authority would have been enough—but it wasn't. Sam left her and went out the door. I did not tell that story, in class.

She was so much like family, that spring—I could not be around her enough, I wanted to spend all of my time in her company. Late nights, when she and Sam were in the den, watching the blue light of the TV, with both of my parents asleep upstairs, I would sometimes crawl on my belly down the hallway to get closer to Sam and Miss Heathcote, and to listen to them.

"This is what I do," I heard Miss Heathcote saying, one time. "It's all I've learned to do, it's all I know. It's too late to change." She was lying in Sam's arms, and neither of them were watching the television. Their faces were blue, their arms.

"You *can* change," Sam said softly. "Come with me to—oh—*Africa!*" I was startled, and did not want Sam to leave, to go to Africa, or anywhere. Miss Heathcote said nothing, but her shoulders began to heave, and

I could see her shaking her head, and I could see big tears rolling down her cheeks, as she continued to shake her head.

Later in the spring, they would have fights. I wanted to patch things—to mend them, to tell Miss Heathcote to hold herself together, that Sam was difficult, but worth it, that he was wonderful, that he saved people—but I could say none of these things, because I had started out telling lies about her, and she would have no reason to believe me.

Sam and I put out a house fire once, a kitchen blaze—the cabinets above the stove flaming, and the rug on fire—the woman and her two daughters out on the front lawn—and another time, we put out a car that was on fire. There wasn't anyone in it, though at the time we thought there might be, and we worked furiously, spraying the extinguishers, one after the other, all over the car's melting body. The tires were exploding, one by one, and the paint and rubber were smoking, filling the night with a horrible stench, and the car was long-ago ruined, but we got the fire put out before the gas tank blew.

Other times, however—most times—we would get there late. The ambulance would have arrived, and a sheet would already be drawn over the victim—or the building would already be in high flames, second-story flames, with sirens, and hook-and-ladder trucks, flashing lights, fire hoses, and loud speakers, bullhorns—and what we did then, which was second-rate, and nowhere nearly as good as the other, but which was the only thing we could manage, was to wander around aimlessly on the lawn of the disaster, clasping our hands over our heads and saying things like, "Oh, God," or, "I'm wounded"—staggering around until one of the emergency technicians, not knowing us from the real victims, herded us over to the ambulance and sat us down, checked our pulse, our throats, our eyes, with flashlights; checked us for cuts, for burns, for bruises.

The questions were always the same—"Where does it hurt?" ("Aww, ohh, I don't know—here, I think")—and we'd lie around like that, getting attention, if no one else was seriously injured, and then, when the atmosphere started to change—when the chaos subsided, and the fire was about to be controlled, or when the ambulance was about to pull away, we would leap up and run off into the night, and hide.

Our hearts would beat like rabbits'. The rest of our life was normal, and our parents never knew we did these things. I felt lucky to have such a brother.

"Are you okay, Jackie?" he'd ask me.

"Hell, yes," I'd say still breathing hard.

"Good," he'd say, and I'd know he was proud of me, that we were partners. "Good."

We'd watch the flames coming out of the windows, watch the roof begin to crash and fall in, then, which is always how it happened: the roof going first. We felt noble; we felt as if we'd *tried* to save the burning house, but had been unable to.

"We tried," I'd say.

"Fucking A," he'd agree, as if we'd been serious in our attempt. "We almost got there."

There were little fights between Sam and Miss Heathcote, at first, but they grew. I didn't know what to do—I felt as if there were some act I could do, some gesture, that would bridge that gap, bridge their troubles—and the fights never grew from anything specific—never "I don't want to go there this evening," or, "You told me that you were going to get a job"—but rather, just from vague fears, I think. They acted, both of them, all that spring, like skittish horses, frightened animals, each afraid to get any closer to the other: enjoying the others' company, devouring it, even—but hypnotized, it seemed, by the other; frightened.

Sometimes I would answer the door, when she came over to our house and knocked, and she was thinner, almost gaunt, and as I led her in the house, I could actually *feel* her dread and her nervousness about the way things were going—Sam would be in his bedroom, working on electronic things; working on the police scanner, perhaps, or just listening to it, waiting for a disaster—because they were sure to happen; even in the slowest of weeks, it was simply a matter of listening, of lying there on the bed and waiting for one to happen—and the feeling I got, when I led Miss Heathcote into the house, was the feeling I might have gotten, leading one of those same frightened horses *into* a burning stall—the smell of smoke—rather than out of it. Sometimes Miss Heathcote seemed near tears.

"I like her," I told Sam. "I sure do like her. Did she tell you I said mean things about her?"

"No," said Sam, looking up at the ceiling—looking up at nothing, there was nothing at all on the ceiling. It was as if he didn't hear me.

"She doesn't want me going out on fire calls," he said. He spoke to me as if I were an adult. "She doesn't like any of those things. She says she just wants to hold on to me and know those things are in me, just below the surface, but she doesn't want to see them." Sam lay there on his bed and looked up at the ceiling.

Even though they fought, he would always try to calm her down, as she had once calmed him. It was always Sam who was running his hand down the back of her hair, rubbing Miss Heathcote's neck and shoulders in the spring, even when they were disagreeing about things, or about nothing; always Sam whispering things to her, reassuring things, as if trying to hypnotize her; but she always seemed to come out of it, and become even angrier than before, and it was an upsetting thing for me to see.

There was a gap between them—a small gap, but a significant one—even I could see that—and in May, almost frantic about the impending loss of Miss Heathcote—the loss of her to myself, for the end of school that year, and the possible loss of her to Sam—a much worse, more permanent loss—I started playing Penetrations in class.

While Miss Heathcote had her back turned to us—writing on the blackboard—or sometimes even when she was facing us—head down, reading something, while we worked on an assignment—I would rise silently from my lab table, and would begin walking to the front of the room—walking so silently, so slowly.

The object, in my mind, was to get as close in as I could. If she looked up, I would stop where I was. She would look at me, puzzled, but also abstracted—and I knew no one had ever behaved in such a fashion, there were no guidelines in the teacher's handbook, on how to deal with this oddity—and strangely, she never said anything—only fixed me with her beautiful, ice-blue eyes, and a strange, stern, almost steely look; watching me as if about to say something, but never saying it.

The class was as puzzled by her silence as I was. I pictured what it would be like if all of us played the Penetrations game—ten or twelve of us moving in on Miss Heathcote, while her head was down, or her back turned, so that when she turned around, there would be a whole herd of us, a dozen perhaps, frozen in mid-step, all gathered around behind her, behind her desk—but it was something I was compelled to do, and something only I did, and perhaps that was why she let me do it; because she could see that I simply had to—or perhaps because she *liked* me doing it.

I never said anything, when she looked up and stopped me in midstep—stopped me from getting any closer. I could never think of anything to say.

She would just open her mouth, as if about to speak—but she never did. I would walk up to within five or six feet of her, trying to see how close I could get before the lights of fear flickered in her eyes. Then I would stand there, quietly, trying to show her that it was all right, that there was nothing to be frightened of—but it never worked, she never lost that initial look, once I had gotten too close—and finally I would go sit back down.

They were seeing each other more frequently than ever—Sam having lost his job, by that time, and having extra time on his hands—and they went on more picnics, watched more movies, but fought more, too. It was all the same as it had been, only there was more of it. One Saturday they had the worst fight yet—Miss Heathcote crying and wrapping herself around Sam's waist again, sliding down to his legs, but then getting angry and getting up and throwing an ashtray through the window and storming out of the house after that, slamming the door.

That Sunday, for the first time I could remember, she did not come over, nor did Sam go over there. We stayed home, sat in his truck and listened to a baseball game on the radio, and to the police scanner—and I thought it was over.

Then that Monday, during Biology, Sam showed up at the window outside our classroom. This would not have been so unusual were it not for the fact that we were on the third floor. Sam was wearing his fireman's hat, and he had on his heavy rubber fireman's coat, and a hank of rope coiled over his shoulder; he was standing at the top of a ladder, tapping on the window, pointing to her, and it was plain to see that he wanted her to go somewhere, to go somewhere with him: It was in the middle of our class. The class, knowing who it was, howled; they cheered. The windows were locked, but I got up and ran over and unlocked them; I was afraid Sam would fall. His balance was not good.

Miss Heathcote looked at me as if she had always known it would be me who would betray her—that I would be the one—and she had that look, by the late spring, had it so well—I did not blame her—and Sam crawled gratefully through the window. He was wearing his boots, his rubber pants, everything. Miss Heathcote ran from him, then, ran out of the classroom sobbing, and my brother followed, running in those high boots, calling her name. Several of the people in the class stood up, to watch, and I felt myself swooning with excitement. He was my brother; he had chased our teacher from the room.

What happened after that—Sam would not, and never has told me. He has been an alcoholic, and has recovered, lapsed, then recovered again; and he has had treatments for depression, and has gotten better. He's told me about all of those things, and more; but he said the other things about Miss Heathcote were personal. He's held that tight to his breast, close to his coat, and told no one. It withers; it dies; the reasons for their fights, their break-up, almost do not even exist any more.

These lives slide by, our lives! Sam is forty-three—my brother, forty-three. And Miss Heathcote—God, Miss Heathcote is past half a century!

I remember Miss Heathcote smiling, as she came up the walk, to go canoeing with my brother, and her with a decade of teaching already a decade of boredom under her belt—like a decade spent under ice, perhaps, until all feelings of the real world are also submerged, and numbed—and she really loved him, even if only briefly. And he made her feel things, for the first time in a while, I think—though again, perhaps, only briefly—and I hate to say this about my own brother, but I think she got off lucky.

I love Sam, but I think he would have made her really unhappy, later in life. I think it would not have been a good idea: though who can say, for sure?

I remember going out with Sam on the fire calls, but even more so, I remember my own game of Penetrations that I played by myself, in class: rising and standing, and then beginning to move closer to her, slowly, carefully, trying to get close enough to touch her, to put my hand on her hand, perhaps, or even up against her face—and I remember how she would look up from across the room, when she saw what I was up to—and how she would just stare at me, saying nothing, but just watching me, the way a hunter might watch an animal at dusk, in the snow; or perhaps the way an animal might watch the hunter, who is moving so clumsily toward it, coming through the woods, right at dusk: wondering, do I let him come closer? How much closer do I let him come?—while all the time, her heart is beating, fluttering, and she knows, without knowing why, that even though it is dusk, and almost safe, that she has to run, must run, or suddenly all will come crashing down around her.

N. SCOTT MOMADAY

AN INTERVIEW

Kathleen Wiegner

"**M**Y FATHER was a great storyteller and he knew many tales from the Kiowa oral tradition," says N. Scott Momaday, Pulitzer-Prize winning novelist. As a writer, artist, storyteller, and teacher, Momaday has devoted much of his life to safeguarding these oral traditions and other aspects of Indian culture. He has been dubbed "the man made of words" and he embraces this identity.

Momaday was born in 1934 in the Oklahoma Dustbowl and spent his childhood on reservations in the Southwest. His father, the acclaimed painter, Alfred Morris Momaday, was a Kiowa Indian. His mother, Mayme Natachee Scott, was of English, French, and Cherokee descent, although she always emphasized her Cherokee heritage. After enduring the rigors of the Depression, Momaday's family settled in New Mexico. In 1946, they moved to the Pueblo of Jemez, where his parents, both teachers, taught for twenty-five years in a two-teacher Indian day school.

He is the author of thirteen books including novels, poetry collections, literary criticism, children's books, and works on Indian culture. His first novel, *House Made of Dawn* (1968), won the Pulitzer Prize in 1969. *The Ancient Child* (1989) and *The Way to Rainy Mountain* (1976) present a picture of Kiowa culture. *The Names* (1976) is a memoir of his boyhood complete with family photos, and *The Man Made of Words: Essays, Stories, Passages* (1997) offers varied "reflections of one who has traveled far and wide in the world, and has recorded the experiences which most excited the days and nights of his journey."

Something of an authority on Billy the Kid, Momaday admits to a life-long fascination for the outlaw. One section of his 1992 book, *In the Presence of the Sun: Stories and Poems, 1961–1991*, is entitled "The Strange and True Story of My Life with Billy the Kid," and a half-life-size, painted wood carving of the legendary wild-west gunslinger by artist Ed Samuels inhabits Momaday's living room.

Today, Momaday and his wife, Barbara Glenn, divide their time between a new home in Santa Fe and the more than century-old Jemez Springs house, which he inherited from his parents. With its original embossed tin ceilings, narrow stairway, worn wood floors, and closets crammed with several lifetimes of possessions, Momaday's country residence provides him with many opportunities to expand on his childhood and the bond he feels for his parents. We conducted our interview there over tea and cookies on February 8, 2003, enjoying his collection of modern art and Indian artifacts that decorate the spacious front room overlooking Highway 4, the main road through Jemez Springs. We also had strawberry jam to sweeten the tea, a custom Momaday picked up on a trip to Russia.

Momaday has said that the landscape of the West is a dream landscape that for the Native American is full of sacred realities. He knows these realities firsthand. He is a member of the Kiowa Gourd Dance Society, and founder and chairman of the Buffalo Trust, which affords the opportunity for elders and medicine people to share their wisdom with others.

"In the oral tradition," Momaday has said, "stories are not told merely to entertain or instruct. They are told to be believed. Stories are realities lived and believed. They are true."

Kathleen Wiegner: To start at the beginning, when did you first start writing? Or when did you even begin to conceptualize that writing was something you thought would be interesting to do?

N. Scott Momaday: Well, my mother was a writer, and so from a very early age, I had her example. And I guess I decided somewhere back in childhood that I wanted to be a writer. I think I announced

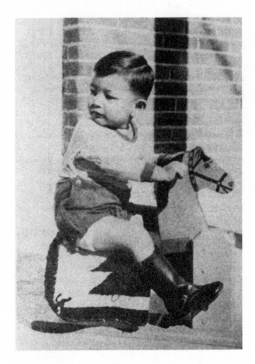

Scott, age 2, ca. 1936

that to her, in fact. I said, "Mom, I'm going to be 'a writer." So, I'm one of those few people who say such things and then do it. It actually happened. I began writing what I think of as seriously when I was an undergraduate, and I was writing poetry pretty exclusively. I entered contests in college and that sort of thing. I published my first poem the year I graduated from college, 1958.

KW: Where was that?

NSM: University of New Mexico. I went there and had an off-and-on career. I dropped out a couple of times, I went to law school for a year, and then back. It took me about six years, I think, to get through the undergraduate school, but then I was published at the end of that year, and so I considered myself a professional writer, and went on from there.

KW: When you were doing poetry, that's usually an age when people are looking for models and they're reading poems with ideas about "am I this kind of a poet or that kind of a poet . . ." Maybe you were different, but if you had influences, who were they at that time?

NSM: As I recall, all of my writer buddies . . . I belonged to a kind of clique. We called ourselves writers. We were all interested in writing, thought of ourselves as writers, and told other people that we were writers, but we read people like Dylan Thomas and listened to Dylan Thomas reading and we could quote him at length. We were mimicking him. Robert Frost, to some extent. D. H. Lawrence was big at the University of New Mexico. I remember reading his poems. And Wallace Stevens. So I don't know about influences. It's hard to say. I can tell you, you know, I can talk about poets whose work I admire, but whether they have been an influence, I don't know.

KW: During this time, in terms of rhythms you were hearing as a poet, were you hearing any of the oral, chanting Indian rhythms?

NSM: I was hearing Indian rhythms, I think, before I knew it, listening to just . . . When I was very little, I lived on the Navajo Reservation. And I heard Navajo, and I heard it at the right time, so that it's in my ear. I can pronounce Navajo. I think I picked up the rhythms of it. And Kiowa, my own language, my father was fluent in Kiowa, so I heard some of that as well. I think these rhythms show up in my writing now, but it wasn't a conscious process at all.

KW: It was just the way your . . . I mean, because when you're writing a poem, you hear something that you've heard, that you liked.

NSM: I have to hear what I write. That's one of the ways I judge it. I listen to it. I guess I listen to it as I write it, and then I do a lot of reading to myself, reading my work back and listening to it. So hearing, finding the rhythms is important to me. I think that's part of my writing process.

KW: Yet the first book you published was actually a book of prose. Is that correct?

NSM: (Hesitates) Yes. First book I published. I'm trying to think what that was. I guess *House Made of Dawn*. Prose. Fiction. And then followed very closely by *The Way to Rainy Mountain,* which is I guess also prose, but it's very lyrical as well, so I was hearing a lot of poetry as I wrote that. Trying to duplicate the sounds that I heard when people were telling me the stories. And, you know, I think I got that into it, which is important to me.

KW: Was there a reason why you chose—if you *did* choose—to do prose as your first major work rather than a collection of poems?

NSM: Yes. I went to Stanford as a creative writing fellow. I was a

Stegner Fellow there for four years. I was doing nothing but writing poetry, and I was learning a lot about the forms of English poetry, and I was trying to take possession of them so that I could write good, solid English poems. The result was that I worked myself into a corner, and I got very tired of doing that. So I felt I needed elbow room, and as soon as I graduated, I started writing a novel. That became *House Made of Dawn*. It is true, though, that I published a number of poems before I wrote the novel. My first publications were poems, and it just happens that *House Made of Dawn* was my first lengthy work in prose.

KW: What effect did it have on you that that very first work actually won a major literary prize, the Pulitzer Prize, in 1969?

NSM: I think it had a considerable effect, and probably one that I can't measure. It certainly made a difference. It was overwhelming in a way, because I got the prize, it was announced to me, and I didn't have any idea that I was in the running, so it came as a complete surprise. All kinds of things happened as a result of that. I was suddenly being interviewed and being feted and getting lots of invitations to speak and to write things. And I think I had to spend some time adjusting to that "new hat." You know, Oliver La Farge once said he was too young to have won the Pulitzer when he won it for *Laughing Boy*. I don't remember how old he was. I was in my thirties, and I think that's an awfully young age to win such an award, so I had to recover from that.

KW: Well, we look at people who get famous when they're young, and what effect does that have then on the rest of their lives, you know, in terms of do they always feel that they need to live up to that? Do they feel that everything after is an anti-climax? Do they feel burdened by it?

NSM: I think probably I felt burdened by it for a short time. Not long. There's always the question, well, what do I do now? But that took care of itself, and I started writing again. I've had other awards, and so I don't take them too seriously, which is probably a good thing. The work is more important to me than the rewards.

KW: You lived on the Navajo Reservation, your background is Kiowa, and yet you chose in *House Made of Dawn* to write about the people of Jemez Pueblo. Was that because of the age you were when you came to the pueblo?

NSH: Right. I think so. I came to Jemez Pueblo when I was 12, and lived what I think of as my most impressionable years there. Got to know the Jemez people pretty well, so it seemed a logical subject for me when I started writing a novel. I knew people who were like Abel in the novel, who came back from the Second World War, and many of them were wounded in their intelligence, and they were psychically disoriented, lost people. I thought this was something one should write about.

KW: Do you have many contacts still down in the pueblo?

NSH: Quite a few, quite a few. I know a number of people there. My parents, of course, had a great influence on a certain generation. They were there for twenty-five years, so a lot of their students are still there. Some of them I know, some of them I don't. Strangely enough, the people of my own age group are largely gone. There are very few people who were in school with me there. I think you can count them on the fingers of one hand, actually.

KW: Do you keep track of them?

NSM: More or less. A couple of them I keep track of. One of my good friends is still there, and he and I get together once in a while.

KW: You've said in a few places that you don't think of yourself as an Indian writer or a Native American writer. You think of yourself as being a writer. Do you find that the *world* thinks of you as being an Indian or a Native American writer?

NSM: I think many people do because they want to categorize you. That's convenient, and it's a natural thing to do. If you're a Jew and you write a novel, you're a Jewish writer. And certainly that's true, but I think it is also true that many writers transcend that kind of identity. They write for the sake of writing. They would write it no matter what their background was. But I think it's perfectly natural for people to pigeon hole you in that way. Label you.

KW: Yet you do work with a lot of native themes like the buffalo, or the bear, and things like that. Correct?

NSM: Right. It's my subject. I spent so much of my life in the Indian world. I grew up on different reservations, but I have a very strong sense of Indian-ness, and it turns out to be a fortunate subject for me. I know a lot about the Indian world and Indian people, and I write about them more easily than I could write about people of another ethnic background.

KW: And yet you move fairly well through the larger world.

NSM: I have had a lot of experience traveling and teaching in different places, and I am fortunate in that respect, too. I have had a lot of different kinds of experience in different places with different people, so I feel fairly comfortable in the world.

KW: When did you start doing your graphic art? Your painting?

NSM: About the middle '70s. I'd watched my father paint as I was a child, but I didn't myself have any interest in painting until I was well into my adulthood. It happened that I was teaching at the University of Moscow in 1974.

KW: Is this Moscow in Russia?

NSM: Moscow in Russia. All of it came out suddenly there. I felt the need to sketch, and I started drawing and all that. Then I guess my father's . . . everything that I'd learned from him suddenly came to the surface, and I started a whole career in drawing and painting. Printmaking, finally.

KW: Do you find that there are themes that run through the written work and the painted work or the drawn work?

NSM: Yes. I would say the subject is largely the same. I've said that I write about the Indian world. That's true. In my poetry, however, I verge from that quite frequently, and I write about things that you wouldn't consider necessarily Indian in character. My paintings are. . . . I like Indian themes. I like Indian icons. I do a lot of masks and shields. Stylized portraits and things like that. But other things as well. I'm not into landscapes much, but . . .

KW: But you do very interesting faces and figures.

NSM: Thank you. I enjoy doing that. I like faces and figures.

KM: Those are the ones I like.

NSM: Good. Okay. (Laughs) I do, too.

KW: There's a book I read once called *The Doubly Gifted,* and it talked about painters who wrote and writers who painted. And, you know, there's this whole idea, that if you're doubly gifted, can you develop any one of those as fully as someone who focuses just on one. It's kind of like if you're bilingual, can you become as fluent in two languages as someone can become in one language? And I'm wondering how you feel about that, being doubly gifted.

NSM: I feel that you can develop both things to, you know, to the extent that you're capable of. I suppose that's a question you

Momaday's parents at the time of their wedding

can't answer if *you* do both things. You never know whether if you did just the one, you'd go farther in it. But if you think about writers who have written in different languages, like Isak Dinesen and Nabokov, they seem to have done remarkably well in one or another or both languages. So I don't know. I would suspect you can go as far as you have it in you to go in either direction.

KW: Have you ever tried to write in Navajo or Kiowa?

NSH: There's no point in that. Some of my students sometimes say to me, "Wouldn't it be wonderful if you wrote in Kiowa?" My answer is, well, in the first place, you can't. There's no written language. And in the second place, no one would read you if you could. The only person I know who writes in an Indian language is Lucy Tapahantso. She does write in Navajo. No one *reads* her in Navajo, as far as I know, but I think it's a good exercise, and I applaud her *for* doing that. But I don't know that I can justify writing in a native language. You can certainly justify *learning* a native language. The oral tradition is, to my mind, as important as the written, tradition. So I'm concerned that people learn their languages and tell stories in them and preserve what stories remain in them, but writing is another question.

KW: I was thinking of Conrad, who wrote in English, even though Polish was his first language, which has always to me been a really big stretch.

NSM: Yeah. Well, Isak Dinesen. You know, someone once asked her, "Why did you write in English? Danish is your language." And she said, "I want to be read." So, there is that practical side of it, which I think is important.

KW: Do you find that your students have a great interest in the oral tradition?

NSM: They do.

KW: This comes in waves. I remember during the '60s, everything was very oral. All the poetry was oral. And then we sort of got away from that, and I'm wondering whether your students are back to that.

NSM: My students, it seems to me, don't know much about the oral tradition. They don't spend time thinking about it. They *have* an oral tradition, they use it, but they don't think what it is. So when they come to my class—and I teach regularly a class in Native American oral tradition—you know, it's as if their eyes are opened to it, and they start thinking about language in a way they haven't before. That's very exciting to me. So by the time they get into it, they understand something about the difference between writing and oral tradition, and they think about it. That's very healthy.

KW: I remember Jerome Rothenberg, who collected that book called *Traditions of the Sacred*, which was sort of a collection of ethnic poetry, but it was really a collection of oral works.

NSM: I know that book.

KW: At one point, that was a fairly influential book . . .

NSM: Right.

KW: . . . and it seems that everyone kind of lost interest in the idea of the spoken word.

NSM: I don't know. I can't gauge that. I think that there's a lot of interest in the spoken word that needs to be awakened. And you can do it in a classroom. You can talk about it and introduce people to what happens when people talk as opposed to what happens when they write or read. It's another dimension of language, and once they are aware of it. I think they develop an interest in it. But sustaining that interest, I don't know. Things conspire against it. We're very deeply entrenched in the written tradition. And writing gives us a false security where language is concerned. We're not encouraged to remember what we hear or to listen carefully. So the oral tradition has advantages of that kind, and that makes a difference. I think we ought to get back to believing that language is magical, which it really is.

KW: Well, in terms of education, I know that when my mother was in school, a great emphasis was placed on memorization of things.

NSM: Yes.

KW: And then when I was in school, there was some. And now there's almost none, as far as I can tell, so that all the old songs and the old poems that were a part of your tradition, of my tradition, who now memorizes big stanzas of "Evangeline"?

NSM: (Laughs) Yes, yes.

KW: And yet somehow that attunes you to the notion that you should memorize some of these things.

NSM: I think it's an awfully good exercise just for the mind to memorize. And you're right. I think people . . . I don't know how many people can even recite the Pledge of Allegiance now. Very few people can recite the Gettysburg Address, which I had to do at one point. And I think it was valuable.

KW: But I know as I said in my mother's case, it's amazing the things she can remember because of course as you get older, you remember back further. I have a theory that when you die, you'll remember the day you were born because you'll have come full circle.

NSM: (Laughs) Interesting theory. I'm not going to put it to the test yet, but maybe when the time comes.

KW: Your choice to come and live in your family house. Can you talk about that a little bit?

NSM: Oh, yes. I love this place. My parents bought this house in 1959, and from that time, I've been in and out of it. And then my father died in 1980, and my mother just a few years ago. When she died, I inherited the house and I decided, well, I'm going to live there. So that's what I've done. I've made it mine, and Barbara has helped me to renovate it and make it what we want it to be. It's a place where I like to spend time.

KW: When you say make it a place you want it to be, does that involve keeping it very similar to the way it was when you got it? What kind of changes do you think of? Maybe it's just a question of shoring it up so it doesn't fall down.

NSM: (Laughs) There's more to it than that. I want to keep as it was, in a certain sense. My parents put their own stamp on it, and I like that. I like what they did. So I try to keep their influence here, but I've done a lot—we've done a lot—with the outside, with the back yard. I've put a kiva out there, and we have it fenced in, and landscaped it to an extent. I'm a cook. I like to cook. The kitchen that was here was very small, and so I moved the kitchen into a downstairs area where it's much larger, and I can look at and talk to people when I cook. That's important to me. And just other changes of that kind. But you know, if you come into the living room, it's pretty much as it was when my parents were here.

KW: Now did they build this house or was it built before they bought it?

NSM: It was built before they bought it. In fact, it is, I think, one of the oldest—if not *the* oldest house—in the village. It was built in 1870. So it goes back a long way. You can see its age in its walls, which are very thick, and there isn't a right angle, I think, in the whole house. It's very distinctive. And that's one of the reasons I like it so much. It has character.

KW: Do you find that . . . one of the things about living in Jemez Springs, is that it's terribly inconvenient if you want to go anywhere and do anything. Going to Tucson every week and coming back. Do you find that's very tiring for you?

NSM: It takes something out of me for two reasons. It's travel, which does cost you something, and in fact, it takes longer for me to drive to the Albuquerque airport than it does to fly to Tucson. And then Tuesday is the day I teach at Arizona. I teach a full load, so I get everything into that one day, and it's a brutal day. But I compensate for it by having long weekends. I like to tell people I have a six-day weekend.

KW: That's very nice. I remember when we were talking during the Jemez Springs Public Library's tri-cultural symposium with Rudolfo Anaya and Tony Hillerman [February 2, 2002], you were discussing your writing schedules. You were talking about how at one time you had this very disciplined schedule, and then not. What is your work like now in terms of either painting or writing?

NSM: It's very undisciplined, I should say. It's catch as catch can. I have become so much involved with traveling and attending meetings—I'm on several boards, and I go to those meetings—and I lecture a good deal. I'm always traveling somewhere to lecture, so all of this takes away from my writing time. I tell myself that I keep my mornings free, which I do as far as I can. I never teach in the mornings. That's when I write. So, you know, when I have a free morning, I try to get to the machine and write. Sometimes it's very difficult to find the mornings, though.

KW: Does it disturb you if you've gone through a whole week and you haven't written anything?

NSM: A bit. But I'm used to that. It doesn't really get me down now. I'm just grateful for time I can find in which to write. I've got projects going. I like the idea of a work in progress, and I think that's a funny concept. I'm going to give a lecture on that at the University of Arizona.

KW: What are you going to say about work in progress?

NSM: (Teasing) That it's a credit card. You know, if you have a work in progress, that's wonderful. You can go a long way on that. You can say, "Well, of course I'm occupied. I have a work in progress." And everybody says, "Oh! Oh, that's good. Yes. Good." It isn't really valuable at all, but people think it is. So you can use it in that way. "I have a work in progress."

KW: Well, that's good. (Laughs)

NSM: (Laughs) Yes.

KW: I look back sometimes on things when I was more active as a poet, at what I said to people about projects . . . works in progress, and sometimes I just laugh out loud. At the time, I really, seriously believed that this was going to go somewhere, and of course it went nowhere. So one wonders whatever happened to those book titles that no longer exist.

NSM: Exactly.

KW: Tell me about your interest in drama. Do you have any interest in drama?

NSM: I love theater, and I think that, yes, I have some kind of interest in and a talent for the dramatic. I acted in a couple of plays when I was in college. I've written a couple of plays, and I love to see plays performed. So I like the theatrical. I like people who are dramatic, and who act out of that pose. I would do more of it, if I could, myself. I think about affecting a personality and gesturing in certain ways, and you know, when it's in mind, I can do a little of it, but it's not always in mind. But I do have that kind of interest.

KW: I thought about you yesterday because I went down to Alamogordo. We went through Lincoln County and Billy the Kid country.

NSM: Ah, yes.

KW: And I wondered if you could speak a little bit on your interest in Billy the Kid?

NSM: Well . . .

KW: For those people who know nothing about the fact that this is an interest of yours.

NSM: Well, Billy the Kid and I are great friends. You know, I spent a large part of my childhood in New Mexico, and so Billy the Kid is a character that I heard about when I was very little. And of course, he's very appealing to a kid. Cowboy. Gunslinger. And so I think most of my generation, anyway, of kids in New Mexico, knew of Billy the Kid and were interested in him. My interest continues to grow, I think. I have researched Billy the Kid. I've read a lot about him. I've written a lot about him. To me, he's a very appealing figure, as a character— I don't know, he was probably worthless as a human being—but he had a way about him. He had good qualities. He was, for example, extremely loyal. And he made people fond of him. He was a kind of magnet. And so the people who really got to know him, came to like him, and to be loyal to him as he was to them. I think he was a kid— he didn't grow to be very old—who was looking for a home, and he came as close as he ever came to finding a home in Lincoln with John Tunstall, the man who came over from England and hired him and who was murdered. And Billy the Kid, that changed his life remarkably. I think he spent the rest of his life avenging his friend, and of course, got into trouble and got himself killed in the process. But he's interesting, and not as simple as most people think. He was even literate, for one thing. He could write and he did write letters to Lew Wallace, asking to be pardoned. Of course, he never was, but we have some of his letters.

KW: And you have the wood sculpture over there. Did Ed Samuels do that for you?

NSM: He did. And this was before I knew Ed, and before I lived here permanently. I was in Santa Fe. And I happened to see this chainsaw sculpture in a gallery, and I said I have to have that. And I bought

Schooldays, Jemez

it, and only later found out that Ed did it. And he did the female figure, whom I think of as Paulita Maxwell, who is Billy the Kid's girlfriend. So they're together again.

KW: They are. Flanking your living room table. So you're going to move into a house in Santa Fe, and then split your time between Jemez, Santa Fe, and the rest of the world?

NSM: Yes. We've been doing that to some extent. Barbara has had a casita in Santa Fe for some years, so we've spent time there. Now we're going to have a condominium there, and so we will continue to divide our time. We have a town house now—or will have—and a country house and any number of train carriages and airplanes. So, we're well sheltered.

KW: Yes, and traveling with all your luggage. How do you relate to New Mexico in terms of the cultures, the landscapes, the antiquity . . . Where do you find your most interesting moments in New Mexico?

NSM: Northern New Mexico is the part of the state that I'm most familiar with. I grew up here, so I have a great fondness for Santa Fe and, I guess, all of the state north of Albuquerque. I like some parts of the southern state, but I don't know it as well. I get a large satisfaction from driving in the northern part of the state through some of the old Spanish settlements like Truchas. You know, when I go north of Santa Fe, I sense a change in the atmosphere somehow. The cultural atmosphere. When you get to Espanola, you're in another part of New Mexico, an older part, and the architecture is distinctive. You get rural features that you don't have south of Santa Fe. I like that very much. I find myself energized by that. I like to take photographs up there and visit people.

KW: Well, it is very distinctive, that area. It really does take you back to another time.

NSM: One of my favorite places is the Hacienda Martinez in Taos, which belonged to a man I also find fascinating, who brought the first printing press into New Mexico, and published the first newspaper. That's Padre Martinez. He was a renegade priest and a fascinating person. That hacienda is a place . . . I would like to have such a house as that. That's my romantic ideal.

KW: What is it about the hacienda that appeals to you?

NSM: It's big. It has an inner courtyard, the rooms are all around it, and they're restored. The house was built, I believe, in 1803. It's pretty much as it was then, you know. And it's just wonderful. It has a large room, which was used for dancing and meetings. A fascinating kitchen with a big fireplace and granaries. Just a fascinating place. All built in a square, with a square courtyard and a zaguan through which you could drive a wagon. And it's just wonderful. It's my idea of early New Mexico. It's probably the last real hacienda in northern New Mexico. There are such places in and around Taos and the north.

KW: Do people ever chide you or confront you on the idea that here you are a Native American, whose land was stolen by the Spaniards, and here you are admiring a hacienda in northern New Mexico?

NSM: No, nobody has chided me on that score. No.

KW: Because there are those, you know. . . .

NSM: Well, I'm certainly aware of the fact that my ancestors were treated badly by the conquerors who came in, the Conquistadores, and the Anglos. But, you know, I think that there's no point in my feeding upon that. I'm aware of it. There are parts of the history of the Indian people in this country that I think are positively shameful. I speak out against that once in a while, but on the other hand, I live in a different time, and they're not trying to take my land at the moment, so . . . And they better not. (Laughs)

KW: I was thinking of Sherman Alexie, for example, who always seems to me to be angry about something.

NSM: Right. Sherman is an angry young man, but he's talented, and I applaud him for speaking out the way he does. I know him, and I've been on the same platform with him a couple of times. He's a hot-blooded young man. I think he'll mellow in time.

KW: He, too, writes poems and fiction and drama. Quite multi-talented.

NSM: Oh, I think so. Yes.

KW: Did you ever have a period in your life when you were angry? Really angry?

NSM: I'm not a political person, so I don't vent my anger. I have anger, but it's not something I express easily. I think I'm more vocally angry in my later years than I was as a young man.

KW: But it's not necessarily a political. . . .

NSM: No, I don't join political groups and protest in public and things like that. I approve of those who do, in many instances, but that's not in my nature.

KW: Would you talk a little bit about the Buffalo Trust?

NSM: Yes. The Buffalo Trust is an organization that I founded five or six years ago. The idea being that I could do something to help young, native people reclaim and protect their cultural heritage. I am alarmed by the loss of that cultural identity. The loss of languages, the loss of ceremonies, the loss of relationship with elders. All of that is happening very suddenly, and the move to urban centers, all of that is costing the Indian his cultural identity. So the Buffalo Trust was founded to do something about that, to reverse that trend. It's an overwhelming task, but I think the trust has been successful on certain fronts, and it continues to exist and do good work. I'm very much involved with that. It takes up quite a bit of time, but I have good people who are helping me with it. We now have some real things going on in Oklahoma, building an archive, for example, at Rainy Mountain. So it continues and, you know, these are hard times for organizations of the kind, but I think we'll survive.

KW: I'm sure that anything requiring money these days . . .

NSM: Difficult. Yes.

KW: Very hard time. You were in Alaska last year. Can you talk about that experience a bit? You were dealing with, again, indigenous populations, but how did that differ from your experiences in the Lower 48?

NSM: There are a number of differences. I had spent time in Alaska before the stint last year. And I've traveled fairly widely in the Arctic. I've been in Greenland and the Northwest Territories, Baffin Island, so I had the opportunity. I was invited to come as a scholar/teacher to Fairbanks last year. I took it. I eagerly accepted it because it gave me a chance to come in contact with Athabascan peoples, and in all my Arctic travels, I didn't meet many Athabascans. I was with Inuit people, largely. So I spent that semester last year at Fairbanks, and they knew of my interest in native cultures, so I was able to travel to native villages, and it was a wonderful experience. I found the Athabascan people very traditional. They still have a kind of subsistence way of life. They still hunt and fish, and they are into traditional crafts. I had a student who came to class with moose hide and was sewing constantly and making moccasins. There's a real investment in the native world there still. So I really enjoyed being there, seeing the villages, and want the Buffalo Trust, as a matter of fact, to establish some exchange programs with groups up there. I think that will happen.

KW: That would be interesting.

NSM: Yes.

KW: Do they have a written language? The Athabascans?

NSM: No. They have a strong language. I suppose it's deteriorating like all other native languages, but it's still very much alive there, and there are still a lot of elders who keep to the old ways and can teach out of traditional knowledge. I went to potlatches there, and I went up to Arctic Village, which is right on the edge of ANWR, the game preserve that they're trying to drill in now. Small village, subsisting . . . 80 percent of their diet is caribou. And what we're doing up there is upsetting the balance of nature and interfering with the migrations of the caribou, so things are changing. And probably for the worse. So a lot of things are happening there, but it's still a place where you can find traditional peoples and traditional culture.

KW: In terms of language, the idea of a language disappearing—there are endangered languages always—no one knows what the

Romans spoke, really, any more. We can read it but we can't pronounce it really correctly. I was in Sicily with my mother, who's Sicilian, and was told that in another generation, no one will speak Sicilian in the way that my mother's mother spoke it because everyone will speak Italian, which is different. When you lose a language, what do you lose? We still can communicate with each other.

NSM: I don't know, I don't know. I'm sure that you lose something, but trying to say what is lost is difficult. I wrestle with that all the time in my oral traditions courses. You know, it is a fact that languages are lost. They die. How many languages have we lost in history and pre-history? Thousands. I believe, though, that it is possible to keep the literature and the spirit of a people alive, even though the language may slip away. There is such a thing as a good translation. All you have to do is read Washington Matthews's translation from the Navajo to know about that. Or Ezra Pound's translations from Chinese or Anglo Saxon. And that, it seems to me, is more important in the long run than keeping a particular language alive. You need to keep the spirit of the literature alive, and I think that's possible to do.

KW: I'm just thinking that words, because they have a certain magic to them and because words derive from our experiences, if we lose the words, do we lose the essence of the experience?

NSM: I don't think so, but as I say, I'm not sure what is lost. I don't know that it's possible to know that. I remember that I interviewed an old Kiowa woman some years ago, and my father interpreted because I didn't speak Kiowa and he did. When we were talking about what she had to say afterwards, he said, "She was speaking a kind of Kiowa that I never heard. There were simply words that I couldn't translate, that I didn't know." And yet, he was fluent in the language. So that says two things to me. One is that languages change, and they change dramatically from time to the time. You lose things even though the language remains vital. The other is that languages themselves can be lost, as so many have been over the years and generations. What does it mean? Cultures persist. They remain alive, even though the languages may not. So, I put my energy into that part of it which remains alive and can be kept alive, I think.

KW: But if the tradition is oral, not written, then all of the oral tra-dition will have to be in translation. Is that correct?

NSM: Well, not for a considerable time, anyway. Yes, oral traditions

N. Scott Momaday

become writing. We preserve oral traditions in writing now. They can exist side by side, but you can't keep records except in writing.

KW: Yes, because if we no longer are an oral people—maybe there are pockets where this is true—but in the beginning, we were all oral people. If we are no longer oral people, then the only way the stories can be preserved is if they're written down, right?

NSM: But the thing is that we are all oral people. We can't help being, you know? And if you stop and think what television means or radio, for example, maybe it's a kind of return of oral tradition. We all have an oral tradition, we're just not all aware of it. You know, with my students, I tell them this the first day. I say, "You all have an oral tradition. Think about that. You don't know that yet, but I can show you that it's true." And it is. So I think the language at the oral level is alive and well. It remains to be seen how writing will affect it in the long run, how the two things will work together. We'll always have an oral tradition. We won't always have the *same* oral tradition.

KW: Did you always think that you were going to teach?

NSM: No.

KW: I know your mother was a teacher.

NSM: No, I didn't consider that I would be a teacher until I was teaching. I wanted to be a writer. I wanted to be a lawyer at one point. I went to law school. But when I won the Stegner Fellowship to Stanford, that changed my whole idea of what I wanted to do. Suddenly, I was prepared to teach at the college level, and I just fell into that, and it has been a real part of my life for many years. I could've been something other than a teacher, though, I think, had things just fallen differently on the table.

KW: Yes. Well, being a writer and a teacher oftentimes go together because it's one way to support yourself while you're writing.

NSM: Exactly. The two things go together quite well.

KW: Right. And somehow, while Wallace Stevens could work in an insurance company and write . . .

NSM: (Laughs) Right. How did he do that?

KW: How *did* he do that? (Laughs) And William Carlos Williams could be a doctor and write, but normally writers by and large tend to gravitate to the teaching professions.

NSM: That's for a good reason. It gives them time. Teaching requires less than my full time by a large chalk, and that's very helpful to me and my writing.

KW: When you told your mother you wanted to be a writer, what did she say?

NSM: I think she was pleased. I mean, you know, what do you say when an eight-year-old comes up to you and says, "I want to be a writer?" You say, "Oh, good! Good for you!" And she did, but she probably meant it a little more seriously because she herself was a writer. So, I think she gave me encouragement.

KW: Because she could have said, "Oh, no! You don't want to be a writer. It's a terrible life. So hard."

NSM: Thank goodness she didn't. She didn't urge me into insurance or some other profession. My parents were very creative, and I think I owe them a lot from their example.

KW: Are you an only child?

NSM: Mm-hm. Yes.

KW: So you would have gotten a lot of attention from your parents?

NSM: Oh, I think I got more than my share. (Laughs) Yes.

KW: And also because they were creative, probably you were encouraged, would you say, to be creative?

NSM: Yes. And the fact they did the kind of work they did, where they did it, because we three, my parents and I, were in some sense isolated much of the time from our own kind. We lived in places where we didn't speak the same language that the populace spoke. And at Jemez, for example, Jemez is an exclusive society, and we got part of the way into it, but not all of the way because there are a lot of secret ceremonies and so on, which we weren't privy to. But I think of that, too, as being, in a way, a good thing in terms of creativity. I think my imagination had to work overtime when I was a kid, and that was probably good for me. I did make good, close friends at Jemez, and got farther into that culture than my parents could, and that was valuable to me. But still, you know, I wasn't fluent in their language. I did pick up enough to get by on, but we were from different experiences and different cultures.

KW: Do you find that your work is infused with a great deal of your own personal emotion? I mean, do you feel that, for example, you write out of your own emotional self? Loneliness? A sense of awe?

NSM: I do, right, because I think that's all I have to write out of. Just my experience. That's all any writer has.

KW: Well, but some people don't go as deeply down into themselves. They can write from what they *know*, at a rational level as opposed to at a deeply emotional level. But having been a poet, I'm wondering whether you . . . that's where you have to go?

NSM: I see what you mean, I think, and would say yes. Yes. I do write out of a deeper emotional level than I would if I were . . .

KW: John Grisham? (Laughs)

NSM: . . . someone else. (Laughs)

KW: Has there ever been a time when you thought you didn't want to be a writer?

NSM: No. No, I think from the time I conceived the idea of being a writer, I've wanted to be that; perhaps along with other things but never instead of other things. I mean, always I wanted to be a writer. There was never a choice of being something else and not a writer.

KW: You have done a number of children's books. Several, I think.

NSM: Three now.

KW: Do you like doing that, and why?

NSM: Yes, I do. I think that children have a greater sense of wonder than adults in general, and it's fun to write to that sense of wonder.

And so, yes, I do love to write children's books. I think I will probably write more, if I can, and I think I can.

KW: You were working on one as a work in progress, it seemed to me, last year. You were doing the drawings for it. Where is that now?

NSM: I was actually, I guess . . . they're both finished as texts. One has to be illustrated still. One is coming out in French right away. I have a wonderful illustrator, a French citizen, who is Chilean, actually, and her style is very much South American Indian. Wonderful colors and forms and shapes. And she lives in Paris and we collaborated on this book, which is actually an adaptation of a play. I wrote a play called *Children of the Sun,* and this is a children's book adapted from that play. So that's imminent. I'm expecting to get copies in the mail any day. And then the other is a children's book, which I've finished, but which I'm still illustrating.

KW: Does it have a title?

NSM: Working title is *Indian in the Garden. The Indian in the Garden.* I'm not sure I'll stay with that, but that's what I call it now.

KW: Okay. I guess the last question I have is was there anything you thought I'd ask that I didn't ask you?

NSM: (Hesitates) Oh, yes. Yes, because it is always incumbent on the interviewer to ask, "Is writing difficult?" (Laughs)

KW: Ah.

NSM: I've adopted an answer that I heard from a writer who was being asked that question, and he said, "No. Oh, no, it isn't difficult at all. All you do is sit in front of a blank page until beads of blood appear on your forehead. That's all there is to it."

KW: (Laughs) That's a good one. I think I didn't ask that question because being a writer, I know what the answer is.

NSM: (Laughs) Exactly.

A BEL WAS suddenly awake, wide awake and listening. The lamp had gone out. Nothing had awakened him. There was no sound in the room. He sat bolt upright, staring into the corner where his grandfather lay. There was a deep red glow on the embers, and the soft light opened and closed upon the walls. There was no wind outside, nor any sound; only a thin chill had come in from the night and it lay like the cold of a cave on the earthen floor. He could see no movement, and he knew that the old man was dead. He looked around at the windowpanes, those coal-black squares of dim reflection. There was nothing. It was a while still before the dawn, before the first light should break in advance of the seventh dawn, and he got up and began to get ready. There was no need for the singers to come; it made no difference, and he knew what had to be done. He drew the old man's head erect and laid water to the hair. He fashioned the long white hair in a queue and wound it around with yarn. He dressed the body in bright ceremonial colors: the old man's wine velveteen shirt, white trousers, and low moccasins, soft and white with kaolin. From the rafters he took down the pouches of pollen and of meal, the sacred feathers and the ledger book. These, together with ears of colored corn, he placed at his grandfather's side after he had sprinkled meal in the four directions. He wrapped the body in a blanket.

It was pitch black before the dawn, and he went out along the corrals and through the orchards to the mission. The motor turned and, one after another, the lights went on upstairs and in the stairwell and in the hall, and Father Olguin threw open the door.

"What in God's name—?" he said.

"My grandfather is dead," Abel said. "You must bury him."

"Dead? Oh . . . yes—yes, of course. But, *good heavens,* couldn't you have waited until—"

"My grandfather is dead," Abel repeated. His voice was low and even. There was no emotion, nothing.

"Yes, yes. I heard you," said the priest, rubbing his good eye. "Good Lord, what time is it, anyway? Do you know what *time* it is? I can understand how you must feel, but—"

But Abel was gone. Father Olguin shivered with cold and peered out into the darkness. "I can understand," he said. "I understand, do you hear?" And he began to shout. "I understand! *Oh God! I understand—I understand!*"

February 28
—From *House Made of Dawn*

Summons

FOR YURI VAELLA

Where is the bear doctor? Where is he?
I have come from the north, and I thirst.
I have come from the east, I hunger.
I have come from the south, I am tired.
I have come from the west in great need.
Where is the bear doctor? Where is he?
In my life I have known the bad things.
In my life I have known the good things.
I have come from the dawn, and I sing.
I have come from the dusk, and I dance.
I have come from the mountains to die.
I have come from my home to go forth.
Where is the bear doctor? Where is he?
Who will outfit me for my journey?

—From *In the Bear's House*
Moscow, 1997

The Khanty Bear Feast

FOR YEREMEI AIPIN

Consign me to ritual
on pretexts of sacred kinds.
Unbutton my coat, and have
children pay me their respects.
Fasten my eyes with bright coins.
Let me hear the singer say,
"Whose house is this?" And reply,
"Behold, this is the bear's house."
And I shall preside with wild,
disinterested kindness.

—From *In the Bear's House*
T'umen, 1997

To an Aged Bear

Hold hard this infirmity.
It defines you. You are old.

Now fix yourself in summer,
In thickets of ripe berries,

And venture toward the ridge
Where you were born. Await there

The setting sun. Be alive
To that old conflagration

One more time. Mortality
Is your shadow and your shade.

Translate yourself to spirit;
Be present on your journey.

Keep to the trees and waters.
Be the singing of the soil.

—From *In the Bear's House*
Santa Fe, 1995

The Indian Dog

WHEN I WAS GROWING UP I lived in a pueblo in New Mexico. There one day I bought a dog. I was twelve years old, the bright autumn air was cold and delicious, and the dog was an unconscionable bargain at five dollars.

It was an Indian dog; that is, it belong to a Navajo man who had come to celebrate the Feast of San Diego. It was one of two or three rangy animals following in the tracks of the man's covered wagon as he took leave of our village on his way home. Indian dogs are marvelously independent and resourceful, and they have an idea of themselves, I believe, as knights and philosophers.

The dog was not large, but neither was it small. It was one of those unremarkable creatures that one sees in every corner of the world, the common denominator of all its kind. But on that day—and to me—it was noble and brave and handsome.

It was full of resistance, and yet it was ready to return my deep, abiding love; I could see that. It needed only to make a certain adjustment in its lifestyle, to shift the focus of its vitality from one frame of reference to another. But I had to drag my dog from its previous owner by means of a rope. It was nearly strangled in the process, its bushy tail wagging happily all the while.

That night I secured my dog in the garage, where there was a warm clean pallet, wholesome food, and fresh water, and I bolted the door. And the next morning the dog was gone, as in my heart I knew it would be; I had read such a future in its eyes. It had squeezed through a vent, an opening much too small for it, or so I had thought. But as they say, where there is a will there is a way—and the Indian dog was possessed of one indomitable will.

I was crushed at the time, but strangely reconciled, too, as if I had perceived intuitively some absolute truth beyond all the billboards of illusion.

The Indian dog had done what it had to do, had behaved exactly as it must, had been true to itself and to the sun and moon. It knew its place in the scheme of things, and its place was precisely there, with its right destiny, in the tracks of the wagon. In my mind's eye I could see it at that very moment, miles away, plodding in the familiar shadows, panting easily with relief, after a bad night, contemplating the wonderful ways of man.

Caveat emptor. But from that experience I learned something about the heart's longing. It was a lesson worth many times five dollars.

—From *The Man Made of Words*

An Encounter in Greenland

ONE DAY LAST SUMMER I traveled by boat along the far northwest coast of Greenland—to the little settlement of Siorpaluk, an Eskimo village about halfway between the Arctic Circle and the North Pole. It was bitterly cold on the water, and yet I could not bring myself to leave the deck, not even for the steaming hot tea below. For the world of that Arctic summer morning was ineffably beautiful. The sun set a glitter on the whole sea. The air was so crisp and clean that it seemed indivisible with the light; it seemed a cold emanation of the sun. The steep land lay off the starboard rail—blue and purple bluffs, and glaciers spilling down. And the whole way we steered barely clear of icebergs. They were huge, fantastic shapes, the size of great ships, the size of skyscrapers, full of iridescences.

At Siorpaluk I walked along a golden, crescent beach until I was just beyond the village. Some of the "calves" of the icebergs had been washed up there. They stood on the sand, creaking, cracking, sweating under the great weight of the sun. I paused at one, within arm's reach. It was the shape of a rabbit's head—about twice my size—its great ears askew and precariously pitched. It creaked and groaned. It would break apart at any moment for sure. But nothing happened. Nothing happened, except that the thing crackled on. At last I decided to take matters into my own hands. I backed off, took up some stones from the beach, and hurled them at the thing. I couldn't miss, I was so close. But nothing happened. After ten minutes of this assault nothing happened. The thing stood shining and impervious before me.

Then I heard someone shouting behind me. Startled, I turned to see an old Eskimo hunter hurrying toward me, gesticulating wildly— carrying a rifle in his hands. I was terrified. He came upon me, talking now, excitedly, in his native tongue.

At last I understood. Did I want him to shoot the iceberg? I was greatly relieved, to be sure. I was humbled. I said yes, please. And he shot the iceberg. In the explosion a part of it went spinning off into the fjord. But still it was the shape of a rabbit's head.

The old man regarded me kindly for a moment, turned, and walked away to his shack. It seemed to me that his attitude was that of having done a good deed.

This is what he said to himself, I believe: "Look at this stranger, this man from some world beyond my ken, beyond my imagination; he comes here to my village, and immediately he tries to kill the icebergs. It seems a strange and futile enterprise. But he is a human being, as I am too. And I shall help him if I can."

—From *The Man Made of Words*

(untitled)

*T*HERE ARE GOOD PEOPLE in the village. They greet each other in the streets; they pause to talk of plain, ordinary things, the things that touch their lives. Good and bad things happen to them in the course of daily events, and these things they share with each other. I have come to know some of the people, and they have come to know me. In no other place have I understood that I could depend upon my neighbors, should real need arise. Everyone, with one or two exceptions, in the village weaves the thread of his or her good will into the fabric of the community. And the one or two exceptions have their place as well. They are here, and there is no village without them. But they keep to themselves.

One of the things that most integrates our lives is the land itself. In this canyon the horizons are very close, and they are very high above the village. We wait longer for the sunrise than do people elsewhere, and the sun sets earlier and strikes deeper colors on the walls around us. The stars seem more concentrated in the space above, and the light of the moon is there on the eastern rim long before the moon appears. The shadows on the cliffs seem to be alive and change in depth and shape even as we look at them.

The canyon enfolds and embraces us, and the spirits of ancient dwellers look down upon us from the towns above. Here we are in the earth as well as on it. We live deep in geologic time, and the river of eternity is just above us.

JUNE 2000

BIBLIOGRAPHY OF
MAJOR WORKS

David Wagoner

Dry Sun, Dry Wind. Bloomington: Indiana University Press, 1953
The Man in the Middle. New York: Harcourt, Brace, 1954
Money, Money, Money. New York: Harcourt, Brace, 1955
A Place to Stand. Bloomington: Indiana University Press, 1958
Rock. New York: Viking Press, 1958
A Guide to Dungeness Spit. Port Townsend: Graywolf Press, 1963
The Nesting Ground. Bloomington: Indiana University Press, 1963
The Escape Artist. New York: Farrar, Straus and Giroux, 1965
Staying Alive. Bloomington: Indiana University Press, 1966
Baby, Come on Inside. New York: Farrar, Straus and Giroux, 1968
New and Selected Poems. Bloomington: Indiana University Press, 1969
Where is My Wandering Boy Tonight? New York: Ballantine, 1970
Working Against Time. London: Rapp & Whiting, 1970
Riverbed. Bloomington: Indiana University Press, 1972
Sleeping in the Woods. Bloomington: Indiana University Press, 1974
The Road to Many a Wonder. New York: Farrar, Straus, Giroux, 1974
Tracker. Boston: Little, Brown, 1975
Collected Poems (1956–1976). Bloomington: Indiana University Press, 1976

Whole Hog. Boston: Little, Brown, 1976

Who Shall Be the Sun? Poems Based on the Lore, Legends, and Myths of Northwest Coast and Plateau Indians. Bloomington: Indiana University Press, 1978

In Broken Country. Boston: Little, Brown, 1979

The Hanging Garden. Boston: Little, Brown, 1980

Landfall. Boston: Little, Brown, 1981

First Light. Boston: Little, Brown, 1983

Through the Forest: New and Selected Poems. New York: Atlantic Monthly Press, 1987

Walt Whitman Bathing. Urbana: University of Illinois Press, 1996

Traveling Light: Collected and New Poems. Urbana: University of Illinois Press, 1999

The House of Song. Urbana: University of Illinois Press, 2002

Denise Levertov

Here and Now. San Francisco: City Lights Pocket Bookshop, 1957

With Eyes at the Back of Our Heads. New York: New Directions, 1959

The Jacob's Ladder. New York: New Directions, 1961.

O Taste and See: New Poems. New York: New Directions, 1964.

The Sorrow Dance. New York: New Directions, 1967.

Relearning the Alphabet. New York: New Directions, 1970.

To Stay Alive. New York: New Directions, 1971.

Footprints. New York: New Directions, 1972.

The Poet in the World. New York: New Directions, 1973.

Voyage. Port Townsend: Copper Canyon Press, 1974.

The Freeing of the Dust. New York: New Directions, 1975.

Life in the Forest. New York: New Directions, 1978.

Collected Earlier Poems. New York: New Directions, 1979.

Light Up the Cave. New York: New Directions, 1981.

Wanderers Daysong. Port Townsend: Copper Canyon Press, 1981.

Candles in Babylon. New York: New Directions, 1982.

Oblique Prayers: New Poems with 14 Translations from Jean Joubert. New York: New Directions, 1984.

Breathing the Water. New York: New Directions, 1987.

Poems 1968–1972. New York: New Directions, 1987.

A Door in the Hive. New York: New Directions, 1989.

Evening Train. New York: New Directions, 1992.

New and Selected Essays. New York: New Directions, 1992.

Tesserae: Memories and Suppositions. New York: New Directions, 1995.

Sands of the Well. New York: New Directions, 1996.

The Life Around Us: Selected Poems on Nature. New York: New Directions, 1997.

The Stream & the Sapphire: Selected Poems on Religious Themes. New York: New Directions, 1997.

This Great Unknowing: Last Poems. New York: New Directions, 1999.

Sonia Sanchez

A Blues Book for Blue Black Magical Women. Detroit: Broadside Press, 1974.

I've Been a Woman: New and Selected Poems. Sausalito: Black Scholar Press, 1978.

Homegirls and Handgrenades. New York: Thunder's Mouth Press, 1984.

Under a Soprano Sky. Trenton: Africa World Press, 1987.

Wounded in the House of a Friend. Boston: Beacon Press, 1995.

Does Your House Have Lions? Boston: Beacon Press, 1997.

Like the Singing Coming Off the Drums: Love Poems. Boston: Beacon Press, 1998.

Shake Loose My Skin: New and Selected Poems. Boston: Beacon Press, 1999.

Richard Hugo

Poems. Portland: Portland Art Museum, 1959.

A Run of Jacks. Minneapolis: University of Minnesota Press, 1961.

Death of the Kapowsin Tavern. New York: Harcourt, Brace & World, 1965.

Good Luck in Cracked Italian. New York: Meridian Books, 1969.

Phoning from Sweathouse Creek. Seattle: Unicorn Bookshop, 1971.

The Lady in Kicking Horse Reservoir. New York: W. W. Norton & Co., 1973.

Rain Five Days and I Love It. Port Townsend: Graywolf Press, 1975.

What Thou Lovest Well, Remains American. New York: W. W. Norton & Co., 1975.

Duwamish Head. Port Townsend: Copperhead, 1976.

31 Letters and 13 Dreams. New York: W. W. Norton & Co., 1977.

Road Ends at Tahola. Pittsburgh: Slow Loris Press, 1978.

Selected Poems. New York: W. W. Norton & Co., 1979.

The Triggering Town: Lectures and Essays on Poetry and Writing. New York: W. W. Norton & Co., 1979.

The Right Madness on Skye. New York: W. W. Norton & Co., 1980.

White Center. New York: W. W. Norton & Co., 1980.

Death and the Good Life. New York: St. Martin's Press, 1981.

Making Certain It Goes On: The Collected Poems of Richard Hugo. New York: W. W. Norton & Co., 1984.

The Real West Marginal Way: A Poet's Autobiography. New York: W. W. Norton & Co., 1986.

Larry Levis

Wrecking Crew. Pittsburgh: University of Pittsburgh Press, 1972.

The Afterlife. Iowa City: Windhover Press, 1977.

Winter Stars. Pittsburgh: University of Pittsburgh Press, 1985.

The Widening Spell of the Leaves. Pittsburgh: University of Pittsburgh Press, 1991.

Black Freckles. Salt Lake City: Peregrine Smith Books, 1992.

The Dollmaker's Ghost. Pittsburgh: Carnegie Mellon University Press, 1992.

Elegy. Pittsburgh: University of Pittsburgh Press, 1997.

The Selected Levis. Pittsburgh: University of Pittsburgh Press, 2000.

Diane Wakoski

Discrepancies and Apparitions. Garden City: Doubleday, 1966.

Inside the Blood Factory. Garden City: Doubleday, 1968.

The Magellanic Clouds. Los Angeles: Black Sparrow Press, 1970.

The Motorcycle Betrayal Poems. New York: Simon & Schuster, 1971.

Smudging. Los Angeles: Black Sparrow Press, 1972.

Dancing on the Grave of a Son of a Bitch. Los Angeles: Black Sparrow Press, 1974.

Trilogy: Coins and Coffins; Discrepancies and Apparitions; The George Washington Poems. Garden City: Doubleday, 1974.

The Fable of the Lion and the Scorpion. Milwaukee: Pentagram Press, 1975.

Virtuoso Literature for Two and Four Hands. Garden City: Doubleday, 1975.

Variations on a Theme: An Essay on Revision. Santa Barbara: Black Sparrow Press, 1976.

Waiting for the King of Spain. Santa Barbara: Black Sparrow Press, 1976.

The Ring. Santa Barbara: Black Sparrow Press, 1977.

The Man Who Shook Hands. Garden City: Doubleday, 1978.

Toward a New Poetry. Ann Arbor: University of Michigan Press, 1980.

The Managed World. New York: Red Ozier Press, 1980.

Cap of Darkness. Santa Barbara: Black Sparrow Press, 1980.

The Magician's Feastletters. Santa Barbara: Black Sparrow Press, 1982.

Greed. Santa Barbara: Black Sparrow Press, 1984.

The Rings of Saturn. Santa Rosa: Black Sparrow Press, 1986.

Emerald Ice: Selected Poems, 1962–1987. Santa Rosa: Black Sparrow Press, 1988.

Medea the Sorceress. Santa Rosa: Black Sparrow Press, 1991.

Jason the Sailor. Santa Rosa: Black Sparrow Press, 1993.

The Emerald City of Las Vegas. Santa Rosa: Black Sparrow Press, 1995.

Argonaut Rose. Santa Rosa: Black Sparrow Press, 1998.

The Butcher's Apron: New and Selected Poems. Santa Rosa: Black Sparrow Press, 2000.

Carolyn Kizer

The Ungrateful Garden. Bloomington: Indiana University Press, 1961.

Knock Upon Silence. Garden City: Doubleday, 1965.

Midnight Was My Cry: New and Selected Poems. Garden City: Doubleday, 1971.

Mermaids in the Basement: Poems for Women. Port Townsend: Copper Canyon Press, 1984.

Yin. Brockport: BOA Editions, 1984.

The Nearness of You: Poems for Men. Port Townsend: Copper Canyon Press, 1986.

Proses: Essays on Poets and Poetry. Port Townsend: Copper Canyon Press, 1994.

Picking and Choosing: Prose on Prose. Cheney: Eastern Washington University Press, 1995.

Harping On: Poems 1985—1995. Port Townsend: Copper Canyon Press, 1996.

Cool Calm & Collected. Port Townsend: Copper Canyon Press, 2000.

Lynda Barry

Big Ideas. Seattle: Real Comet Press, 1983.

Everything in the World. San Francisco: Harper & Row, 1986.

The Fun House. San Francisco: Harper & Row, 1987.

The Good Times are Killing Me. Seattle: Real Comet Press/Sasquatch Books, 1988/89.

Down the Street. New York: Harper & Row, 1989.

Come Over, Come Over. New York: HarperCollins, 1990.

My Perfect Life. New York: HarperCollins, 1992.

It's So Magic. New York: HarperCollins, 1994.

The Freddie Stories. Seattle: Sasquatch Books, 1999.

Cruddy. New York: Simon & Schuster, 1999.

The! Greatest! of! Marlys! Seattle: Sasquatch Books, 2000.

One! Hundred! Demons! Seattle: Sasquatch, 2000.

Yusef Komunyakaa

Copacetic. Middletown: Wesleyan University Press, 1984.

Dien Cai Dau. Middletown: Wesleyan University Press, 1988.

Magic City. Middletown: Wesleyan University Press, 1992.

Neon Vernacular: New and Selected Poems. Middletown: Wesleyan Press, 1993.

Thieves of Paradise. Middletown: Wesleyan Press, 1998.

Talking Dirty to the Gods. New York: Farrar, Straus, and Giroux, 2000.

Pleasure Dome: New and Collected Poems. Middletown: Wesleyan Press, 2001.

Marilyn Chin

Rhapsody in Plain Yellow. New York: W. W. Norton & Co., 2002.

The Phoenix Gone, the Terrace Empty. Minneapolis: Milkweed Editions, 1994.

Dwarf Bamboo. Greenfield Center: Greenfield Review Press, 1987.

Ivan Doig

Winter Brothers: A Season at the Edge of America. New York: Harcourt Brace Jovanovich, 1980.

The Sea Runners. New York: Atheneum, 1982.

This House of Sky. New York: Atheneum, 1983.

English Creek. New York: Penguin Books, 1985.

Dancing at the Rascal Fair. New York: Atheneum, 1987.

Ride With Me, Mariah Montana. New York: Atheneum, 1990.

Heart Earth. New York: Atheneum, 1993.

Bucking the Sun. New York: Simon & Schuster, 1996.

Mountain Time. New York: Scribner, 1999.

Prairie Nocturne. New York: Scribner, 2003.

William Stafford

Down in My Heart. Elgin: The Brethren Press, 1947.

Traveling Through the Dark. New York: Harper & Row, 1962.

The Rescued Year. New York: Harper & Row, 1966.

Friends to this Ground: A Statement for Readers, Teachers, and Writers of Literature. Campaign: National Council of Teachers of English, 1967.

Allegiances. New York: Harper & Row, 1970.

Temporary Facts. Athens: D. Schneider, 1970.

Someday, Maybe. New York: Harper & Row, 1973.

Notes for the Refrigerator Door. Binghampton: Bellevue Press, 1976.

Stories That Could Be True: New and Collected Poems. New York: Harper & Row, 1977.

Writing the Australian Crawl: Views on the Writer's Vocation. Ann Arbor: University of Michigan Press, 1978.

Smoke's Way. Port Angeles: Graywolf Press, 1978.

Passing a Creche. Seattle: Sea Pen Press, 1978.

Around You, Your House and a Catechism. Knotting: Sceptre Press, 1979.

The Quiet of the Land. New York: Nadja, 1979.

Things That Happen Where There Aren't Any People. Brockport: BOA Editions, 1980.

Sometimes Like a Legend: Puget Sound Country. Port Townsend: Copper Canyon Press, 1981.

A Glass Face in the Rain: New Poems. New York: Harper & Row, 1982.

Segues: A Correspondence in Poetry. Boston: D. R. Godine, 1983.

Smoke's Way: Poems from Limited Editions, 1968–1981. Port Townsend: Graywolf Press, 1983.

You Must Revise Your Life. Ann Arbor: University of Michigan Press, 1986.

An Oregon Message. New York: Harper & Row, 1987.

Passwords. New York: HarperPerennial, 1991.

Getting the Knack: 20 Poetry Writing Exercises. Stephen Dunning/William Stafford. Urbana: National Council of Teachers of English, 1992.

The Animal that Drank Up Sound. San Diego: Harcourt Brace Jovanovich, 1992.

The Darkness Around Us Is Deep. New York: HarperPerennial, 1993.

Crossing Unmarked Snow: Further Views on the Writer's Vocation. Ann Arbor: University of Michigan Press, 1998.

The Way It Is: New & Selected Poems. St. Paul: Graywolf Press, 1998.
Every War Has Two Losers: William Stafford on Peace and War. United States
    Milkweed Editions Publishers, 2003.
Brother Wind. Rexburg: Honeybrook Press, 1986.

Sharon Olds

Satan Says. Pittsburgh: University of Pittsburgh Press, 1980.
The Dead and the Living. New York: Alfred A. Knopf, 1984.
The Gold Cell. New York: Alfred A. Knopf, 1987.
The Father. New York: Alfred A. Knopf, 1992.
The Wellspring. New York: Alfred A. Knopf, 1996.
Blood, Tin, Straw. New York: Alfred A. Knopf, 1999.
The Unswept Room. New York: Alfred A. Knopf, 2002.

Rick Bass

The Deer Pasture. College Station: Texas A & M University Press, 1985.
Wild to the Heart. New York: W. W. Norton, 1987.
Oil Notes. Boston: Houghton Mifflin Company, 1989.
The Watch: Stories. New York: W. W.Norton, 1989.
Winter: Notes from Montana. Boston: Houghton Mifflin/Seymour
    Lawrence, 1991.
The Ninemile Wolves: An Essay. Livingston: Clark City Press, 1992.
Platte River. Boston: Houghton Mifflin, 1994.
In the Loyal Mountains. Boston: Houghton Mifflin Company, 1995.
The Grizzlies: A Search for Survivors in the Wilderness of Colorado. Boston:
    Houghton Mifflin, 1995.
The Book of Yaak. Boston: Houghton Mifflin Company, 1996.
The Sky, the Stars, the Wilderness. Boston: Houghton Mifflin Company,
    1997.
Fiber. Athens: University of Georgia Press, 1998.
The New Wolves: The Return of the Mexican Wolf to the American Southwest.
    New York: Lyons Press, 1998.
Where the Sea Used to Be. Boston: Houghton Mifflin Company, 1998.
Brown Dog of the Yaak: Essays on Art and Activism. Minneapolis: Milkweed
    Editions, 1999.
Colter: The True Story of the Best Dog I Ever Had. Boston: Houghton Mifflin
    Company, 2000.
The Hermit's Story: Stories. Boston: Houghton Mifflin Company, 2002.

The Roadless Yaak: Reflections and Observations About One of Our Last Great Wilderness Areas. New York: Lyons Press, 2002.

The Ninemile Wolves. Boston: Houghton Mifflin Company, 2003.

N. Scott Momaday

The Journey of Tai-me. Santa Barbara: Privately Published, 1967.

House Made of Dawn. New York: Harper & Row, 1968.

The Way to Rainy Mountain. Albuquerque: University of New Mexico Press, 1969.

Colorado, Summer/Fall/Winter/Spring. Chicago: Rand McNally, 1973.

Angle of Geese and Other Poems. Boston: Godine, 1974.

The Gourd Dancer: Poems. New York: Harper & Row, 1976.

The Names: A Memoir. New York: Harper & Row, 1976.

The Ancient Child: A Novel. New York: Doubleday, 1989.

In the Presence of the Sun: Stories and Poems, 1961–1991. New York: St. Martin's Press, 1992.

Circle of Wonder: A Native American Christmas Story. Santa Fe: Clear Light, 1994.

The Man Made of Words: Essays, Stories, Passages. New York: St. Martin's Press, 1997.

In the Bear's House. New York: St. Martin's Press, 1999.